FAR JOURNEY:
A PSYCHIATRIST'S
CHRONICLE

BY
Yitzhak Hanu

Old Rugged Cross Press
1160 Alpharetta Street, Suite H / Roswell, Georgia 30075

For Wu, daughter of Chen Mao-Fu

my wife . . . from the land where the Min River flows,
companion of the heart,
and spiritual alter ego

ACKNOWLEDGEMENTS

I am indebted to the many patients it has been my privilege to treat over a career spanning some 25 years. They have taught me more about the work I have dedicated myself to than the many textbooks and journals I have studied and lectures and conferences I have attended. I hope that in the telling of some of their experiences the public will come to understand the nature of mental illness and what it is the psychiatrist actually does.

In particular, I wish to express my gratitude to Reverend Mother Maria Dolores of the Carmelite Order in Melojloj on the island of Guahan in the Marianas, who, in life and in death, quietly encouraged me to complete this work.

I also owe a debt of gratitude to M.L. Jones of Atlanta, Georgia, whose unswerving faith in the manuscript helped me to persevere until it finally emerged as a book. Blessed with a sense of ecumenism and focused insight, he sees the spiritual emptiness of American life today and the need to start filling that void with true substance in these the final years of the second millennium of the Christian Era. That he believes *Far Journey* can contribute toward this end does me honor.

AUTHOR'S PREFACE

Far Journey: A Psychiatrist's Chronicle is not a work of fiction. The events depicted in these pages are true. However, some names have been changed in the interest of preserving individual privacy, both patients' and others. The same consideration may help explain the exiguities of certain passages. Much of the dialogue, especially that from the psychotherapy sessions, has been reproduced from notes and represents the words actually spoken at the time.

A number of patients are presented, drawn from both my private practice and from my work at the Gotham Psychiatric Clinic. But *Far Journey* is more than a collection of case histories. It chronicles a year in the life of one particular psychiatrist. Before the book concludes, seemingly unrelated threads coalesce and the purpose of the book becomes clear: the thoughtful and involved reader will come to see the Divine Hand in human events. The unconvinced will have to look to Volume II, *Interlude In Paradise* (the second part of a proposed trilogy), for further "proof" that Providence is keenly concerned with and participates in events on earth.

Names, especially those buried in history, hold relevance for some. The cover and title page bear the ancestral name of the author.

Alexandria, Louisiana
September 20, 1992

CHAPTER ONE

He saw the Magi, robed in Oriental splendor, making their way along the Judean hills. "There ahead," said the tallest to the other two, "is the town with the blessed infant." As his fellow travelers nodded, a child's blackboard glided past them as though floating through air. Scrawled upon it was an address: 379 *Köln Strasse*.

The telephone rang, and he awoke with a start. He fumbled for the receiver.

"Five a.m."

It was the voice of the desk clerk at The Adams, a fashionable residential hotel in Manhattan's Upper East Side where he made his home.

"Thank you," he mumbled, and quickly hung up.

Before any time could pass, he jotted down the essence of his dream: "Magi" and "Cologne street address." He also wrote the numbers "3-7-9" and underlined them.

An interesting way to start out the day, he mused. A mystery address in Deutschland and the Three Wise Men of the East passing across my mind's sleeping eye.

He was now fully awake and on his way to the shower, the dream still turning over in his mind: I think they were the Magi . . . But Christmas is past . . . Why would those three famed Persians of old creep through my unconscious at this particular moment?

It was Wednesday, the 10th of January, 1973. Nothing special about January 10th in history or in my own history as far as I can recall, he cogitated on the way down in the elevator. He walked in the early morning darkness to his office several blocks away.

Rex Cordis, M.D., psychiatrist, was in his forties. He carried his 6′1½″ frame well, successfully concealing the chronic pain he suffered from osteoarthritis centered in his neck. Although his left hand was considerably weakened by nerve-root irritation originating in his cervical spine, he would, nevertheless, painstakingly loop his tie in a Windsor knot each morning.

His scheduled 7 a.m. patient was on time. While writing up his notes following the psychotherapy session, he found his mind wandering back to his early morning dream. He phoned Father Dominic.

There was a pause on the line after he had described the dream. "Unusual, what?" Father Dominic finally said.

Father Dominic Raynes was a scholarly man who had been educated

1

at Oxford in the twenties. His crisp, clear English accent stood out sharply against the distinctive vocal sounds uttered by New Yorkers.

"I do my share of dreaming," Dr. Cordis said, "but this dream is definitely out of place in my repertoire; in fact, it's so out of the ordinary for me, I wonder if it isn't . . . numinous."

He had paused dramatically before delivering the final word of the sentence.

"You Jungians!" Fr. Dominic said. Dr. Cordis could almost see his approving smile. "Why don't you stop by for breakfast."

Cordis was grateful for the invitation. "I only have a few minutes," he said. "Make mine coffee."

He hung up, and outside his office building took a cab to St. Alvin Catholic Church, not far from the synagogue he attended.

Cordis had met the churchman years earlier, and what had started out as a chance meeting had solidified into a warm friendship.

Fr. Dominic's lean physique was a testament to judicious nutritional monitoring, but he smoked too much. On this cold January morning, he greeted the doctor warmly while coughing vigorously. He dismissed his younger friend's concern with a wave of his hand and the minimizing words: "It's a minor catarrh."

When they were settled into Father's living room, each with a cup of hot coffee in tow, Cordis said, "Why in the world I would dream of the Three Wise Men of the East is a mystery to me. In no way are they part of my particular ancestral tradition."

"How about a down-to-earth explanation?" offered the aged priest. "We have only just celebrated the Feast of the Epiphany in commemoration of the Three Kings. Perhaps you saw something about it that affected you."

"Perhaps," Cordis conceded. "Maybe something on the evening news or in the paper."

"However," the priest went on, "the Koln—Cologne—street address certainly warrants closer inspection."

"Tell me more."

"The Magi are sometimes called the Three Kings of Cologne because their relics are in the Cologne Cathedral."

"You know something," Cordis said thoughtfully, wrinkling his forehead, "I've been there . . . with Antje Haag when we were medical students struggling our way through anatomy and physiology, she at the University of Cologne and I at St. Andrews in Scotland."

"Cherchez la femme," said Father jokingly.

"Met her in Amsterdam in the summer of sixty," Cordis responded,

2

smiling. "Now she's a psychoanalyst practicing in Hamburg. We're just . . . well, friends these days."

"What about *those* days?" father asked laughingly, with a twinkle in his eye. "No, don't tell me," he added, just as the doctor was about to respond.

It was close to 9 a.m. and Cordis had to start seeing patients at the state-run Gotham Psychiatric Clinic in Manhattan's Soho district. "You've given me more to consider," he said, quickly sipping the remainder of his coffee. "As usual."

The priest smiled. "Always happy to oblige."

"Maybe you can check out those numbers—three, seven, nine—in the *Köln Strasse* address for some hidden significance?"

"I will look into it," the priest promised.

Cordis arrived late at the clinic and immediately found himself engulfed with patients and paperwork. Things didn't slow down until mid-afternoon, when he was finally able to sit for a quiet moment at his desk. He was going over the dream in his mind when the telephone rang. A youthful-sounding woman who gave her name as Renata Delacross wanted to make an appointment to see him.

"You don't need an appointment," he said politely. "All you have to do is come down to the clinic and register."

"You don't understand," she said fretfully. "I want to see you as a private patient in your own office."

After obtaining the customary basic data—address, home telephone number, manner of payment, referral source—he offered her a 9 o'clock appointment for Saturday morning. "Is that okay with you?"

"I will be there," she answered, sounding relieved.

The brief conversation lingered in his mind. He was intrigued by her soft, refined voice and her accent, which he was unable to place. The referring physician she named, a Park Avenue internist, was not someone he knew. She had singled out depression as her major problem, a common enough one attracting patients to private therapy. Just then someone rapped on his door, jarring Renata Delacross from his thoughts.

The name of Renata Delacross came up again that evening when he had dinner with A. Hashimoto, whom he had known since 1944. Hashimoto had left his native Japan for the United States on Christmas Day, 1926, the day the Showa Emperor Hirohito had succeeded to the throne.

There was talk among his friends that Hashimoto—Harris to them— had worked in the OSS during World War II. The suspicion of intelligence work simply added to the aura of this friendly, elusive, mys-

3

terious man.

In all the years Cordis had known him, Harris had never discussed personal matters, except on one occasion when he related how his grandfather had survived the atomic bombing of Nagasaki in August, 1945. Grieved and depressed by the sight of the holocaust all around him, the old gentleman had turned to saki as his special solace, and in the juice of the fermented rice brew had found, so he had claimed, the elixir of life.

As strange as the story sounded, Cordis could discern a kernel of truth in it. Ethanol, with its antioxidant properties, has the capacity to neutralize the highly reactive free hydroxyl radical produced when ionizing radiation reacts with water (splitting it into hydrogen and hydroxyl radicals). There is scientific support for the concept from another quarter. The Argentinian Nobelist in physiology Bernardo Houssay was able to destroy the insulin-secreting cells of the pancreas in his laboratory animals with the drug alloxan. This diabetic agent also generates hydroxyl radicals, and one can suppress its diabetogenic properties with alcohol.

Harris drank saki with the same apparent enthusiasm his grandfather had shown for the beverage. He sipped it slowly, which, as any biochemist can tell you, would tend to prevent intoxication.

"I want to alert you to a young lady who will come to you for treatment," Harris said during dinner. His speech was clear, devoid of the lambdacism, the *l-r* inversion, often found among Orientals speaking English. "Her name is Delacross."

Cordis stared silently at his friend. "She called this very afternoon," he said after a few seconds had passed. "She's coming Saturday morning."

Harris smiled. "I'm relieved to hear that. I've been trying to get her to do that for months now." There was a brief silence, and then Harris added, "Take good care of her. She's my goddaughter."

When Cordis arrived home that evening there was, among his day's mail, a letter from the Manhattan physician Renata Delacross had mentioned:

January 9, 1973

Dear Dr. Cordis:
    This will introduce Miss Renata Delacross, a 24-
year-old unmarried, overseas Caucasian who suffers
from hypochondriasis, marijuana addiction, and schizophrenia. Extensive workups have failed to reveal any
organic pathology, and she is referred to you at the

4

request of a family member for psychiatric treatment.

Sincerely yours,

_____ _____ , M. D.

Sweet and to the point, Cordis thought. Maybe even sour. The overseas bit would explain her accent. Referred by a family member? Hmm. The doctor accepts Harris, the godfather, as a member of the family. Schizophrenic, huh. Maybe and maybe not. Internists aren't the best psychonosologists.

In the background, the radio was playing a medley of Sammy Cahn songs. Frank Sinatra was halfway through "Three Coins in the Fountain" when the phone rang. It was Fr. Dominic.

"Your dream intrigued me when you shared it with me," the older man began. "Now I am even more intrigued."

"How's that?"

"During the Middle Ages, I found out, it was common practice on Twelfth Night to write the names of the Magi on doors or doorposts with chalk which had been blessed. This gives us insight into the chalkboard in your dream. But that isn't all. Do you know the names of the Magi?"

The dream that had gripped Cordis all morning into the afternoon had receded from his consciousness—lost its emotional luster for him— by the time he had arrived home. But now Fr. Dominic had rekindled his interest in it.

"No, I can't say that I do," Cordis replied.

"Gaspar, or Caspar—the difference is of no consequence in our context—Melchior and Balthasar. They were the ones who followed the star of heaven to the infant Jesus. Now, back to the practice of writing their names on doorposts. Sometimes only their first initial was inscribed in chalk: G, M, B."

"I think you may have sounded the call letters of the stars!" Cordis blurted out.

"Or perhaps of heaven," said the old priest.

Cordis had been busy with pen and paper with Father's mention of the letters. "The letters translate into seven, three and nine," he said excitedly.

They were both familiar with the basic mnemonic system of translating letters into numbers, and vice versa. They had learned the Bruno Furst code, but any other system, such as Harry Lorayne's, would have yielded the same results in this instance.

5

Cordis' interest in mnemonics dated back to his days at William Howard Taft High School in The Bronx, when students were encouraged to develop mnemonic pegs as an aid to learning. ROYGBIV was a well-known mnemonic for recalling the colors of the visible spectrum. PEACE RELATIONS was one developed by a clever classmate to remember Wilson's Fourteen Points: P for Poland restored, E for evacuation of and self-determination for Russia, A for Alsace-Lorraine returned to France, et cetera.

"Rearranged, the very numbers in the street address — 3-7-9 Cologne Street," Fr. Dominic added.

"Amazing!" commented Cordis.

"God works in mysterious ways," the old priest said simply.

At that point, Cordis told Father Dominic about Renata Delacross, adding, "She just happens to be Harris' godchild. What do you make of that?"

The priest drew a deep breath. "She may very well be what this is all about."

"You never know."

"You will keep in touch," Fr. Dominic said softly.

"Of course," the doctor responded. "I may even need your help, especially if my new patient, it turns out, belongs to your ancient undivided Christian church."

Father Dominic didn't reply to that directly. He said only, "Treat her as you would any of your other patients, only more so."

CHAPTER TWO

Renata Delacross was late for her Saturday morning appointment. To pass the time, Cordis set himself a challenge — to come up with ten reasons why patients are late for their psychotherapy sessions.

Exhibitionist behavior is one, he said to himself, jotting it down on a blank note pad. This type, the hysterical personality, will keep the therapist waiting a suitable length of time and then make a dramatic entrance accompanied by an outpouring of excuses.

Then there's the passive-aggressive type, he continued musing, unloading her misdirected hostility. What about the person who needs to be in control? That's something rooted in the oral, anal or phallic stage of development. Right up the psychoanalyst's alley. That's three.

Ah, castration anxiety. No, I had better leave that one out, because the analysts generally state it as the male's problem, even though little girls can also experience fear of genital injury.

He thought of the need for atonement for a real or imagined past sin. This would lead the patient to cast the psychiatrist in the role of castigator and thus to be avoided.

He included the phobic patient unable to leave her dwelling place. The process of forgetting was an acceptable mental mechanism, since it involves the use of repression as a means of diminishing anxiety. A medical emergency would constitute a legitimate reason, but he crossed it out after writing it down, for he was limiting himself to psychological reasons.

The repetition-compulsion, which is the compulsion to repeat an earlier emotional experience even though it is counter-productive or destructive, was another consideration. Lateness as a depressive equivalent brought his list up to eight.

Negation seemed appropriate for inclusion. What is unpleasant or threatening to the ego gains access to consciousness by proclamation as the negative. Thus, if Renata Delacross had been treated previously by a psychiatrist, she could now assert, 'How fortunate that I have not had to see a psychiatrist for so long,' and she would convince herself that her present need was hardly a need at all.

The classic reason Cordis saved for last, the high point in the whole panoramic view of the lateness theme: *resistance*, the patient's surfaced expression of the negative, inhibitory and self-defeating dictates of the unconscious.

With his self-imposed task at an end, Cordis turned to his book shelves and tuned in to WQXR for background music. He picked up where he had left off previously in Anna Burr's *Weir Mitchell, His Life and Letters*. Silas Weir Mitchell occupies a significant place in the history of American neurology, but it was his intellectual excursions into the nascent psychiatry of his day which intrigued Cordis. For instance, in a letter to his son John in 1873, he wrote: "Just now we will drop the ego." That in 1873? Before Freud popularized the term! And from a letter of 1897: "I have egotized for you at sad length." As a guidepost to time, Freud's great work, *The Interpretation of Dreams*, came out in 1900. Burr's book was published in 1929. Cordis wondered if Burr had edited Mitchell's letters, substituting what had become the fashionable Freudian language where she felt it fitted. Or did the neurologist Weir Mitchell actually use the

7

term "ego" in his letters to his son. "Something else for me to research," he muutered under his breath.

Renata Delacross arrived at 9:40.

"I'm so sorry to have kept you waiting," she apologized.

"Don't let it worry you," Cordis said, shaking hands with her. Her grip was weak and her hand cold.

"I must apologize," she said. Her voice was soft and her speech, with its elusive accent, unhurried.

She was an attractive young woman with long, dark hair and brown eyes. He gauged her height to be 5'5" or 5'6" and her weight about 110 pounds. She was dressed well, to the point of elegance, and she carried herself with poise and a quiet dignity.

The deportment and carriage is very European, he said to himself, maybe Mediterranean. He noticed a certain sadness about her, the mien of the melancholic.

"Please come in," he said, leading her from the waiting room into his office. He motioned for her to choose either the psychoanalytic couch or the armchair in front of his desk. "Please, make yourself comfortable."

"Are you a psychoanalyst?" she asked, choosing the armchair.

Cordis detected a note of perplexity, with a dash of anxiety, in her voice. He shook his head. "I'm a psychiatrist who mixes psychodynamic psychiatry with biological or organic psychiatry."

She frowned. "What does that mean?"

Cordis smiled reassuringly. I'm a physician who has specialized in psychiatry, one of the branches of medicine."

"Do you practice Freudianism?" she asked, making it sound like a religion.

"My approach is eclectic," he explained. "I take a little bit from several approaches in order to achieve an integrated, harmonious whole."

"Oh, smorgasbord therapy," she said, smiling for the first time.

Cordis smiled, too. "That's a good way to put it."

"But why do you have the couch?"

"So I can have a place to take an occasional nap," he replied.

She laughed. "Really? No!"

"Actually, it's here so that you can have a choice. I always give you choices. Some patients do prefer the analytic couch."

"Ah, then I am to be your patient?"

"That is also your choice."

She remained silent and looked the office over. "That painting on your east wall, what is it?" she asked as she got up to view it at close range.

Cordis noted her orientational facility. She had quickly, almost

8

automatically, alligned herself spatially.

"It's a print of the Moshe Castel painting *The Synagogue*." He watched her studying the print. "On the main wall of the synagogue is a Menorah," he went on, "the symbol of Hanukkah, the Festival of Lights, a holiday celebrating the Hasmonean triumph over Antiochus, the Syrian, in the second century B.C.E. If you look closely you can see above it the Tetragrammaton, the four Hebrew letters that signify God's name, transliterated as YHWH, Yahweh, without the vowels."

She nodded her approval. "What period . . . what movement does he belong to?"

"Castel?" Cordis shrugged. "Pure Hebrew. His work bridges the span of man's history. It is steeped in his ancient Hebrew heritage, with something drawn from Sumerian, Assyrian and Canaanite art, and his roots may go all the way back to archaic man creating art with his cave glyphs."

She nodded approvingly again. "I sensed an antiquity about him." Turning from the print to face the doctor she asked, "Are you Hebrew?"

"Yes, I am of the Hebrews, an ancient race."

She smiled. "I am Catholic, of a not-so-ancient race."

"Roman Catholic?"

"Yes," she replied, once again absorbed in the Castel.

"Do you have a favorite artist, a favorite among favorites?" he asked.

Renata Delacross was quick to respond. "Artemisia Gentileschi, the seventeenth century Florentine painter," she said, making eye contact with Cordis. "I consider her *Jael and Sisara* and *Judith Decapitating Holofernes* among the finest paintings of her period." She continued to hold his eyes.

"Hmm," Cordis muttered. Hebrew women of the Bible engaged in acts to save their people, he mused. But she is so . . . retributive. "Why Artemisia?" he asked aloud.

"Like the Count of Monte Cristo, she proved that revenge can be sweet." With that she broke off eye contact.

"In what way?" Cordis asked, after she failed to say more on the matter.

"At the age of eighteen," she responded, "Artemisia had been raped by one of her artist father's apprentices, and her androcidal paintings are her triumph and her revenge."

This was interesting material, but before Cordis could develop it further, Renata Delacross moved along to the north wall to examine the art work there.

"What is this?" she asked, and laughed loudly.

9

He leaned back in his swivel chair, the palms of his hands interlocked over the back of his head, and said, "The Moulin Rouge."

She was gazing at a framed poster from the early fifties advertising the movie *The Moulin Rouge*, with Zsa Zsa Gabor the central figure.

"Why is Zsa Zsa Gabor on your wall?" she asked, trying to stifle another urge to laugh.

"She's the patron saint of femininity. While American womanhood rushes headlong into jeans and sloppy men's shirts, she clings to her fluffy dresses and long, flowing gowns."

"You're a *vive la différence* proponent," she commented.

Cordis sat up straight. "You can say that."

She continued to the west wall, which was dominated by two large bookcases stacked high with volumes upon volumes of books and medical journals. The south wall, at Cordis' back, was dissected by the entry door. The two halves flanking it were bare.

"Is there a reason the wall behind you is barren? Does it have anything to do with the door being there?"

He smiled. "We come into the world with nothing and we take nothing with us when we leave it."

"But if you enter this chamber through its portal, with your problems of the heart and mind, shouldn't you leave with something tangible?"

The doctor nodded, impressed by her reasoning. "Hopefully, everyone goes out a little happier, a little wiser and less burdened."

"I catch what you are saying," she said softly in that elusive accent of hers. She turned her attention to the bookcases where she was standing and read some of the titles aloud. "I like to read prose," she went on to say, "but my love is poetry."

"Fair enough," Cordis said, seizing a therapeutic opening. "Then quote me something in verse that summarizes your mental state."

Renata Delacross became pensive and returned to the armchair. After collecting her thoughts she said, "Samuel Rogers, a nineteenth century English poet, said it for me:

> *Go! You may call it madness, folly;*
> *You shall not chase my gloom away!*
> *There's such a charm in melancholy*
> *I would not if I could be gay.*"

"That is how you perceive yourself?" he asked.

"Melancholy—I think your profession refers to it as melancholia—runs in the Delacross family," she responded. "Several of us suffer from terrible depressions," she added before falling silent.

"Including yourself?" he finally asked. "You said 'us'"

"Oh, I'm only mildly depressed."

"Have there been any suicides among your family members?"

She nodded. "Mother took a fatal dose of poison." She hesitated momentarily. "Grandmama is fearful I will follow her example one day. Mother was an alcoholic." She looked directly at Cordis. "Rather than continue with that slow-acting poison, she chose a more powerful one, something from the gardener's tool shed," she added, her voice filling with anger.

"She disappointed you," the doctor commented softly.

"Yes!" she screamed. "Yes! I was an only child. Just seven years old. I needed a mother, not a house full of nannies, maids and servants to occupy me while she was away in a sanitorium somewhere."

"You were reared by others."

"I may be overdramatizing," she said, regaining her composure. "I was raised by strict sexagenarians—my grandmother and two great-aunts. You see, I never experienced childhood. I grew up old."

"And your father?" he asked as he jotted down his impressions, concluding with an old Yiddish saying, loosely translated into English as: 'Dying while young is a boon in old age.'

"I adored him," she replied. "But he was gone a good deal of the time. Away on engineering projects in distant lands. I . . . I was only ten when he died. I believe I've been depressed ever since."

Cordis was pleased with the session's progress, but he realized time was becoming a factor. He had to gauge her suicidal potential before letting her go.

"Tell me, Miss Delacross, have you—?"

"Please call me Renata," she said, interrupting him.

"Then tell me, Renata, have you ever attempted suicide?"

"Yes, three times," she answered easily. "I took pills. All kinds—sleeping, stomach, head, menstrual."

"I see," he said slowly, cautiously. "Did you ever lose consciousness after overdosing?"

She shook her head and wiped away the tears now sliding down her cheeks. He slid a box of Kleenex on his desk closer to her, and she pulled out a handful of tissues.

"No," she answered and sighed. "I would phone my doctor and he would tell me to go directly to the hospital emergency room. There I would be made to vomit or they would pump my stomach or both for all I remember. Afterwards, my doctor would lecture me on my dreadful, un-Delacross-like behavior."

"What do you think you were really trying to achieve with those

11

attempts of yours?" he asked. In her chart he wrote:'(?) Gestures, not suicidal attempts. (?) Cries for help, not checking-out notices.'

"I suppose I wanted someone to hear my desperate cries for help," she answered.

"And did anyone hear?" he asked as he crossed out the question marks.

She shrugged. "Each time I was shipped off to a nice, quiet, private and discreet hospital—we are wealthy, you know—where I was diagnosed as schizophrenic and dosed with Thorazine."

"Thorazine?" he said, raising the level of his voice. "That's pretty powerful stuff."

"If I resisted I was threatened with shock treatments. So, I swallowed my pills and sank deeper and deeper into depression and what lies at its bottom, despair."

"Hmm," he murmured, conveying his disapproval of her treatment. "When was your last hospitalization?"

"Last year," Renata replied. "If you wish, I will sign a release so you can get my records—"

He shook his head. "I doubt if I'd want to write them," he said firmly. "Records like that would only throw us off the track."

"I'm . . . I'm sorry. I don't understand."

"Well, it sounds to me as though you've been misdiagnosed for a long time. As a result, the treatment hasn't fit the malady. I would rather start from scratch and form my own conclusions."

Renata leaned forward. "Do you think . . . do you consider me to be . . . schizophrenic?" she asked fearfully.

The doctor smiled sympathetically. "You want an instant diagnosis. I understand." He took a deep breath. "I don't think you're schizophrenic. You suffer from depression, which is a different mental problem altogether."

On hearing this, Renata burst into tears, relieved and grateful that someone *finally* believed her. "Thank you," she managed to whisper while dabbing at her eyes with the Kleenex and blowing her nose several times.

As she regained her composure, Cordis said, "We're almost out of time for this morning. Before you go, I'd like to get a little more personal data from you. Why don't we start with your place of birth."

"I was born in Switzerland," Renata said, dabbing one more time at her nose with the facial tissues. "But I was raised in Egypt and Iran. My father was French and my mother Italian. After the Second World War, my father was granted American citizenship—General Eisenhower decorated him for his service to the Allies during the Normandy landing—so

12

I acquired multiple citizenship at birth. I didn't come to America until five years ago, when I was nineteen years old."

Cordis was impressed by what he heard about her father and nodded several times in approval. "What about your mother?" he asked.

"Mother never came here during my childhood, as far as I know. My father spent some time in the States, I was told."

Cordis checked his watch. "By the way," he said. "I don't usually see patients on Saturdays except for an initial ninety-minute workup. Generally, working patients prefer seven a.m. or come later in the evening. Right now, I have a Tuesday evening opening at eight o'clock. And all of these sessions are for fifty minutes, the now-famous fifty-minute hour."

Renata made a face. "I could never make it for that early morning appointment. I take too much Thorazine to be able to wake up on time."

Cordis narrowed his eyes. "How much of that Thorazine do you take?"

"I'm supposed to take eight hundred milligrams three times a day—"

"A zombie's dose," he interjected.

"But I never take it during the day. It knocks me out completely if I take it in the daytime. I only take it when I go to bed, and even then I can barely make it out of bed in the morning." Renata paused and looked squarely at him. "Actually, and I have to confess this, I take only two hundred milligrams—"

"At two hundred, there's no chance of a withdrawal reaction," the doctor said, mostly to himself. Then he looked at Renata. "Some patients on large doses do develop flu-like symptoms if they stop abruptly—"

"You mean I can stop?"

Cordis nodded once. "Yes, I think you should. Thorazine is not an appropriate medication for you. However, should you have trouble sleeping, you can take one of those two hundred milligram tablets tonight, but just for tonight."

Renata smiled broadly. "I'll have no trouble sleeping. Why, I'll sleep like an angel."

"I don't believe angels ever sleep," he said good-naturedly.

"You know what I mean," she said exuberantly. "Doctor, you have given me a new lease on life! Ohh!" She wrapped her arms around herself joyfully.

"Good," he said, genuinely pleased with how she had perked up. "Now, who in your household do I talk to when they call? In other words, how private do you wish these sessions to be?"

"I live with my grandmother and two great-aunts," she replied, " and I'm sure they will want to know what's going on."

"They're sisters?"

"Yes."

"Okay, the three sisters." He entered the datum into her chart.

She laughed. "That's what everyone calls them, 'the Three Sisters.' Oh, you may receive a call from my cousin in Casablanca. She's devoted and very nosy."

"Nosy relative in Morocco," Cordis said aloud, writing that down, too.

"Yes, I have lived in the Maghreb also."

"You've been around, as they say. Next time just tell me where you haven't lived. It would be simpler."

Renata smiled and said, "I feel I have been on a merry-go-round all my life."

"And now you have the chance to choose your own starting point."

Renata seemed elated. She clapped her hands together and said, "Oh, Dr. Cordis, I don't know how to thank you!"

"Don't get carried away," he advised. "There's still a great deal to be done. We've only chipped away at the tip of the iceberg."

"It feels like a big chunk to me," Renata said glowingly.

"Come, I'll walk you out," Cordis said, standing up.

As they were passing through the waiting room, Renata said, "So my next appointment is for Tuesday at eight."

"Right. If you should get here early you can grab a bite to eat in the coffee shop downstairs. It stays open late. Or you can use the waiting room, of course. My seven o'clock appointment will be leaving at seven fifty. Never later. Remember that some patients don't want to have to see one another, so you handle it any way you want."

"I'm not squeamish or self-conscious," Renata said.

"Good. That's just fine."

As she was about to enter the corridor, Renata paused to ask, "Why do you have that horseshoe over your door. Is it for luck?"

"It's not mine," Cordis answered. "It came with the office. Of course, it is a symbol of good luck. Among Arabs in years gone by, whenever a female camel died, they cut off the yoni, which was then tied over the door or tent entrance to ward off evil or bring good luck. In medieval Europe, where camels were scarce, they cut off the genitals of a dead cow or mare for the same reason. And today, rather than a mare's yoni, people hang the inoffensive horseshoe."

"Yoni—an interesting word," Renata said reservedly.

"It's a very old Sanskrit word for the female organ."

"You believe in symbolism," she said, her cheeks now a little red.

14

He noted her reaction to his last comment. "Symbols are universal," he said, responding to her statement. "To understand symbols is to penetrate into the primeval mind of mankind."

"You are an antiquarian also," Renata added. "I noticed all the many rare books in your bookcases. No doubt full of arcane symbols."

Cordis shrugged. "Symbols mark out one of the royal roads into the unconscious, which is where we'll be doing most of our work together. There is also a road that goes through dreamland and another that meanders down the byways of childhood memories. We shall travel a long road together before we have finished here."

She nodded and smiled. "Thank you."

"And now it is time to say good-by for today," Cordis said. He handed her a folded sheet of paper he had been carrying since getting up from his desk.

"For me?" she asked.

"It's just a general information sheet," Cordis responded. "You can bring it back on Tuesday."

She tucked it into her purse. "Thank you," she said. "I . . . I must confess, I don't know what to say . . . how to bring this enchanting hour to a close."

"Since it's my sabbath, you can say *Shalom*."

"*Shalom* then," she said.

"*Shalom*," he repeated.

When she was gone, Cordis returned to his desk and reviewed the abbreviated session. This woman doesn't exhibit any significant signs or symptoms suggestive of a schizophrenic disorder, he said to himself. An affective disorder, yes. They've missed the diagnosis.

He checked through several desk references to run down the term "Maghreb" she had used, and discovered that *Maghreb* was an Arabic word meaning "setting sun" or "west," in common use in medieval times to designate the territorial expanse encompassing modern-day Morocco, Algeria and Tunisia, but apparently not Egypt.

"Lady of mystery," he heard himself say aloud as he filed her folder.

Cordis had dinner at Mama Leone's that evening with a few friends from Ghana, and when he returned to The Adams a little before eleven there was a message for him that Mrs. Celine Delacross had called at 8 p.m. and was going to call again later on.

Ah, the grandmother, he said to himself. The one who's paying for her treatment. She may be a night owl, so I better stay up a while.

15

Her call came right after the 11 o'clock news.

"Dr. Cordis? This is Renata Delacross' grandmother." The accent was distinctly French.

"How do you do?" Cordis said.

"Dr. Cordis, I don't care to mince words. I want to know if my granddaughter is mentally deranged."

He thought he detected a slight slurring of her speech, as though she had not completely recovered from a stroke. Cordis focused on the content of her statement.

"If by deranged you mean schizophrenic, my answer is no."

"Then tell me why on three separate occasions she has been diagnosed as schizophrenic."

"I can't answer that," the doctor responded. "I can only tell you that I do not find any evidence to support a diagnosis of schizophrenia."

"Why don't you want to review her hospital records?" she asked, the message delivered accusatorily.

"If you think it will help clarify the situation, I can review them," Cordis said, trying to be agreeable.

"And you think it prudent to take her off her medication without being sure of the diagnosis?"

"Mrs. Delacross," he said, reacting to her anger, "I understand you doubt my diagnostic re-evaluation of her case; however, in my judgement, and a judgement is all I can offer at this time, Renata is suffering from an affective, or mood disorder, not schizophrenia, which is a thought disorder. Therefore, it is terribly inappropriate that she should be on a powerful medication like Thorazine, designed for the treatment of schizophrenia and other psychotic states."

He had aimed to countervail her statement and felt he had succeeded.

"I don't want her going from the frying pan into the fire—the very hellfire where her Italian mother is!"

He heard the venom in her anger. "I understand," Cordis said.

"You had better be very sure of yourself, Doctor," Mrs. Delacross said by way of good-by.

Cordis was bothered by the telephone conversation, and for the next fifteen minutes found himself considering and reconsidering his session with Renata. Each time he came away with the same impression: Renata Delacross is not schizophrenic.

He received a second phone call from the family early in the morning, awakening him from a deep sleep. This one was from Beatrice Delacross, one of Renata's great-aunts.

"I am very concerned about Renata's well-being, poor child," she

16

said in a shaky voice, one weakened by the infirmities of old age. Her accent, too, was clearly French.

"As am I," Cordis responded, yawning. He stared at his bedside clock. My gosh! he said to himself. Four thirty in the morning, and Sunday at that.

"Young man, do you worship that god of psychoanalysis, Freud?"

"Ma'am," Cordis said, startled, "the only God I worship is the God of my fathers, the God of Abraham, Isaac and Jacob—Yahweh—and Freud was not one of his prophets."

"Then you reject his message?"

"Whose, God's or Freud's?"

"That Antichrist Freud!" she yelled.

"Freud has his place in the pantheon of psychology," he responded calmly.

"He's an atheist!"

Cordis was about to remind her that Freud had been dead since 1939, but decided not to prolong the conversation. "Ma'am," he said, sighing, and then with exaggerated politeness added, "why don't you call me during office hours sometime this week, and we can pursue this matter further then?" With that he hung up.

Awake now, he got out of bed. Before he could step into the shower, the phone rang again. It was Renata's other great-aunt, Edith.

"I'm sorry my sister disturbed you," she said in a dulcet tone that revealed not the slightest accent whatsoever. "I guess we're a sorry threesome of crabby old dames."

Ah, a possible ally in that household, Cordis thought. "It's a pleasure to speak with the third of the Three Sisters," he said warmly. "No, she didn't bother me. I like to rise and shine early on Sunday morning." It was a little white lie.

"Thank you, Dr. Cordis," Edith Delacross said graciously. "I want to tell you that I for one think you have already helped Renata. Immensely. You see, we have been so worried about her. However, I agree with you: she does not suffer from schizophrenia. Renata is a fallen-away Catholic. Why, she has not been to mass since her father's death in nineteen fifty-nine. Hers is an illness of the spirit, not of the mind."

"I'll remember that," the doctor said.

"I am sure you will when the time comes."

"I'll do my best for her," Cordis added.

"I know you will. I will pray for you at mass today."

"I'd appreciate that," he said with sincerity. "Thank you."

17

CHAPTER THREE

That evening Cordis had dinner with Harris at Lüchow's on 14th Street, and during dessert Harris brought up Renata. "Is she really mad?" he wanted to know. "After all, two-thirds of that trio of relatives of hers think she is, and they have a few doctors agreeing with them."

Cordis looked at his friend. "She suffers from a depression of the nonpsychotic type, not madness."

"Can she recover?"

"With the right kind of help she can," the psychiatrist replied.

Harris nodded. "You know, those old ladies are dyed-in-the-wool French Catholics from the old school. They still believe Jews have horns."

"Shades of my youth!" Cordis cried out jovially. "And black people are made from pancake mix!"

Harris smiled. "They'll look at your head and swear you have protrusions there."

The doctor shrugged. "That's what we refer to as a visual hallucination."

"They'll never let go of the idea that you have two bumps on your head—in other words, a pair of horns."

"That, my friend, is delusional," Cordis rejoined, still jocular.

"Meaning what?" Harris asked, inquiring.

"A delusion is a false belief that can't be corrected by resorting to reason. Not by argument, persuasion, nor by the evidence of one's own senses."

"Which would make the old ladies what?"

"Half way to being schizophrenic themselves," Cordis said laughingly. Then he added, "No, I'm only kidding."

"That peculiar term you psychiatrists use," Harris commented, shaking his head. "One day you will have to explain it to me."

They retrieved their coats on their way out of the restaurant. Harris had also checked a walking stick. Now, as he removed a tough, fibrous covering from its top, the doctor could see the metallic figure of a hawk with curled wings spanning about four inches. Curious, he ran his fingers over the shape and realized with a start that the alar flanges and the claws were sharp enough to cut flesh.

As they strolled along 14th Street, Harris asked, "This mental disease Renata is supposed to have, schizophrenia, which you say she doesn't have, exactly what is it?"

"That would take more time than a night stroll will allow," the doctor replied. "Suffice it to say that it is a profound mental illness involving disordered thinking. To focus on just one aspect of it, it is a matter of logic gone astray. You see, Harris, most of us make use of Aristotelian logic in our thinking, whether we realize it or not. For example, All men are mortal. Richard Nixon is a man. Therefore Richard Nixon is mortal. That's identity based on identical subjects. Strictly Aristotelian."

"I follow," Harris said. He held the walking stick firmly in his right hand, a few inches below the crowning metallic emblem.

"Now, a schizophrenic with grandiosity," Cordis continued, "distorts the mechanism by seeing in it identity based on identical predicates. Jesus Christ is a man. I am a man. Therefore, I am Jesus Christ. The thinking is paralogical, not Aristotelian."

"So life's an illusion to him?"

"Delusion," the doctor said, correcting him. "An illusion is a false interpretation of a real sensory image. The kind of thing your mind will correct for you with further probing. A delusion isn't rooted in any reality."

"Now I understand something of this illness, " Harris said, rubbing his chin with the fingers of his left hand.

"I picked out one type of schizophrenia for you," Cordis said. "The paranoid type."

"Why that type?"

"Because in the kingdom of the mad, the clever paranoid is king," the doctor said laughingly, patting his friend on the back.

The night air was fresh and invigorating as they continued their stroll in the direction of Tompkins Square Park, a small patch of green with several concrete benches. There they were set upon by a young black mugger armed with a nasty-looking switchblade.

They were a Mutt-and-Jeff-looking pair. The doctor, at 6'1½", towered over his diminutive friend, who looked a lot like the Hungarian character actor Laszlo Loewenstein, known in the United States as Peter Lorre. Lorre starred as Mr. Moto, a Japanese Charlie Chan, in a series of pre-War films. In his youth, the doctor and his friends used to compare Harris to Mr. Moto, especially when it came to his jujitsu skills. At 74, 30 years older than the doctor, he was as spry as ever.

"Watch yourself, Harris!" Cordis called out, but it was unnecessary. The mugger, in what appeared to have taken only a second, found himself lying face down on the ground, securely pinned with Harris' walking stick lodged against his nape and a foot planted in the middle of his back. The

19

knife, only a moment earlier so threatening, lay just beyond the grasp of the mugger's right hand, which was pinned beneath the doctor's foot. Between them, they gave the mugger a short lesson in Pavlovian conditioning—whenever he attempted to move, he felt the pressure—and he quickly learned to remain perfectly still.

"I've given a lot of thought to this case," Harris said softly.

"Which case is that?" the doctor asked, showing as little attention to the man under his foot as Harris.

"Why, Renata's."

"Ah, that one."

"Do not hesitate, my friend, to call upon me for any assistance I may be able to render you in your efforts to save her."

Cordis nodded graciously. "Thank you, Harris."

Meanwhile, the mugger underfoot was whimpering and his breathing was labored.

"Discourteous fellow, wouldn't you say?" Harris pointed out. "What do we do with him?"

"Turn him over to the gendarmerie?"

"That's too easy for him," Harris asserted. "He'd be back on the streets in no time at all trying to mug someone else."

"Maybe cut off a finger with that knife of his," Cordis voiced. "In the manner of the yakuza."

"A mere finger?" Harris thundered. "This man tried to deny us the peace and pleasure of the evening! He deserves to lose the whole hand, at least."

Cordis nodded. "Ah, yes, Islamic law—sharia. I appreciate the suggestion, Harris, but from a surgical point of view, it may prove messy. Severing the hand is a very bloody procedure, as I'm sure you know. The dry cleaners will charge an arm and a leg—pardon the pun—to get the blood stains out of our clothes. A finger would be a whole lot easier on us than a hand." He ignored the weeping of the mugger and continued, "Of course, you have a point, the talion law might be more applicable here."

"What Italian law?"

"The law of the talion. You know, that biblical thing. An eye for an eye, et cetera. It follows that a man who threatens my life forfeits his own—"

"Aha! Now you've said it."

"Just like in that other time in Old Mexico," the doctor added, a memory from the past stirring in his mind.

"Yes, I agree. Justice in the absolute."

To an onlooker the scene might have appeared surreal. But their

20

apparent indifference to the situation was deliberately theatrical. Having overcome the danger posed by the mugger, they reacted by exhibiting a degree of playful lightheartedness reserved for the victor in such circumstances. For Harris, it was old hat. For Cordis, a former pupil of the jujitsu master during his high school days, now restricted physically by his osteoarthritis, it was a reminder of past adventures. Something of that past nevertheless carried over to the present: the quiet confidence he exhibited in handling the occasional violent or dangerous patient at the clinic—staff members had been shot and stabbed there on more than one occasion.

By this time the mugger was begging for mercy.

Seeming to ignore his pleas, Cordis picked up the knife and cut through his jacket and shirt sleeve, exposing an arm marked by numerous needle pricks. "Ah, we have a junkie on our hands," he said.

"Did you have any doubts, my friend?"

Cordis put his face close to the man's ear. "Look here, my good fellow, if we were to spare your miserable life—"

"And equally miserable hand," Harris piped in.

"You must promise upon your sacred honor to enter a heroin treatment program."

"Yes, yes, God, anything, yes!" the mugger babbled.

"Let him go," Cordis said to his friend. The mugger clamored to his feet and darted away, ignoring the knife still in the doctor's possession. "A lost soul," he lamented, watching the man disappear into the dimly lit distance.

"He seeks to wreak his own vengeance on society for his predicament in life," Harris intoned, "just as we would exact our measure of retribution upon him."

"Which of course is not ours to do. Vengeance is the Lord's responsibility."

Harris sighed. As they turned toward the darkened street that had swallowed up the mugger, he said, "It is not vengeance but deliverance which is the subject of the night. It has fallen to you to deliver Renata from the darkness of her soul. May the same Lord be with you."

Harris could be melodramatic at times, as though he were an actor in a Japanese movie. But the doctor was keenly aware that this was the second time he had heard Renata Delacross' problem couched in the language of theology rather than psychiatry.

21

CHAPTER FOUR

Although the clinic had been set up primarily to follow chronically ill patients discharged into the community from the state mental hospitals, it accepted everyone who walked in, and the conditions treated there ran the gamut from alcoholism to zelotypia.

Monday morning found the clinic swarming with patients, both scheduled and unscheduled. Wintertime always saw the day's roster of patients swell, just as it would shrink in summer when the homeless-inclined took to living in the streets or traveling to unknown destinations.

The Gotham Psychiatric Clinic served the greater part of Manhattan and was itself divided into three separate divisions, each in turn further subdivided into catchment areas. Cordis was attached to Division III. His clientele numbered lower middle-class apartment dwellers, numerous poor tenement residents, single room occupancy (SRO) patients who had literally taken over a number of hotels in town and some transients.

Before he was able to get started with his own workload, one of the social workers from Division II asked him to see an elderly man she had found on the clinic's doorstep and with the help of several of the clinic's personnel had carried him up in the elevator to the waiting room.

None of the Division II doctors had arrived as yet, so he was asked to take a look at the patient. It was common practice for the doctors and social workers to help out on the other divisions, especially in cases of emergency, such as this one.

"Mrs. Rosenberg, you've got to stop dragging waifs and orphans in from the cold," Cordis chided her playfully, as he walked with the social worker down the corridor designated as Doctors Row toward the waiting room. "We're not an emergency room."

It was an "in" joke, because the clinic had recently been reprimanded by the head office in Albany for handling too many emergencies instead of "concentrating"—the word used in the memo from upstate—on the more familiar work of an outpatient facility, as though the clinic staff had control over such events. 'We might as well be getting orders from Timbuktu,' one staff member had wailed, throwing her hands up in the air, when the notice had arrived. Routine administrative matters were handled from the central office at Gotham State Hospital in uptown Manhattan, which exercised direct daily control over the clinic.

"*Shah!*" said the big, fat social worker. It was Yiddish for 'Quiet!'

"Just do me a favor and see the poor wretch." She was the motherly type.

No one from the clinic staff recognized the man, who only mumbled incoherently in response to questioning. They had propped him up in a chair in the quietest corner of the huge waiting room, with the security guard and a clerical worker on either side of him to keep him from falling onto the floor.

"No identification on him," the burly, black security guard said.

"Phew!" said the clerical worker. "He stinks!"

"What's the matter—you never used your nose before?" Mrs. Rosenberg said, addressing the younger woman. "That's the way winos smell. So what!"

Cordis shone his pocket flashlight into the man's eyes. "His pupils don't react to light," he said. He leaned even closer to the bedraggled, bearded man to whiff his breath.

"He probably has nits," the young clerical worker said nervously, inching away so that now only her fingertips were in contact with him.

"That's not the odor of alcohol," Cordis commented. He whiffed again. "It's not ethanol."

"Do you think he's a druggie?" the guard asked.

"It's methanol," Cordis said. "The man got his hands on some wood alcohol. Probably couldn't find any booze."

"O God!" Mrs. Rosenberg exclaimed. "That can cause blindness."

"Yes, it chews up the optic nerve," Cordis said. "And five ounces of the stuff can kill you unless treated aggressively. We had better call for an ambulance and get him to the E.R."

By this time, the group gathered around had expanded into a small crowd of kibitzing onlookers, including staff members and curious patients.

"Grab a cab and take him to the hospital," a voice offered.

"Call the fire department," came another recommendation.

"Give him first aid," someone suggested.

"What kind of hospital is this," bemoaned a confused patient in the gathering, "that you should let a patient die in your waiting room?"

"Come away, Mr. Santucci," his social worker said. "Come on, it's time for you to see the doctor."

Cordis stepped back from the throng, his eyes casting about for sight of the clinic nurse. "Let's get our nurse here to take his vital signs," he said.

Pete, the security guard, hastened off to find her.

The crowd of onlookers grew larger, blocking entry to Doctors Row. It was well past 9 o'clock, and some of the other psychiatrists had arrived and were trying to see their scheduled patients. One or two of them peeked in to see what was going on. They were so used to such events that, seeing another doctor handling the problem, they went about their own business.

"Okay, break it up," a voice shouted. It was Joe Mansoni, M.S.W., the clinic director. He made his way through the bystanders to the patient. "What's going on here?" he demanded.

"We've got a sick drop-in on our hands," Cordis said. "Looks like methanol poisoning."

"Has anyone called for an ambulance?" he asked. When no one answered he shouted, "Maria, call Beth Israel for an ambulance." The switchboard operator heard him and shouted back, "I'm doing it now!"

"Which unit does he belong to?" Mansoni asked.

Cordis took it upon himself to respond. "He's not registered with the clinic. I sort of inherited him."

"What do we do until the ambulance gets here?" the director asked Cordis.

"Well," Cordis started to answer, "someone can run downstairs to the liquor store across the street for a bottle of booze, preferably vodka."

"What the hell for?" Mansoni asked angrily.

"To try to get the methanol out," Cordis replied. "Standard treatment for methanol ingestion is to start an i.v. drip of alcohol. We're not set up to get alcohol into him intravenously, so at least let's try to administer it via his gullet."

Pete returned with the nurse, who showed herself to be reluctant to get involved in what was going on.

"I won't be able to get him to keep a thermometer in his mouth," she said objectingly. "He'd probably chew it, anyway."

"Death from mercury poisoning sounds more attractive than death from methanol," someone said facetiously.

"All right," bellowed Mansoni, "let's not get frivolous."

The nurse, Miss Jones, was taking the patient's pulse. "Does anyone know who he is," she asked.

"Yeah, he's Danny," one of the social workers chimed in.

"Danny who?" the director asked.

"Danny X," came the response from the same quarter.

"We used D the last time," Miss Jones said. "Let's call this one Edward. He makes the fifth no-name derelict we've had since Halloween." She looked squarely at Cordis and added coldly, "His pulse is eighty-six with occasional premature contractions." She started to walk away.

"What about his blood pressure?" Cordis asked. "Do you plan to

24

take it?" He was annoyed at her indifference.

"I'll get my cuff," she said detachedly, her back to Cordis as she continued walking.

Before she returned and before anyone had acted on Cordis' suggestion to purchase a bottle of vodka, the ambulance arrived and Edward X was carried off on a stretcher.

"You know, Doc," Pete said when the episode was over, "I liked that idea of yours of plying the guy with alcohol to wash out the methanol. Does it really work?"

"It was the best choice at the moment," Cordis answered.

Joe Mansoni was not at all pleased by the incident. A little before noon he rapped loudly on Cordis' door and swung it open before being invited in. Fortunately, Cordis was alone working on a chart; otherwise, there would have been a row—Cordis would not tolerate being embarrassed in front of a patient.

"What the hell were you trying to do out there, encouraging the staff—in front of all the patients—to buy booze for a sick patient?" he yelled. "We're trying to develop an alcohol treatment program and you're advocating its use."

Cordis remained calm. "An intravenous drip of ethanol is what's employed clinically to treat methanol poisoning," he explained. "Alcohol administered by mouth—for a conscious patient who can take fluids p.o., that is, who isn't vomiting—would do as well. The suggestion was offered as a treatment, not as a treat!"

The director was calmer now. "Really?" he said. "You medic guys really prescribe it for methanol?"

"That's right," Cordis said, ignoring the "you medic guys" put-down. "Alcohol—ethanol—is oxidized in the liver to acetaldehyde, just as methanol is broken down into formaldehyde and then formic acid. It's the formaldehyde and the formic acid that cause the toxic amblyopia, the blindness, and quite often death. The biochemical rationale is to block the methanol from going to formaldehyde, and you do this by forcing ethanol to compete with methanol for the enzyme alcohol dehydrogenase which they both need for metabolism. The more acetaldehyde you can produce, the less formaldehyde you generate. And then you merely blow off the methanol."

"Blow off?"

"Yes, breathe out. Exhale. The portal of exit for methanol is the mouth or nose—the stuff is coming up from the lungs."

The director went away satisfied that the doctor was not sabotaging his alcohol program. Cordis, however, was irritated. It was incidents like

25

this one—and there had been a number of them involving the director in the 1½ years the psychiatrist had been with the clinic—that was making the job distasteful for him.

Cordis saw the issue from an historical perspective. The Joint Commission on Mental Illness and Health had published a turning-point report, *Action for Mental Health*, in 1961, which was critical of the outmoded state hospital system and recommended a program stressing treatment in the community. The Kennedy Administration got Congress to pass Public Law 88-164, the Community Mental Health Act, in 1963, but the act had a fundamental flaw. It allowed for nonmedical staff—social workers, psychologists, nurses—to serve as directors of clinics in areas where psychiatrists were not available: rural locations. There was no shortage of psychiatrists in New York, but an opening had been found for nonphysicians to become heads of community mental health clinics (CMHC's). The irony of it all was that the state system had adopted the federal philosophy, so now even the Gotham Psychiatric Clinic had a social worker as its director.

The act had another flaw: financing. Just as soon as he assumed office, Nixon started phasing out federal suppost of mental illness. On the other hand, the New York State system was still flourishing in 1973, but cracks were beginning to show in its financial structure.

Community mental health clinics had started out as medical facilities, but were steadily being converted into nonmedical centers staffed by so-called mental health professionals. For Cordis there was a special meaning in being a physician, and to be called a mental health professional was a denigration. When they gave him his diploma and called him "Doctor" for the first time in 1965, he had entered the hallowed profession of Hippocrates, Avicenna and Maimonides.

At the Gotham Psychiatric Clinic the doctors were slowly but surely dwindling in numbers. Their utility, as far as the powers that be were concerned, was in having them sign prescriptions. The mental health professionals were taking over the task of doing psychotherapy, whether they were properly trained or not. Most of the psychiatrists at the "Soho House of Madness," as some called the clinic, were psychoanalysts working part-time, and they couldn't care less. They did their share of psychotherapy elsewhere, in their private offices.

Joe Mansoni was trying to come up with a name for the clinic which would disassociate it from its medical moorings. At a meeting of the staff just to discuss a name change, he had proposed 'The Refuge.' "Why not 'The Asylum,'" one of the psychoanalysts had suggested sardonically. "It's a synonym for refuge," he had added sophistically. The Mansoni forces had had to retreat from the meeting, but the doctors knew they were only staving off the inevitable.

In the afternoon, Cordis saw another alcohol-related problem. An old medical saw states that rare cases of a disease usually come in two's and three's. The very first two patients Cordis had examined as a medical student in 1961 suffered from syringomyelia, a rare disease of the spinal cord. He was yet to see another patient with syringomyelia.

The patient now before him was a middle-aged lady with a long history of alcohol abuse. She was a Division III patient, but she was not scheduled to be seen that day: she was a walk-in. Actually, she had staggered in, according to Pete's account, and he had had to carry her to Cordis' office.

"I've seen Sarah Kay drunk before," he said to Cordis shaking his head, "but never this bad."

The woman sat limp in the chair where she had been placed, her head bent forward.

"Sarah," Cordis said. "Sarah, this is Dr. Cordis." He lifted up her head so that he could see her eyes. She smelled of cheap wine, and her eyes remained closed. "Open 'em up, Sarah," Cordis continued coaxing. "Come on, Sarah, you're at the Gotham Psychiatric Clinic, on the second floor of the Pyramid Building, and you just came up in the elevator."

"Wha'? Wha'?" she mumbled, straining her facial features.

"That's right. Open up your ocular windows to the outside world."

"Who . . . who?" she mumbled, peering at him through her half-opened eyes.

"Dr. Cordis, I'm Dr. Cordis."

"Dr. Cordis," she said feebly, recognizing him and reaching out to touch his chest with an emaciated hand.

"Yes, you know me." She nodded weakly, patting him several times. "Do you know where you are?"

"Clinic, I'm at the clinic," she said slowly.

"And how did you get here?"

"Elevator."

"That's right. And our security guard here helped you get to my office."

"Hello, Sarah," Pete said warmly.

"Pete?" Sarah said.

"Yeah, you got my name right," Pete said. "You recognize me." Pete had gone off briefly to get a wash cloth and now he washed her face.

Sarah nodded. Her eyes were wide open, and Cordis could see her eyeballs darting back and forth ceaselessly, and she was unable to get them to follow his upright held finger as he moved it slowly in front of her.

"Pete," he said, "we've got another medical emergency on our hands. I'm going over to the pharmacy."

"Sure, Doc," the guard said. "Do you want me to get something for you there?"

"No, I had better take care of this personally. You just make sure Sarah doesn't fall out of that chair and fracture her skull or something."

The clinic dispensed its own medication free of charge, and the R.N. did double duty, also functioning as the pharmacist. Cordis didn't approve of the arrangement, because by law only someone with an R.Ph. degree was authorized to dole out medicine.

He had trouble with Miss Jones, who was more interested in the next beauty contest she was entering than in doing the work of the clinic. She was young, attractive and intelligent, but her main asset was that she was Mansoni's favorite, perhaps as some gossiped, his mistress. Whatever the relationship, she could do no wrong.

"Do we have any parenteral thiamine, Miss Jones?" Cordis asked in a no-nonsense tone. He was in no mood for another one of her passive-aggressive displays.

She saw the serious look on his face and heard it in his voice. "I think we do," she answered politely. "Yes, I think we do." She started looking through her drawers.

"Give Sarah Kay, who's in my office with Pete, one hundred milligrams i.m. Stat."

"Yes, here it is," she said, holding up a vial.

"Good, get right to it."

Cordis returned to his office. He looked at the somnolent figure of Sarah Kay, and shaking his head in a sign of despair said to Pete, "She needs to be hospitalized. Let's call for an ambulance."

"Again? Two in one day?"

"Yup, again."

"All right, but the brass don't like this—you docs practicing medicine in this social service club," Pete said in mock derision. He picked up Cordis' receiver and relayed the order to the switchboard operator.

Miss Jones came in, carrying a syringe and a thermometer in one hand and her blood pressure cuff in the other.

"I'll need her to lean over on her side in order to get this into her buttock," she said.

"Never mind the gluteal route," Cordis said. "Use the deltoid. And mark the time."

28

It was 1:30. What could be done for Sarah in an outpatient psychiatric clinic setting had been done. The rest would be up to the hospital medical and nursing staffs.

"Temp is ninety-six four and B.P. a hundred over sixty," Miss Jones said.

"A little hypothermic," Cordis commented. "Not unexpected."

"What's going on with her, anyway?" the nurse inquired.

"Wernicke's encephalopathy," he answered. "She's got a lateral nystagmus, gaze paralysis and an ataxic gait. The classic picture."

"O my Gosh!" she exclaimed.

"In her favor," Cordis continued explaining, "there's no evidence of an impairment in her memory, retentive memory. In other words, she doesn't have Korsakoff's."

Cordis and Pete supported Sarah between them and moved her to the nursing station, where they stretched her out on a cot. She seemed oblivious to what was happening to her.

"How serious is her condition?" Pete asked, observing the slumbering form.

"Plenty serious," the doctor responded, also eying the patient. "She could suffer some permanent brain tissue damage. Wernicke's syndrome—cerebral beriberi—is grief enough, and even if she recovers from it, she can still go on to develop Korsakoff's syndrome—a kind of brain damage that prevents the registration of new memories in the mind."

"Jeez!" said Pete, and he let out a low whistle. "And the injection she got, is that gonna help?"

"I gave her a hundred milligrams of thiamine," Miss Jones offered.

"It's vitamin B_1," Cordis said. "It's the antidote for Wernicke's, and she's going to have it poured into her."

"How much do you have in mind?" Pete asked.

"For nutritional purposes," Cordis started to say, "the body only requires a milligram or two of thiamine a day. She's going to get a hundred milligrams every hour."

Cordis had half a dozen scheduled patients to see that afternoon, and he found himself moving back and forth between his office and the nursing station for the next hour. At 2:30 he had Miss Jones give Sarah a second 100-milligram injection of thiamine hydrochloride, and shortly after that the ambulance attendants arrived.

"This is getting to be a regular milk run for us," one of them said.

"Here," Cordis responded, handing him an envelope containing a writeup of his findings and standby treatment. "Make sure the doctor treating Sarah Kay reads this. It's my report."

Cordis saw three more patients, each in for a Prolixin decanoate injection. Prolixin is one of the major tranquilizer drugs, or neuroleptics, used to treat schizophrenia, and for those patients who are too unreliable with pills there is the decanoate form, a special preparation which, by being released slowly into the blood, works for 2-3 weeks.

His last patient of the day was George, a young man suffering primarily from auditory hallucinations: he heard voices—those of his dead parents—coming from a pair of cockroaches he kept under glass. His landlady found him in his room one evening prostrated before two jars, each with a cockroach, muttering prayers all through the night. The following morning he was still at it, so she called his family, who had him readmitted to Gotham State Hospital for the fifth time in six years. He could function in the community as long as he stayed on his medication, but his compliance was poor, which invariably led to a relapse. He was the type of patient who did better on the long-acting injectable form of Prolixin.

"We've stretched it out to twenty-five milligrams every three weeks," Cordis said cheerfully. "You're doing just great."

As long as George could perform his ADL's, activities of daily living, i.e., brush his teeth, change his clothes, attend to his meals, et cetera, the staff at the SRO hotel where he was now living didn't mind listening to his talk about cockroaches, but they wouldn't let him keep any in his room.

"Do you want to see my cockroaches, Dr. Cordis?" he asked.

"Not really," came the doctor's reply. "I thought you weren't allowed to have them where you're living."

"They're dead cockroaches. I pickled 'em."

"How many do you have?"

"Two. One in each jar—one for my mother and one for my father."

"What are they saying to you?" Cordis asked, the critical question.

"Nothin'. They're dead. They can't talk."

As long as the medication kept the voices at bay, Cordis was not about to try to strip George of his roach fetish.

Between patients, Cordis bumped into Dr. Brown in the corridor. He, along with Cordis, was the only other nonpsychoanalyst among the psychiatrists at the clinic, and like Cordis was medically oriented, although both did psychodynamic psychotherapy in their private practices.

The encounter gave Cordis the chance to engage in some "pure" doctor talk with his colleague, something he rarely had the opportunity to do in that setting. They discussed Sarah's encephalopathy—the ophthalmoplegia, or paralysis of the eye muscles, she presented, her ataxia explainable as a lesion in the superior cerebeller vermis, and how the enzyme transketolase binds its cofactor, thiamine, less effectively in patients with Wernicke's disease, probably determined on a genetic basis, making some people more vulnerable to this biochemical disorder than others — five minutes of hallway psychotherapy to reaffirm for them their identity as physicians.

Cordis tried several times to reach the doctor treating Sarah, and it was not until a few minutes before 5:00 that a Dr. Ehrlenberger returned his calls.

"Thank you for the detailed note," Dr. Ehrlenberger said. He was a first-year resident in internal medicine at the NYU School of Medicine.

"Keep up the thiamine, whatever you do," Cordis said commandingly. The nystagmus may clear up early, misleading you into believing that you've pulled her through. If you stop thiamine prematurely, she's a sure candidate to go on to develop a Korsakoff's."

"I'll keep it flowing."

"I had that happen to me when I was a psychiatric resident at Big Charity in New Orleans. The internists thought my patient didn't have a Wernicke's because she didn't have nystagmus when they first examined her, so they discontinued thiamine treatment. Well, the next day they saw it, but it was too late. The patient recovered, but her mind was a blank."

"I'll follow your outline," said Dr. Ehrlenberger. "Big Charity? Is that the famous Charity Hospital of Louisiana that Huey P. Long built in the thirties?"

"The very same."

Dr. Ehrlenberger now sounded animated. "My father interned there in the forties! He used to refer to it as Mother Charity."

"Some of the patients called it that—those who had been born there."

The reference to Charity Hospital lit a spark.

"Don't worry, Dr. Cordis, I'm going to take good care of your Sarah Kay."

Cordis found that the personal touch was an effective bonding agent, and even in New York's oversized and overworked hospitals, it often led to some good where his patients were concerned. Now he could smile inwardly and say to himself, It's dinner time.

CHAPTER FIVE

Renata Delacross was late for her appointment the following day. Cordis sat at his desk leafing through a volume of Jung's works dealing with his concept of synchronicity. Whereas Freud believed in psychic determinism, suggesting that actions were always explainable through unconscious causality, Jung favored an acausal principle that linked human events by their coincidence in time and not in some sequential or necessarily logical fashion.

Is this Renata woman's sudden appearance upon the scene—how shall I put it?—Jungian? he asked himself. Other patients come to therapy through usual channels, but Renata Delacross comes not as a stranger but as the godchild of my oldest friend.

He switched to A.M. Hamilton's *Recollections of an Alienist*, opening to the page where he had left off the previous week.

Does she really tie into that strange dream I had? he continued pondering. Do these events belong to the realm of—do I dare use the word?—the numinous?

He started reading, and in the process his elbow accidentally shoved what looked like a note sheet onto the floor, which he retrieved. It was a condolence card, beautifully but simply designed with a brief message of sympathy printed in ideogramic Japanese as well as in English. It had been sent to Harris by a friend upon the death of his father in 1971, who had succumbed to a heart attack. Under the lettering his friend had added a written message: "No Man in his sphere, has left fewer enemies or more friends." The friend attributed the quotation to one "Jonas Green in the *Maryland Gazette*." Harris had wanted Cordis to have it when he recognized his friend's deep sorrow following the death of his mother a few months after his own father's passing.

Cordis had come across the name of Jonas Green while reading about Dr. Alexander Hamilton (not the Alexander Hamilton who had been George Washington's Secretary of the Treasury). This Hamilton was a pre-Revolutionary War figure who achieved fame in his day for a remarkable journey he made from Annapolis to faraway York in what is now Maine, which he described in a celebrated book of the 1740's called *The Itinerarium*. It was a time when overland journeys of such a scope were remarkable adventures simply for being undertaken and completed.

What Dr. Alexander Hamilton had witnessed on his trip to the north was the ending of medieval class structure and the beginnings of the liberation of the common man. In the 18th century, people belonged to one of three ranks in Colonial America: the better sort, the gentry; the middling sort, yeoman farmers and artisans; and the inferior sort, black slaves, indentured servants, laborers and sailors. As he progressed northward, Hamilton observed less and less subordination of inferiors to superiors, and he conceded that the people of Boston were more civilized than his own in the southern parts.

That was pre-America then, Cordis mused. Now it's turning into a two-layered society: the White Anglo-Saxon Protestants, dwindling in numbers, whose European forebears created the United States of America out of Colonial America, and the fast-growing *minorities* so-called, dominated, curiously, by a majority group: women.

Recently the city had put out a call for construction workers—for minorities. Irish-Americans, Jewish-Americans and Polish-Americans were excluded from consideration, for they were now lumped in with the WASP's. "Such is the new American mentality," Cordis muttered half-aloud.

He was drumming his fingers on Hamilton's *Recollections of an Alienist*. This Hamilton—Allan McLane Hamilton—stemmed from a distinguished line. His grandfather was Alexander Hamilton, Washington's cabinet member. His maternal grandfather was Louis McLane, Ambassador to the Court of St. James during the administration of President Andrew Jackson. McLane's personal secretary in London was Washington Irving of *Sleepy Hollow* fame. Later McLane became Jackson's Secretary of the Treasury and then Secretary of State. His paternal grandmother, the widow of Alexander Hamilton, used to read letters from Dolly Madison to him when he was a boy—he was born in 1848, when the country was at war with Mexico. His older brother, a captain in the Seventh U.S. Cavalry, was killed in a raid on Red Kettle's band in Wichita during November, 1868. General George Custer wrote of his death: " . . . he has gone where there are neither wars nor rumors of wars, where the soldier is at rest and all is peace."

George Custer wrote as well as his friends, Generals Lew Wallace and Ulysses S. Grant, Cordis thought. The 19th century was a literate time in American history . . . All these Hamiltons. Hmm. And then Jonas Green . . . who ties in with Harris . . . And there's George Washington and Washington Irving . . . Synchronicity at work. Of course, the slide-rule-carrying scientists would have us believe that there are billions of coincidences occurring all the time throughout the universe. What an unimaginative way to view the human experience!

33

The phone rang at 8:30.

"We've decided not to continue Renata's treatment with you," came the harsh voice of Celine Delacross. "We'll find another doctor for her."

"I'm sorry to hear that," Cordis said, struggling to keep calm. "May I ask how Renata feels about this decision?"

"No, you may not!" Mrs. Delacross answered angrily. "This is a family issue. It is neither discussable nor negotiable. Do not worry. You will be paid for your time," she added, hanging up.

Cordis stared at the silent receiver for a moment and then got a dial tone. Quietly, he dialed Harris' number.

"I will be gone today. Please leave your name, message and date of your call after the beep. You have thirty seconds. Sayonara."

Cordis smiled, knowing it to be one of Harris' cryptographic messages. He hung up and dialed again. This time he wrote the message down verbatim, careful to underline stresses and inflections.

'I will be gone today.' Six syllables, stress on the word 'will.' The closing word, 'Sayonara,' with its four syllables, was comically pronounced.

"Okay, Harris," Cordis whispered to himself. "let's see what you're about." The six syllables of the first sentence gave him the number *six* which, in the Furst mnemonic code, corresponded to the letter *J*. So, he's gone to Japan. By stressing the word 'will,' Harris was indicating that he would be gone for 'w' eeks. The four syllables in 'sayonara' indicated that he would be gone *four* weeks. "Too bad," he said aloud. "I would have liked your input on this one."

The next afternoon, Edith Delacross phoned him at the clinic. "I was outvoted, outshouted and outraged by the anti-Jewish forces in the house," she blurted out.

"My concern is solely for the patient," he responded.

"I'm sorry to say that Renata is no longer your patient."

He could hear Edith sigh at that point. "That is a fact of life," she added.

Cordis hid his disappointment. "What's next for her?"

"I don't know. I really don't. Celine and our family physician will most likely find another psychiatrist, a Catholic psychiatrist as in the past, for her."

"Is that the way you do it?" he said wryly. "You pick 'em by religious affiliation?" He managed to keep his tone level.

"That and other factors were considered," Edith said simply in response. "In any case, that is that. Thank you, Doctor, for your time and interest." Her voice had turned suddenly cold. "Good-by and good luck."

The following Tuesday, January 23rd, Cordis discovered an en-

34

velope under the door to his office waiting room which contained the fact sheet he had given Renata Delacross at the conclusion of their first and only meeting together.

"I see Renata doesn't consider the matter closed," he mused aloud. He noted her signature and the current date at the bottom of the sheet. "She's still crying out for help from me." He sighed. "But my hands are tied, lady of the Maghreb. They want a Catholic shrink for you. Someone to squeeze you down to recognizable dimensions and strip you of that precious individuality which is your greatest birthright."

Suddenly, he recalled something Edith Delacross had said to him during their first telephone conversation. She had referred to Renata as a fallen-away Catholic, one who hadn't been to mass in fourteen years. Similia similibus curantur. Like is cured by like. A Catholic for a Catholic. Only she is no longer a professing Catholic. He shook his head several times and threw up his hands in a gesture of disgust.

The phone rang as he was getting ready to leave the office. It was Fr. Dominic.

"How is your patient doing, the one who came to you when you had your unusual dream?"

"She's gone. The family decided she should see someone else. A Catholic psychiatrist."

His tone was clearly censorious, and Fr. Dominic had no difficulty picking it up. "I'm sorry to hear that," he said softly.

There was a pause, and Cordis, changing the subject, said, "I wonder if we should really be trying to attach any special significance to those numbers—three, seven, nine—in the Cologne street address from that dream I had. One can get carried away . . . maybe too far. For instance, Antje Haag had lived in Cologne, but I don't connect her to the dream."

Fr. Dominic recognized that Cordis was attempting to dissociate Renata Delacross from the dream, something he himself had linked together only moments earlier.

"There's numerological gibberish, of course," the priest started to say, "and then there's the hidden meaning in numbers, on occasion, coming up from the great ocean of the unconscious, as you very well know. Don't abandon Jung so quickly because of a momentary setback."

"It's more than a momentary setback," Cordis intoned. "She's no longer my patient."

"For the moment," Fr. Dominic stressed. "If this patient has come to you through the numinous, then Jung, the spiritually oriented doctor of the mind, should remain your guide. And I do not believe for a moment that you have heard the last of this young lady."

Cordis reflected on what he had just heard. "Thanks, padre, for your comforting and inspiring words." Jokingly, he added, "My check for your psychotherapeutic services will be in the mail!"

CHAPTER SIX

The practicing physician is locked into a one-to-one relationship with humanity. He gives five minutes or fifty minutes or a greater amount of time to his patient, depending upon the nature of the problem. Whatever his own religious affiliation, he is constantly renewing what the sages of the Talmud proclaimed: "He who saves a life, it is as though he has saved all of mankind." These words remain at the core of the physician's dealings with his fellow man.

Even at the dickensian Gotham Psychiatric Clinic in the very bowels of Manhattan Island, where the depths of despair, mental derangement, deprivation and bureaucratic-fostered degradation heaped upon an already overburdened patient population plummet to grotesque lows, the act of salvation occurs more often than happenstance would have it.

Late Friday afternoon, February 2nd, Joey Dee popped up at the clinic. He had to wait a while until Cordis could see him, since he was unscheduled and the doctor had two other scheduled patients ahead of him. Joey had been diagnosed as schizophrenic six years earlier when he was 17, and by this time he was well known to the clinic staff. He sat quietly in the smoke-filled waiting room, waiting patiently, for time held no meaning for him.

His clothes were wrinkled, tattered in places and dirty, his face bore a week's growth of beard at least, and he smelled like he hadn't had a bath in a month.

"Please don't be angry wit' me, Dr. Cordis," he pleaded, flashing an incongruous smile. It was a typical opener for him. "You didn't gimme 'nough med'cin last time, so I gotta come back," he added. "You're not angry wit' me, are you, Dr. Cordis?"

Although the psychiatrist had seen him the week before and had prescribed a month's supply of haloperidol, another one of the antipsy-

36

chotic agents, for him, Joey was out of medication again, typical of him. Cordis had to repeat several times that he was not angry over his unannounced clinic visit and untimely need for more pills.

"The clinic is open to serve its patients, those who come on time and those who come any time," Cordis said reassuringly.

Joey's guilt was mollified. "T'anks," he said.

With that matter out of the way, Joey proceeded with a ritualistic offering he had developed: handing his doctor six oranges and three BIC pens. This was a pattern he had established during his five previous sessions with Cordis. Cordis now thanked him on behalf of the clinic for his gifts, which he would turn over to a member of the staff. When Joey first learned that his doctor didn't keep his oranges and pens, he took it as a mark of rejection. "They raffle off your gifts in the day center," the doctor had told him. "It's all for a worthy cause, and you've become a local celebrity to the patients over there. They want to meet you." It would go no further, for Joey did not mingle with people. His offering to Cordis was the unsure hand of a very sick mind reaching out for friendship. No one could tell when he would be ready to hold out both hands and to more than one individual. Cordis would not try to hurry him out of the dereistic world he had occupied for so long.

Joey now launched into a monomaniacal verbal junket which was to monopolize the remainder of the session. "Four is a magic number," he began. "Like in Aristot's t'eory o' da four elements." He had a way of sounding like Lenny, the gargantuan, dim-witted protagonist in John Steinbeck's Of Mice and Men. However, Joey's was not a case of mental retardation. On the contrary, he was slightly above average in intelligence, and until mental illness had forced him to quit high school in his junior year, he had been a star pupil. He was indeed familiar with some of Aristotle's writings, despite his reference to him as Aristot. The mispronunciation is an example of schizophrenic metonymy, the use of approximate but related words in place of more precise and definite terms. "You know Aristot's four elements?" he asked.

"Earth, fire, air and water," Cordis rattled off without giving the matter much thought. Then he wondered if wood or iron should have been listed in place of one of the others.

"Yeah, you know 'em!" Joey bellowed. "Eart, fur, ear an' woder." His pronunciation didn't quite echo what the doctor just said. In this instance it wasn't a matter of metonymy—Joey's maternal language was deep Brooklynese.

"All dem Greeks had four eminents," Joey emphasized.

Eminents instead of elements? In the non-schizophrenic world this

37

would be interpreted as a malapropism, but in Joey's schizophrenese it was nothing out of the ordinary.

"Eminently correct," said Cordis. "They had four elements." With Joey assuming a self-satisfied pose, as though he had uttered an ultimate profundity, Cordis decided to challenge him. "The Chinese had five . . . elements," he said.

"Da Chinese had five," Joey said slowly and carefully. Unruffled, he continued firmly, "Yeah, but even da Indian Buddhists had a system of da eminents more like da Greeks wit' four. Da penta-ementalism o' da Chinese was da exception. Four and t'ree are da magic numbers o' da universe. When da Paracelsians gave up da four classical elements, dey substituted da *tria prima*."

For a few moments Cordis didn't move a muscle. Finally, he sat up straight, arms akimbo, and stared at Joey, trying to take in all that he had just heard. No one, he said to himself, but no one, patients or staff, walks into the Gotham Psychiatric Clinic and starts talking about penta-elementalism and the Paracelsians.

For the sake of the purist, Joey had committed only one metonymic mispronunciation—he had left out part of penta-*e*lementalism.

"What about the *tria prima?*" Cordis probed.

"Salt, sulfer an' mercury," he responded, thinking his doctor was testing him and never suspecting that he might not know what they were.

The Paracelsians may have been close to Carl Jung's heart, alchemist scholar that he had been, but Cordis was not about to become involved in an alchemical dialogue. Nevertheless, he felt it necessary to respond to Joey's train of thought.

"Well, my young scholar," he said, "the Greeks could only associate their elements with the planets, whereas the ancient Chinese had a more elaborate system of symbolic correlations, linking the elements with specific organs of the body. That these could counterbalance each other and be generated from one another were workable ideas they incorporated into their system of medical knowledge."

What he said sounded impressive, even though it was a bit of verbal sidewinding.

Joey was not put off by his little spiel, not for a moment. Unperturbed, he came right back with his number four concept, this time with the four humours of the ancient Greeks: blood, corresponding to air; yellow bile, to fire; black bile, to earth; and phlegm, to water. The four elements were still pronounced in Joey's inimitable manner. What surprised, even amazed, Cordis was the ease with which he disseminated the information, as though he were discussing something as commonplace as

38

basketball.

Cordis' response to Joey's discourse on the four humours was a mumbled, barely audible, "Oie, yoie, yoie."

Although Joey was showing himself to be knowledgeable far beyond Cordis' prior assessment, the doctor wondered if his paradoxical display of intellectuality was goal-directed or just random.

Now Joey explained how these humours were connected with the liver, gallbladder, spleen and lungs, respectively. Here I will spare the reader a repetition of this fascinating yet tedious mishmash. In all fairness, it should be noted how well Joey did in countering Cordis' bit about the ancient Chinese with their symbolic correlations.

"Healt' depends on da right balance o' da four humours," he said, not so much in summation but as though he had put his finger on the very pulse of the universe.

Cordis was about to say something like, 'Thank you, Professor Aristotle,' or 'We now know a little more concerning health than the theory of the four humours,' when Joey began in again with the number three, that is, "t'ree."

He gave Cordis the theory of the three primary vitalistics which the Taoists had developed during the Europeans' Middle Ages. These vitalistics Joey referred to as three essences: *ch'i*, *ching* and *shen*. Cordis recalled that he cited the last-mentioned as mental essence, but he missed what he had to say about the other two, which he garbled in his metonymic manner. Cordis was familiar with *ch'i* as the vital energy or life force of the acupuncturists, but he didn't want to go off on that tangent with Joey.

Theoretically, Joey's current verbal productions fitted in well with his recent cultivation of medieval European mysticism ersatzed with Eastern religion. What surprised Cordis was the finesse with which he delivered it all, seemingly inconsistent with the severity of his mental illness, which prevented him from saying hello to anyone else in the clinic. Out of step with what he had to say was how he said it: his speech pattern was decisively moronic-like.

Soon Joey got on to the fundamental forces in the natural philosophy of the Chinese pervading the universe, Yin and Yang: female and male, darkness and light, wet and dry, cold and hot. "Disease is a consequence o' da imbalance between da two forces in da body, an' da doctor must help da patient restore nature's equilibrium," he said, with a wisp of Oriental sagacity.

Pari passu, from a psychoanalytic point of view both doctor and patient were in *resonance*, which could account for Joey's fluency in session and non-communication when out of session.

Cordis now had to respond to the deeper communication or to the one Joey presented on the conscious level, and at that moment the psychiatrist chose the latter. He nodded appreciatively, realizing that his own professor of medicine couldn't have closed out a lecture with more grace. Then he contributed a few appropriately selected words by the noted British biochemist F.G. Hopkins: " 'Life is a dynamic equilibrium in a polyphasic system.' "

The discussion had moved from Joey's philosophical ruminating to Cordis' epigrammatic distillate taken from the realm of basic science; and even though Joey couldn't grasp the full meaning of the epigram, he seemed to grasp its essence with the intellectual apparatus at his command.

"Da Chinese developed numerology to da level ob an exact science," he said, after a short silence, picking up where he left off.

Although Cordis enjoyed mulling over such Chinese concepts as the unity of the spiritual and corporeal worlds, yin-yang balance, and the macrocosm-microcosm approach to the universe, he was not prepared to place Joey's views on numerology in the same domain as mathematics, the ultimate and utilitarian tool of science.

"Numerology is at best a figure of a good imagination," he said, pleased with the metaphor he had delivered.

"Joey smiled and asked, "Dr. Cordis, wha' about my med'cin?"

His question was not a non sequitur nor a schizophrenic detour. For the moment Joey was content, perhaps dazzled or overwhelmed, by what and how much he had said so far in the session.

The clinic was primarily a medication clinic for discharged hospital patients, and the amount of psychotherapeutic work done depended upon the outpatient's tolerance and the physician's time. Some patients came only for their medication and could not tolerate even five minutes of talk, while others were suited for a fifty-minute hour. The limiting factor was the unpredictable number of daily drop-ins, both unscheduled and emergency patients, who would cut into the scheduled patients' time. Others came on the right day but would drop in at any hour, again throwing the timetable off. The general inability of many of the patients to handle time was part and parcel of their mental and emotional state. But then again, even people who are normal or healthy will play their special games with time as a psychological ploy.

Medicating Joey was a never-ending problem. He had been discharged from Gotham State Hospital on Haldol, Taractan, Thorazine, Stelazine, Valium and Cogentin. Cordis was opposed to polypharmacy, prescribing more than one psychotropic drug from any one class. Combining Haldol, Taractan, Thorazine and Stelazine constituted polypharmacy. At first he had tried to maintain Joey on Haldol plus Cogentin, an anti-parkinsonian agent which holds in check some of the side-effects patients can develop to antipsychotic medication. But Joey was never satisfied with the doctor prescribing only one major tranquilizer, and constantly asked, actually begged, him to prescribe Taractan in addition. When it came to discussing medication, the adult in Joey would vanish, and what would come out sounded like a whining child. "Please, Dr. Cordis, please, please gimme Tractan," he would say, unable to pronounce Taractan. "I need Tractan an' Hadall," he would add, unable to pronounce Haldol either.

Cordis would repeat over and over that there was no indication for using this particular combination of what were in effect potent medications. One or the other was sufficient, but Joey would continue to whine for both of them. Since he never took his pills according to the schedule prescribed, Cordis wanted to put him on the injectable Prolixin decanoate, but Joey always resisted the suggestion. The doctor brought it up again on this occasion, which only made his patient angry and excited. His huge frame jumped right out of the chair, and his bulky body headed for the door, clenched fists flailing the air menacingly.

"No, sir, nobody's gonna inject me," he howled. "I'm no reject to be inject. Injections are for rejections wit' infections."

This was an outburst of metonymic distortion. Here he was employing clang equivalence with a rather bizarre form of coded word rhyming.

"Where did you get the idea you are being rejected?" Cordis calmly asked him.

"Please, Dr. Cordis, gimme da Tractan an' Hadall," he pleaded, stopping in his tracks. "It won't hurt you ta give 'em ta me."

This was his statement that injections hurt *him*, that he didn't want to be hurt physically as well as emotionally. Then he clarified his reference to infection.

"I didn't get V.D. from da prostitute," he said penitently.

"Well, we've already gone over that ground," Cordis said, "and we determined the only thing you contracted was pubic lice, which we treated successfully."

During a previous session Joey had talked about his fears of having contracted syphilis from a hooker he had shared a third-rate hotel room with for ten minutes. He hadn't escaped scot-free, for he did pick up a case of pediculosis.

"Lice was da price o' my vice," he rhymed. "But you zeroed in on da lice and fractioned dem."

Joey's thinking was getting quite loose, but Cordis could sense the direction he was taking. A more appropriate word for Joey to have used for "fractioned" would have been "fractured," meaning wiped out. His use of two mathematical terms, zero and fractions, moved Cordis to say, "What it adds up to is this. The price, in round numbers, for over-the-counter sex is too high."

"Da price is too high?" Joey said quizzically, now returning to his seat.

"Right," Cordis said reassuringly. He got the feeling he was on the right track. Joey had mathematized his language, so develop the theme further. Trying to make use of the mathematician's concept of whole numbers, he continued, "You wanted a piece of *tochis* when in fact you were really looking for a whole woman who would help make you whole. A wholesome woman."

He had used the Yiddish word for "ass."

Joey sat with a forefinger pressed against his chin. After a few moments he asked, "How will I find her? Girls don't like me, Dr. Cordis. I don't move in circles where dere are nice girls."

Joey spoke native Brooklynese, as already stated, but he didn't say the expected "goils"—he could pronounce "girls."

"What you are now asking is a function of time, place and of chance," Cordis responded. "One day you will find a woman and she will help make you whole."

"Da last time I stuck my neck into a hole I got lice," Joey said.

"You didn't get nuchal lice," Cordis came back, "but pubic lice, so you didn't use your neck. There's a price to pay when you dip your wick in dirty waters—you got off easy."

"Everybody's got a girl except me," Joey wailed.

"Not everybody," Cordis responded. "When it comes to finding the right woman, every man is on his own."

"I'll never find one on my own."

"Sure you will, pal. There are places where you can meet women, and that's how it begins. Go to a dance, visit a museum, attend a party, take a boat ride—"

"A boat ride!" Joey let out. "Dat's a terrific idea, Dr. Cordis. I always wanted ta go on da Circle Line aroun' New York."

"Go on the Circle Line around New York then," Cordis said.

"I bet I can find a nice girl on da Circle Line!" Joey exclaimed. His face beamed and even his yellow-stained teeth seemed to glitter for a moment. "T'anks, Dr. Cordis. You're a good man. You're my friend, Dr. Cordis."

Cordis thought of Erik Erikson's psychosocial schema of development, framed as the Eight Ages of Man. The first, the oral-sensory, equivalent in time and substance to Freud's oral stage, centers around the issues of trust versus mistrust. Its successful resolution leads to trust, whereas failure at this level breeds mistrust. Joey had failed to navigate his way successfully through that first stage, and ever since has been in deep water, as everything else backed up.

As for his medication, Cordis decided on a compromise. Breaking his rule on polypharmacy, he prescribed Thorazine and Stelazine, a combination of antipsychotic drugs popular with a number of psychiatrists at that time. It seemed a realistic compromise. Joey was insisting on two major tranquilizers, and he appeared to accept the two his doctor now offered hm. He did, however, make one more feebly voiced plea for "Hadall" and "Tractan," but did swallow his day's dose of Thorazine and Stelazine in Cordis' presence—the doctor wanted to make sure his patient got started back on neuroleptic medication before leaving the clinic. Cordis scheduled him for an appointment in a week's time—routine would have been a month—to monitor him more closely.

When Joey left the clinic that afternoon, his thinking seemed somewhat improved, his mood was one of rare buoyancy for him, and his ruminative insistence for Haldol and Taractan was held in check. For Cordis the session's success, and he saw it as a successful one, revolved around a series of linguistic associations falling into place. The thought linkages were: wholesome (woman)—whole (unity)—hole (vagina)—circle (unity). Joey had promptly transposed boat ride into Circle Line. A line once curved and continued will eventually form a complete circle. The circle is the symbol of Joey's prime concern: that total unity of the self is achievable, or that his current fragmented ego can be made whole. Hole and zero are also symbolic representations of the circle. Joey was dabbling in mysticism at the moment, and at one point in a previous session had brought up the name of Jung. It was the Age of Aquarius, and Jung was enjoying something of a renaissance, with his books on sale in bookstores everywhere in Manhattan. Cordis had helped Joey see the magic circle of Jung, the mandala, symbol of the totality of the Self, if but for a fleeting moment.

CHAPTER SEVEN

Cordis' private practice was growing steadily, and he had to add Monday evenings to his already busy schedule. He was expecting a new patient at 7:00 p.m. on Monday, February 12th, an Orthodox Jew who had rejected a Saturday appointment because he kept "the sabbath holy," as he had explained to Cordis several days earlier over the telephone.

He had been deliberately noninformative, or minimally informative, making it difficult for the psychiatrist to decide in his own mind if he wanted to offer the caller an appointment at all.

When Cordis had asked him what his problem was, he had answered with one word, "Depression." Cordis had tried to find out who had referred him, and he had answered, "The County Medical Society." Cordis' question, "How old are you?" had elicited the incomplete response, "In my late fifties." "Do you have a name?" Cordis had asked wryly. "Chaim Cohen," the caller had replied.

This guy is just name, rank and serial number, Cordis had said to himself. Not my kind of patient. But if the County Medical Society gave him my name and phone number, I had better see him at least once.

Cordis had been put off by Cohen's communicated hostility and verbal parsimony, but nevertheless had patiently proceeded to the next step: "What's your home phone number, please?"

"I'll call you if I can't keep my appointment."

"And I would have to call you if I must for any reason change your appointment," Cordis had retorted. With that Chaim Cohen had surrendered up a home number.

Matching his parsimony with words was his punctiliousness: he arrived on the stroke of the hour.

Chaim Cohen was of medium height, thin with greying hair, and he was wearing a three-piece business suit which bore the mark of expensive London cloth.

Cordis offered him a choice of either the analytic couch or the armchair near his desk, pointing to each with an open hand, but he brushed him aside with a fluttering wave of his own hand as he selected the least comfortable piece of furniture in the office to sit upon, a plain, wooden chair close to the doctor's bookcases which Cordis used only as a footstool or one-step ladder to be able to reach the uppermost shelves. Chaim Cohen scrutinized his collection and then focused his attention on one shelf which contained a dozen copies of Cordis' book, *A Psychiatrist*

"It's not much of a work," Chaim Cohen said, "but for a first book I suppose it will have to do."

Cordis could have asked him how he knew it was his first book, or even challenged his patient's assessment of his brainchild, but he said simply, "I'm pleased to hear that you're familiar with it."

"An author is certainly entitled to express his sundry opinions," Chaim Cohen said, "and you happen to find it convenient to have an opinion for every letter of the alphabet." He spoke in a nonchalant manner bordering on indifference, which nevertheless didn't conceal his sarcasm. "But you must not present facts incorrectly."

Cordis ignored his patronizing airs and asked calmly, "Oh, how so?"

"In your chapter on zirconium," he said, sneering at the mention of the word, as though accusing Cordis of perhaps not being able to find anything else under the letter Z to write about, "you state that the property of resistance to high temperatures is the reason zirconium alloys are used to make nuclear reactors. That is alloying the facts, if I may say. Rather, these particular alloys are employed because of their low neutron absorption rate."

"Thank you for the information," Cordis responded, jotting down what his patient said. "I'll notify my editor that we have to make a correction should the book go to a second printing."

Chaim Cohen continued with his controlled small talk for ten minutes, revealing nothing personal about himself.

Cordis thought, Maybe the guy's a physicist.

He wanted to gather some solid history, but was prepared to let his patient dillydally his way through the session. No other strategy appeared appropriate at the moment.

Here and there he managed to break through Chaim Cohen's intransigence to gather up bits of data. His patient revealed that he was married and his wife's name was Marsha. Adroitly interrupting his idle chatter from time to time, which Cordis had noted as "drivel," he uncovered that he had four children, in their twenties and thirties. He wanted to know something about their lives, but his patient was not obliging.

At half past the hour, Chaim Cohen looked at his watch and in his calm manner, with an imperious touch, said, "I have given you enough of my time for today." He then promptly stood up and prepared to leave.

"How you spend your time is your affair," Cordis said. "However, before you go I need to know your address."

"Why?" he asked coolly. "You have my telephone number."

"I can't mail your bill to a telephone number."

45

Chaim Cohen did furnish him an address on Long Island, and added, "The Medical Society's quote of your fee is disproportionately high. I still haven't determined to my satisfaction if you are worth it. Regardless, I am prepared to see you again next week."

Cordis tried to ignore the condescending manner in which he announced his willingness to return for another session. "I can see you again next Tuesday at the same time," he said, checking his appointment book and straining to sound pleasant.

Before he left, Chaim Cohen had a final comment for Cordis. Seeing a copy of Jolande Jacobi's *The Psychology of C.G. Jung* on his desk, he said, in his supercilious way, "At least your reading material is worthy of note."

When he was gone, Cordis sat chewing on his pen, trying to figure out who he reminded him of. It came to him. "Why, of course," he uttered aloud, "Clifton Webb as Mr. Belvedere."

Cordis' 8 o'clock patient was Pat O'Connell, a 45-year-old muscular ex-Marine who had become a soldier of fortune following the Korean War. His most cherished exploit was an attempt to rescue the doomed Patrice Lumumba in the Congo in 1961. His rogue band had failed in their mission, and Lumumba, the first prime minister of Zaire, died at the hands of a rival group in Katanga.

"We almost got the commie bastard out," he had said in September when Cordis first saw him.

The communist label stemmed from the founding of Lumumba University, or the People's Friendship University, established in Moscow in 1960 for third-world students.

Now he was planning to go to Northern Ireland to help the IRA in their struggle against the British. But that very afternoon Cordis had had to get him out of jail for being drunk and disorderly.

"You're lucky today's a legal holiday and the clinic was closed, Cordis was saying to him. "Otherwise, I wouldn't have been available to have arranged your release so readily."

The clinic was closed for Lincoln's birthday, just as it would close the following Monday, the 19th, for Washington's birthday (moved up from the 22nd to create a 3-day weekend).

"How did you manage it?" Pat asked in his southern drawl, impressed that his doctor had been able to get his charges dismissed.

"The precinct sergeant is a friend of mine," Cordis answered. "Besides, he's a shillelagh clansman of yours."

Actually, Sgt. O'Meara's son was in private treatment with him.

"Thanks, Rex. I'm not gonna be a bother to you much longer. I'm going off to Belfast."

Pat had never accepted the patient role, choosing instead to deal with Cordis as a friend and not as his psychiatrist. It was a contributing factor in his failure to make any significant progress in therapy.

"You were released on the understanding you would take the cure—Antabuse."

"You've been a good friend, Rex, but I gotta get on with my life."

"What about all your talk of returning to North Carolina to patch things up with your wife, as you've discussed so many times?" Cordis said. "Given your current emotional state, Ireland may prove a disaster—worse than the Congo."

"But I almost pulled it off in the Congo," Pat said, clenching a fist.

"Just like you almost pulled it off in Hobart last year and nearly got your head blown off."

Cordis was referring to Pat's effort to bring back a divorced California woman's 3-year-old son, abducted to Tasmania by the boy's father.

"Ireland should be easy. With my genes, I'll blend into the countryside."

"The Irish don't need another alcoholic fighting their battles for them."

After half an hour of this sort of dialogue, Cordis prevailed, and Pat agreed to give Antabuse a try. Explaining the manner in which the drug was used and what it was like to experience an Antabuse-alcohol reaction took another fifteen minutes.

Cordis heaved a sigh of relief following Pat's departure. Just trying to keep his patient alive from session to session took so much effort that there was hardly any time to do definitive therapy with him, which he was resisting strongly in the first place. The man wants to self-destruct, the doctor said to himself. Why do I insist on trying to defy the law of entropy?

His 9 o'clock appointment, a Medicaid patient, failed to show. That's two weeks in a row, he mused. Three strikes and you're out of my ball game.

It was lost income, for he never billed Medicaid for no-shows, nor was it tax-deductible as income owed but not collected. A friend and colleague of his, Edna Paxton, M.D., had sat in her office for four hours one evening and all four of her scheduled Medicaid patients had failed to keep their appointments. She, too, did not bill Medicaid for such hours wasted. Psychotherapy is labor-intensive, and unbillable no-shows are the bane of the practitioner.

Medicaid paid poorly as well, only thirty dollars an hour. Private paying patients were being charged anywhere from fifty to one hundred dollars an hour in New York City at the time. Cordis' fee was fifty dollars. His clinic salary of $37,500 represented substantial income for 1973.

47

CHAPTER EIGHT

Wednesday, February 14th, was a particularly busy day at the clinic for Cordis. Dr. Schlosberg, the only other full-time Division III psychiatrist was out, and his scheduled patients' charts lay heaped upon Cordis' desk. They were arranged in two piles, alongside Cordis' own charts for the day.

Dr. Schlosberg had scheduled 32 patients, and Cordis had 12 of his own to see. The maximum number of patients for which the clinic could be credited was 28 per doctor per day, determined on the basis of a minimum time of 15 minutes per patient for a 7-hour work day. Since phone contacts, which occurred regularly, could also be logged for clinic credit, about 25 would be all any one doctor could theoretically, and humanly, handle in a day. And these calculations did not take into consideration drop-ins and emergencies, some of which required extensive attention.

Mansoni heard the chart clerk mischievously describing the mountainous piles of charts on Cordis' desk to her co-workers. He marched into the psychiatrist's office to see for himself what was going on. Taking in the scene, he roared, "Where the hell is Schlosberg?"

"How do I know?" Cordis responded, hidden from view behind the charts. "Am I my colleague's keeper?"

Dr. Schlosberg was known for his absences, but never before had he bequeathed such a huge work load to his fellow doctors. Usually, Cordis assumed the bulk of the burden, with several of the Division I and II physicians helping out. On this particular morning the medical staff was in full force, and Mansoni managed to distribute Dr. Schlosberg's charts around so that Cordis only had to take on 6 additional patients. Still, 18 represented a heavy day's schedule.

He had to see 6 patients who were in for their Prolixin decanoate injections. Depot neuroleptic medication represented a significant advance in the treatment of the deinstitutionalized schizophrenic patient. The manufacturer's chemists had succeeded in adding a long-chain fatty acid group, i.e., a decanoate, to the water-soluble oral form of Prolixin and suspended it in sesame oil. Such a depot agent is absorbed slowly into the general circulation when injected into a muscle because the affinity of the fat-soluble drug for the oil is greater than its tendency to diffuse across cell membranes into the bloodstream. When it oozes into the blood, enzymes split off the decanoate side-chain, and the released Prolixin is the

48

same as the drug taken orally.

When Cordis had arrived at the clinic in 1971, patients on PD, as the clinicians refer to it, would line up at the nursing station for their shot without having been seen by the doctor. Cordis had insisted that each Division III patient be evaluated by him first before automatically getting his or her routinized injection. He wanted to chart his patient's progress to see if he could stretch out the interval between injections, perhaps from two to three weeks or from three to three-and-a-half weeks and, if possible, lower the dosage. The starting point, or average, was 25 milligrams every two weeks. Some needed more, perhaps 50 mgs or even 75 mgs every 2-3 weeks. The only way to judge was to note the patient's mental status from clinic visit to clinic visit. Out of the 6 PD patients for the day, 3 were doing well on 25 mgs every two weeks, or q. 2 wks., in the doctor's shorthand; 1 was able to have his dose lowered to 12.5 mgs q. 2 wks.—PD is put up as 25 mgs per milliliter (ml), so that this patient was cut down to 0.5 ml; 1 patient Cordis stretched to 3 weeks; and 1 patient on the standard 25 mgs q. 2 wks. needed to have Cogentin added because he had developed side-effects, i.e., a hand tremor and muscular stiffness.

Mid-morning found the clinic with a crisis: a patient was out of control—had gone berserk. She was a young woman, only 5 feet, weighing 80-85 pounds, but the 200 pound security guard, Pete, could not subdue her. She bounded about Dr. Schlosberg's empty office, leaping over furniture and darting out of the grasp of those trying to restrain her—she had attracted a crowd of staff workers. The police finally had to be called, but she threw two of New York's finest plus Pete back against one of the walls, with glass-encased wall paintings falling and smashing all about. After a sustained effort, with five powerfully built males on top of her, she was under control. Cordis was standing by with a syringe loaded with sodium amytal.

"We can't bare her skin anywhere for you to inject her," one of the five managed to say through his labored breathing.

"Don't bother yourself," Cordis responded, plunging the needle through her dress and underclothing right into her hip and quickly squeezing the plunger.

"What happens if she develops an infection?" one of the many onlookers asked.

"That's what we've got penicillin for," Cordis retorted testily. To himself he added, My God, don't these people know what you do when charged by a tiger—you shoot!

The police were subsequently able to take the sedated patient off to Bellevue Hospital without further incident.

49

"Schlosberg would be gone today!" someone commented angrily a bit later.

"Whew! What strength!" someone else exclaimed. "It took five muscle-bound guys to pin her down. If I hadn't seen it with my own eyes, I never would have believed it."

"That's the fabled strength of the schizophrenic in catatonic excitement," Cordis commented. "We were lucky the place wasn't shattered. Thank God we're all still intact."

Pete, however, was showing signs of developing a black eye, and one of the social workers involved in the fracas had a cut and swollen lip. The two police officers had more than their uniforms ruffled as well.

Before he went to lunch, Cordis saw an elderly lady in for a one-week followup. She had appeared confused, mentally dulled and delusional on her previous visit, and he had started her on a little Mellaril, another much prescribed antipsychotic agent. Now she was back with her brood—her daughter, granddaughter and her granddaughter's five small children—all crowded into Cordis' office. Cordis was flabbergasted to find the old woman smiling, alert, oriented and thinking rationally.

He had chosen a starting dose of 25 mgs three times a day for her. The neuroleptics psychiatrists had begun using some twenty years earlier, beginning with Thorazine, are not like the standard drugs of medicine with their fixed dosage schedules. Most patients on a tetracycline, for instance, take 1-2 grams a day. But Mellaril might be administered anywhere from 30 mgs to 800 mgs per day, and Thorazine from 75 mgs to 3000 mgs. How the psychiatrist zeroes in on the right dose for a given patient is through a process of dosage adjustment referred to as titration. Cordis had a flair for finding not only the effective dosage of a psychotropic agent quickly, but also the right drug for his patient.

In the afternoon, Cordis saw Madam Anna Bee, a graceful lady in her late sixties. She was originally from Kazakhstan, one of the 15 Soviet republics. Madam Bee had been married to an Indian government minister and had lived much of her adult life in comfort in Uttar Pradesh in the north of India. Her husband had taken his own life after losing his fortune, and her only child, a grown son, had met with a fatal accident. She had suffered a "nervous breakdown," a term patients frequently use for their mental or emotional illness, during her final hectic years in India. Somehow she had found her way to New York, where, alone and penniless, she had wandered into the Gotham Psychiatric Clinic one day and met Cordis.

Madam Bee spoke Russian, Kazakh, German, Mandarin, French and English. Cordis had voiced some complimentary words about her fluent

English on meeting her and she had responded, "As a child I was taught English by nuns." "Good for them," he had said. "But they were such dreadful, I might even say, horrible, women," she had added. Cordis then cemented the therapeutic bond in those opening moments by commenting, "Imagine what they would have been like had they not been nuns."

She was one of only two clinic patients Cordis saw regularly for psychotherapy who were not on any medication. Getting her on her feet had been a joint effort with social service. She now had her own apartment with her own furniture and a dignified job. She could even afford to pay for her psychotherapy, not the full amount private care would have entailed, but a reasonable fee based on her income—the clinic had a sliding scale for such patients.

As an avocation, Madam Bee was writing her memoirs, with Cordis' encouragement. At first she doubted she could do it. "I can't take pen in hand or sit at the typewriter keys and write," she had complained. "Nothing flows." She was a good conversationalist, and Cordis coaxed her into investing in a tape recorder and an ample supply of tapes. The words began to flow. "Some people are neurologically routed from fingers to brain," he had explained, "others from mouth to brain."

Madam Bee was grateful to America for allowing her to enter the country after her difficult life abroad. She had a nephew, her sister's son, in Milwaukee, and from time to time would visit him. The only other person she felt close to was Cordis.

She was approaching the end of her seventh decade, and her own mortality was beginning to weigh heavily upon her frail body. Cordis saw it as his task to shore up her ego defenses in the hope of staving off an end-of-life depression.

"There is a saying in the Upanishads," she said. "Abundance is scooped from abundance, yet abundance remains."

Cordis thought for a moment and then commented, "It sounds Helmholtzian—his conservation law."

"But isn't that in conflict with your next law of thermodynamics, which has the universe slowly but surely running down?" she asked.

"The entropy law." Cordis nodded. "But that only operates under certain conditions."

"Ah, the Western mind is too complicated for its own good," the wizened lady said. "For the Indian liturgist of old, the universe was imbued and derived from eternal being, and no matter how much of it is used up, or scooped out of its reservoir, the abundance remains."

"Yes," Cordis affirmed, "some things go on forever." His statement was equivalent to saying that some things, like one's memoirs, live forever, bestow immortality.

"The tree of knowledge divides," she said, "into a major branch called theology and another, science."

"And somewhere down the road the twain shall meet," Cordis added, smiling.

She liked to poke fun at the Soviets. "Khrushchev was a fool," she said, "banging his dirty shoe on the table at the United Nations like an imbecile and boasting, 'We Communists will bury you.' " She let out a laugh. "Nonsense, sheer nonsense. Don't fight the Russion bear. Feed him what he hungers after. Grant him half the world—two-thirds of the world—three-fourths of the world—and let him try to feed it."

"You have a point."

"Of course!" she exclaimed, raising her hands in the air to affirm her point. "General Mikhail Kutuzov," she continued, "gave Napoleon Moscow and all the surrounding landscape his hungry Corsican eyes could take in. And then the master of the Grand Armée saw that he had swallowed more than he could chew, and was himself consumed. So will be the fate of the Ruskies."

Cordis would try to schedule Madame Bee for 3:30, when the clinic had usually thinned out and he could give her fifty minutes. She used to come weekly, then twice monthly and now once a month. As she prepared to leave she said, "Remember what the Wife of Bath said."

"I don't," Cordis confessed.

"Oh, you must reread your Chaucer then," Madam Bee said advisedly. "In her words you will discover what it is that drives this new America which has emerged since the sixties."

Cordis always found himself looking forward to her next visit.

CHAPTER NINE

Harris was back in New York by the latter part of February, proving the cryptographic message to have been correctly interpreted. He phoned the doctor at his office on February 20th.

"Compañero, how have you been?" he asked.

Cordis smiled, pleased his old friend once again shared a common geography with him. "Fine, fine," he replied. "Listen, old friend, about your godchild—"

"I know," Harris said. "I know. I've kept in touch. I swear, those old women are soft in the head."

"With sclerotic vessels in those mushy heads," Cordis tacked on.

"The damage to Renata can be repaired," Harris said, focusing on the main issue. "On my way back from Tokyo I stopped in Casablanca and—"

"Ah, yes! Renata mentioned having relatives there."

"Distantly related but very close to her. Descended from Huguenots—French Protestants. The three sisters don't even talk to them. Well, Simone and her husband Pierre will be coming to New York next month to help out. They have the same family name, but it's not Anglicized. Delacroix. They will prove a big help when they get here."

"What do you hear from Renata?" the doctor asked.

"She's holding up well . . . considering. You know that they found a psychiatrist for her, a Catholic one. They had him lined up all the time, actually. After you, Renata started seeing him three times a week. Into the second week, he started pawing at her, so that was the end of that."

"Hmm," Cordis mumbled, unable to think of anything to say for the moment.

"When the cousins arrive from Morocco, we'll work out some plan for getting Renata back to you."

"Why does she stay, Harris? She's of age. Why does she allow herself to remain a prisoner?"

"You would probably be able to answer that better than I, but I imagine it has much to do with her being a Christian with a Muslim woman's mentality. That comes from living too many years in the Middle East without . . . let's call it . . . proper direction."

"Plausible," Cordis conceded. "Well, keep in touch, amigo. It sounds like things are getting interesting again."

"What do you mean *again*?" laughed Harris. "I didn't know they'd ever ceased."

Cordis had scheduled only Chaim Cohen for the evening, and he arrived at exactly 7 o'clock. Once again he held on tightly—the psychoanalyst would say anally—to the essential data that would have to pass from him to the psychiatrist if Cordis were to be of any help to him.

After devoting twenty minutes to a discussion of the weather, featuring a minor treatise on why he considered meteorology an esoteric art

53

rather than a science, touched off by Cordis' acquisition of several scarlet pimpernels for his office, he said, "I want to give you a dream."

His meteorological discourse was an attempt to weigh the art of psychiatry against its scientific base. Cordis was also aware that with his patient's unexpected offering of a dream for interpretation he was hurling down a personal challenge.

"Did you have this dream last night?" Cordis asked, opening a bottom drawer of his desk where he kept a tape recorder.

"It doesn't really matter," Chaim Cohen retorted. "The dream is the dream."

"Of course," the doctor said. "Do you mind if I tape this part of our session?" he added, setting his Panasonic on the desk top. Cordis seldom taped sessions, preferring to take down essentials in his own shorthand system, but he felt that what was coming up would require careful analysis.

His patient responded, "Be my guest."

After maneuvering in his chair to gain the greatest degree of comfort, Cordis said, "Okay, we're ready to go."

Chaim Cohen was a remarkably lucid speaker, and he recited his dream with such emotional intensity and clarity of voice, it would have pleased the most self-demanding actor.

"I saw the sun rise in Jericho," he began, "and before the day was done I saw it set in Babylon. The voice of Moses rose above the wailing multitude: 'Death is born; I die with life.' One white cloud draped the sun, and tears poured down upon the promised land. And when the red orb of heaven had heated up the day, Yahweh spoke to the stock of Abraham: 'I have given to you this day he whom I have saved to lead my people against the Canaanites.' And the wailing was done, for the future had come. 'By din will the walls of Jericho tumble down and by glory shall the land be taken,' shouted Joshua to the Israelites. And it was done." Chaim Cohen took several deep breaths at this point before continuing. "I saw a mighty warrior cry by the water's edge, a sword of strength at his side. He who had set out to learn the secret of eternal life and who with Enkidu had defeated the bull of heaven sent by Ishtar. Now he wept where the waters flowed; for the herb of youth was lost forever, swallowed by the dragon of the deep, and he knew at last that when the sun does mark the noon, death is born." He paused again and shook his head from side to side several times before resuming. "O Babylon, O Babylon, where the tears of my fathers flowed with the river which cradled man. The sun went down, and I saw the reach of darkness upon the world. 'What time is it?' I cried out. 'You have time,' said Nabu-Rimmanu. 'For you the world flows beyond Babylon,' spoke Kininnu. Thus I heard the stargazers of Babylon who

54

marked the eclipses when most men thought the sun a god." ·

At this point, his mouth was dry and he was licking his lips.

Cordis rose from his chair and filled a glass with cold water from a mini-refrigerator tucked between his bookcases. "Here, try this," he said.

Chaim Cohen nodded appreciatively, and after a few swallows continued with his account.

"I awoke while there was still darkness upon a new day, my heart pounding and my breathing labored. Marsha was already up. 'Welcome to the morning,' she said. 'I dreamt too much,' I said to her, 'just now at the moment when autumn ends and winter comes. Come, let us share with Ra the mystery of his parabolic journey.' "

He was finished with his recitation. Cordis pressed the stop button on the tape recorder and sat quietly, fingering his chin.

Chaim Cohen smiled, a triumphant smile as though successfully concluding a game of chess with an unspoken 'Checkmate!'

He stood up—it was only 7:40—and said, "When you have figured out my dream, call me, and we will set up another appointment."

With that he left. Cordis sat motionless for a minute or so and then began to replay the tape.

CHAPTER TEN

March blew in with the usual winds. On Friday, the 2nd, Joey Dee dropped in at the clinic unscheduled, having missed his followup appointment several weeks earlier.

"I'm outa pills, Dr. Cordis," he lamented, which could have meant that he lost them, discarded them or even that the bottles were lying around somewhere unopened.

"Outa, or never used?" Cordis asked, doubting that he had used them as prescribed.

Patients were issued a month's supply of each medication, and if taken as directed would run out of pills by the time of their next monthly visit.

55

"Gimme Hadall an' Tractan, Dr. Cordis," Joey said pleadingly, ignoring the doctor's question. "Please, Dr. Cordis, it ain't gonna hurt ya t' gimme Tractan an' Hadall."

"Stick with the Thorazine and Stelazine for a while," Cordis advised. "You haven't given them a chance yet." Immediately he wished he could retrieve the verb he had used, for *stick* could suggest *inject* to Joey, which might launch him on a wild and frantic spree . . . or physical outburst. Fortunately, it slipped by his semantic filtering apparatus and Cordis was able to add, "We can always change the medication in the future if it becomes necessary."

"All right," Joey responded, much to Cordis' surprise.

Cordis was relieved that they had settled the medication problem for the moment. Maybe there has been some therapeutic carry-over from our last session after all, he thought. But before he could finish savoring the recollection of that successful hour, Joey returned to discussing yin-yang theory.

"Dey complement each oder, Dr. Cordis," he summarized after a lengthy discourse.

"And Thorazine and Stelazine complement each other in their way," the doctor chipped in.

However, Joey continued with his line of thought, ignoring what Cordis considered a well-placed comment. "Dey complement each oder," he repeated, "dus restorin' inner order. Chaos yields t' serenity an' fulfillment."

Gone again for the moment was the infantilism and in its place Cordis heard the adult intellect giving voice. With that, and prescriptions for Thorazine and Stelazine, Joey left the office. Cordis was satisfied that his patient had departed the clinic looking and sounding serene.

His next patient was an elderly woman he had seen only the previous week who was back as an emergency. She had been maintained on 10 mgs of Mellaril three days a week—Monday, Wednesday and Friday—for five years, and Cordis thought she might be able to manage medication-free. He wanted to check her in a month to determine whether she was holding her own, and he was shocked to see her so floridly psychotic after what had been only a few days without medication.

She was accompanied by her daughter, who seemed solicitous of her mother's health, and Cordis was satisfied that his patient was in good hands. He put her on 25 mgs of Mellaril three times a day, with the admonition that if she did not improve over the weekend, the daughter was to bring her back Monday morning.

Afterwards, Cordis had a brief postmortem with Miss Jones.

"My gosh," he said, "she was only on thirty milligrams of Mellaril a week. A week! That's just about a homeopathic dose. Who would have ever believed she would decompensate like this almost overnight!"

"You doctors have a lot to learn about the workings of the human mind," was the nurse's unsympathetic response.

Cordis then spent thirty minutes with Larry Teek, a 22-year-old with a family history of Huntington's chorea—his mother and her two sisters had died of this hereditary disease in their thirties. Choreiform movements and mental deterioration are the hallmarks of Huntington's, and every time he had a muscle twitch Larry feared he was exhibiting early signs of the disease.

Huntington's chorea is passed on as a genetic dominant, meaning that if you acquire one gene from either parent you go on to develop it, usually beginning in your forties. In Larry's case, his mother and aunts had already begun showing signs in their twenties, and death had followed quickly, in less than the 15 years Huntington choreics usually have from onset to the end of life.

Psychotic episodes or mental deterioration sometimes precede the development of abnormal movements. Larry had already had several hospitalizations for transient psychotic episodes, thought to have been related to drug abuse along with marked anxiety when he contemplated his bleak future.

Cordis maintained him on a little Mellaril and Valium plus vitamins. Most of the neuroleptics can induce a movement disorder, and so Cordis prescribed Mellaril for him, the one with the fewest effects on the musculature. Valium was a good muscle relaxant, which might forestall the development of a neurotic tic-like disorder, brought on by anxiety, readily confused with the initial jerky movements characteristic of Huntington's. Vitamins, especially the B's, were thrown in because of Larry's poor nutritional status.

There was no treatment for Huntington's, except for palliative measures. A diagnostic test was close to development in 1973, but Larry didn't want to register with the Woody Guthrie Foundation, which the clinic saw as his best resource for diagnosis and assistance. He had no other living relatives and lived like a waif on the streets.

Every time he left the clinic, the staff had some clothes and a bag full of sandwiches for him. Cordis could only shake his head and sigh as Larry went off on his tortured way.

A secretarial error allowed a nonpatient to gain entry to Cordis' office soon after Larry left. Cordis found himself with an adult black male and his 9-year-old son, leaving him to wonder what was going on when

57

the adult said the meeting was not for him but for his son. The clerk doing the processing paper work had managed to mistake the father for the patient. Gotham Psychiatric Clinic was an adult clinic, and children were followed elsewhere within the organizational structure of the state-run system.

When it became clear that there had been a mix-up, Cordis said to the youth's father, "We'll have to refer the boy to our facility on Theiler Street."

At that the lad's father blew up at Cordis. "Don't call him *boy*!" he yelled. "You can call Tarzan's son *boy*, but don't call mine *boy*! We're a hundred years past the Civil War, and nobody calls us *boy* anymore! We've taken all the shit we're gonna take from Whitey!"

Fortunately for Cordis, Pete was walking down Doctors Row and overheard the commotion—the doctors and social workers always saw patients with their office doors open. Pete tactfully interceded, avoiding any further verbal carnage, but the incident left Cordis shaken.

He had no time to recover, for a few minutes later he received a phone call from Gotham State Hospital demanding his immediate presence in the superintendent's office. He rushed through his next four patients to clear out his morning appointments, but at noon he got another call from the hospital director's secretary instructing him to drop everything and come at once without further delay.

Cordis ate lunch at the Horn and Hardart Automat on 14th Street, one of the few left in New York, and took the subway to Harlem. He disliked going to the hospital for two reasons: he disliked the hospital and he didn't like moving about Harlem even in daylight.

He had no idea why he was being summoned. From the secretary's tone he got the impression he could be on the carpet for something. It can't be the incident with the black youth, he thought on the ride up. Not enough time for news of the incident to have reached their ears up there. But who knows?

The clinic answered to the hospital director, who in turn answered to Albany—to the commissioner of mental health. Dr. Irving Kissel, the hospital's head, had risen steadily in the state system to his current position of command. He was old-fashioned, refusing to change the hospital's name to Gotham Psychiatric Center in keeping with the trend throughout the country—psychiatric center sounded less 19th centuryish—and retaining his title of superintendent rather than adopting something more modern such as director, which in the 1980's would become CEO à la the business world.

Cordis was surprised when he learned the reason for his summons to the Harlem facility. He had recently recommended hospitalization for a black woman he thought too ill to be at home. Normally, he would have arranged for her to go back to Gotham State Hospital, where she had been admitted any number of times in the past. When he discovered that she had Medicare, that is, Social Security disability, he presented her with the option of going to Gotham Square Hospital, a private hospital, where the level of care was far above that of the state hospital. She thought it was a good idea and asked Cordis to attend to it for her. He had his social worker make the necessary arrangements, and she was scheduled to enter Gotham Square the following day.

Such a simple situation became complicated when the patient's sister, an R.N., phoned Mansoni to complain that Dr. Cordis was improperly trying to make extra money by treating her sister at a private hospital. Mansoni relayed the complaint to Dr. Kissel, stretching the facts of the matter still further. Only now did Dr. Kissel explain the reason he had asked Cordis to his office.

"We don't treat the patients we refer to Gotham Square," Cordis explained to the hospital superintendent. "Whenever any of us at the clinic refers a patient to Gotham Square, he or she is assigned to one of the hospital's psychiatrists not affiliated with the clinic. The administrator then gives us a credit, and the next patient admitted there without a psychiatrist goes to one of us. It's a fair swap and there's no conflict of interest."

It was a straightforward matter requiring no more explanation than what he had furnished. Yet, he felt uncomfortable all the while he was explaining himself. These hospital command calls—drop everything, come immediately—had that kind of effect on him, just as they did on the other clinic personnel.

Cordis was relieved that the problem had been cleared up so readily to the superintendent's satisfaction. By way of small talk, or driven by a burst of nervously released energy, to state it more accurately, he mentioned the morning's incident involving the 9-year-old.

"You've got to be so careful these days," the aged and gray-haired Dr. Kissel counseled. "The racial issue is a hot potato, and more so up here in Harlem than at the clinic downtown. I'll give you an example. Only this morning we were discussing the case of a black patient whose treating psychiatrist thought needed ECT. The matter came before the treatment team, which voted on it. They split along racial lines, four white staff members, two doctors and two nurses, in favor, and four, all black, an LPN, psychologist and two psychiatric aides, against. The deciding vote was cast by a black psych aide called in as a consultant. I, by the way, was one of the doctors outvoted."

"You vote on a medical treatment decision?" Cordis asked, incredulous. "It sounds like the way they do things in Communist China, not the U.S.A."

"Well, that's what things have come to," Dr. Kissel said softly. "ECT*—electricity to the layman—means punishment, not treatment. These people here can't understand that ECT is a valid therapeutic modality in well chosen cases, and this was one of them."

"God save us from little brother and little sister," Cordis intoned.

"We doctors no longer call the shots here," the superintendent said barely above a whisper.

Cordis pondered the changing sociological scene on his ride home later in the afternoon.

*Electro-convulsive therapy

CHAPTER ELEVEN

Cordis didn't hear from Harris again until March 5th, when his phone rang at 4 a.m.

"Renata is in the hospital," Harris said.

"What's happened?" the doctor asked, half awake.

"She was in a car accident."

"Bad?"

"She suffered minor injuries. Nothing more, fortunately, but they decided to keep her for a few days as a precaution."

"They call that observation, Harris, and it's usually just overnight."

"Well, you know how it is with her and that family."

"Was it deliberate?" Cordis asked, fishing for details.

"I don't think so. Renata told me it was caused by lack of concentration. Simone and Pierre arrived yesterday, and the sparks began to fly immediately. They're still fighting the battle of the Reformation or whatever it was."

"I see."

"I think the family is about to use the incident to have her transferred

60

to that special little hospital in the hills again. And I don't believe that would be in her best interests."

"I'm listening," the doctor said.

"Simone, Pierre and I will check her out of the hospital at six forty-five this morning, during the nursing shift change. We want to get her out before the family doctor or the three sisters can counter our action. I think we can pull it off."

"She is an adult, Harris. She can sign herself out. It's her legal right."

"With her background . . . ," Harris began, his tone alone making clear that the case was not as simple as Cordis was suggesting.

"Ah, yes. So you'll get her out and stash her away in a hotel with the Moroccans."

"The hotel will hardly be necessary. They have an apartment on the East Side. She'll be comfortable and with good people. Then, if there's a sanity hearing, it will be your statement against whatever the family chooses to present."

"Harris," Cordis was frowning as he asked, "this isn't a poor-little-rich-girl scenario, is it?"

"No, nothing like that. This isn't about money. It's about possessiveness and individuality."

Cordis was in agreement with what he had just heard. "Okay," he said. "Keep me posted, Harris. And good luck with your rescue mission."

"Thanks, but I think it won't be luck we'll need so much as good timing."

On March 9th, Cordis received a telephone call from Renata. It was several days after Harris and his party had "successfully relocated her to the East Side," as Harris had phrased it to him.

"I'd like to continue with my therapy," she stated calmly.

Whatever psychic trauma she might have endured since he had seen her on January 13th wasn't detectable in her voice. Two months was a long time between sessions, so he decided to have her come in the next morning, Saturday, at nine.

"Is that too early?" he asked.

"No. I threw away the Thorazine weeks ago."

Renata was late by some ten minutes.

"I walked," she said by way of apology. "Next time I shall be on time."

"Good," Cordis responded. "So tell me," he continued, taking the lead, "are you comfortable in your new surroundings?"

"Very much so," Renata answered placidly.

"And at peace with yourself?"

A cloud passed over her calmness. "No, I'm torn between my own needs and trying to please my grandmother and aunts."

He noted the distance she was now placing between herself and her grandmother, whom she had previously referred to more intimately as "Grandmama."

"What will you do?"

She sighed deeply. "Try to save myself and also mend fences as best I can."

He noted that she had said *save* rather than find.

"And how do you plan to proceed?"

"I wish to continue in therapy with you. You've already helped me immeasurably. Thank you." She smiled. "Having the burden of that horrible diagnosis off my shoulders has been positively liberating."

Cordis was pleased to hear that. He sensed in her the capacity to become truly involved, or "engaged," in therapy. The transference was good. He was equally pleased to note that she elicited a strong positive counter-transference from his quarter. There was no apparent evidence as yet of resistance. Probably on the subject of sexuality, if I read the signs correctly, he mused.

"I had a dream last night," Renata announced, abruptly changing the general mood. "I dreamt of Snow White."

"With or without the seven dwarfs?" Cordis asked seriously.

Renata tilted her head, confused. "What . . . what did you ask?"

"It can be important whether or not the little elves were in the dream."

"Oh. No, they weren't in it. It was a simple scene, really. You know the part where the handsome prince comes in and plants a kiss on her lips, waking her from the deep sleep of the drugged?"

"Of course." Cordis looked at her expectantly.

"Well, that is what occurred in my dream. He kissed her and she awoke at long last." Renata paused several seconds. "That was my dream."

"Anything else?"

She lowered her eyes. "No. I'm afraid that's when I woke up." She seemed disappointed.

Cordis looked at her for a moment and then said, "Now here's what I want you to do next time you have a dream you want to relate. Keep a pen, pad and pocket flashlight at your bedside, and write your dream down right away, even though it means waking up, of course, to do so. Then you can go back to sleep."

"Oh, I see."

"Now," the doctor coaxed, "Renata, I want you to go over the dream again to see if you've left out anything, any details you might have overlooked."

She thought for a few moments and then repeated her dream, this time providing a clear picture of the cottage's furnishings. "And one other thing," she added. "It was me. I was asleep. I was Snow White."

"Anything else you can remember?"

She forced herself to concentrate hard. "The dwarfs were there," she said after a while. "Oh, I never saw them. But I heard them singing in the background: 'Hi ho, hi ho, it's off to work we go,' and when Snow White, I mean, I, woke up after being kissed, I could hear: 'I'm wishing, I'm wishing, for the one I love, to find me, to find me,' and so forth." She blushed slightly for having sung aloud.

"You have a lovely voice," Cordis said. "Yes, a lovely voice." He paused a moment before asking, "Tell me, what was the prince like? Prince Charming?"

"Yes, the prince." She frowned. "Well, he wasn't tall and blond. He appeared to be of average height and had dark hair and dark eyes, and when he smiled, he smiled like . . . like, well, Mona Lisa. An inscrutable smile."

"How did his kiss make you feel?"

She leaned back against the chair. "I don't know. I woke up before I could react to it."

"You know that fairy tales are one of the royal roads through the unconscious," Cordis said, preparatory to going into an analysis of her dream.

"You said that about symbols," Renata pointed out.

Cordis smiled. "Yes, I did. Fairy tales are one of the royal roads precisely because they use symbols so effectively. For example, Snow White. The story of Snow White symbolizes a specific developmental-phase conflict—"

"Is this going to be an eclectic interpretation of my dream?"

"No, just a basic, Freudian rendition. Just to get your feet wet. You've got to start somewhere, and education is part of the process."

"Freud is a blank for me."

"That's okay," Cordis said. "We'll do it in simple steps. You see, in Freud's grand design of psychological development, the individual advances along recognizable stages—through succeeding phases of childhood development he termed oral, anal and phallic/oedipal, the so-called formative stages; then latency, the in-between years; and adolescence with its sexual awakening."

"Sounds very technical," Renata said demurely.

"You need only know that it was at the age of seven—the end of the oedipal stage and the formative years—that Snow White fled from the wicked stepmother by escaping through the forests of the deep and over the seven mountains—symbolically one for each of the seven formative years of development."

"But why should seven be so important?" Renata asked.

"It is the magic number of childhood, the watershed of development. Europeans recognize this by not starting their children in school until they reach the age of seven, the end of childhood and the beginning of what Freud termed latency."

"What happens to the child at that age?" she asked, curious.

"There are alterations going on in the brain, recorded physiologically as an abrupt change in the pattern of the electroencephalogram."

"But how do you apply all this to interpreting my dream?" she asked impatiently.

"Well, those seven dwarfs," Cordis went on, "who do not figure in your dream except as an echo, symbolize the seven years of latency. Snow White lives with them for seven years, during which time she cooks and cleans and cares for them. At fourteen latency ends for her. Puberty, meaning sexual awakening, is ushered in when she bites into the red apple—symbolically the breaking of the hymen with the gushing forth of the first menstrual flow. At this point in the tale she falls into a deep sleep until finally awakened to adolescence by the kiss of the young prince."

"Why does she need the deep sleep—other than to be awakened eventually by her hero so that the two of them can proceed to live happily ever after?" Renata asked somewhat facetiously.

"A thoughtful question," the doctor replied. He was monitoring her responsiveness, and he could see she was ill at ease with his sexual talk. "Snow is ill prepared for adolescence," he continued, "what with her childhood history of deprivation and abuse at the hands of her wicked stepmother, and the purpose of the long sleep is to effect a psychological process of repair. The prince's kiss awakens her to the meaning of adolescence, which in her time signaled social as well as sexual awakening and an early maturity."

"All this psychological talk takes my breath away," Renata said, her cheeks slightly flushed.

"Well, you're involved in the process," Cordis said, and that's what matters. Now, *en fin*, back to your dream—"

"*Oui*, my dream—at last."

"In your dream there was no wicked stepmother and only a faint

64

reminder of the dwarfs. Time-wise, therefore, your dream belongs to the end of latency and the beginning of sexual awakening."

"I don't think I follow that entirely," Renata said.

"Well, this tale is entitled *Snow White and the Seven Dwarfs* and not *Snow White and the Wicked Stepmother*, which would have meant an oedipal-stage story, or *Snow White and the Prince*, which would be an adolescent-stage story."

"Um, I see."

"The author was writing about the period of latency, glossing over what preceded Snow White's seven years with Grumpy, Sleepy, et al."

"And somehow all of this applies to me?"

"What we have in your dream is not a Prince Charming but rather a shadowy and possibly malevolent figure."

"I can't imagine who that might possibly be," Renata said quickly.

Looking steadily into her eyes, Cordis stated, "Discovering the identity of the prince in this dream will become an important, if not pivotal, goal of therapy."

After a lengthy pause, Renata muttered, "I . . . I'm sure it's obvious to you that I'm not . . . comfortable, that is, at my ease, when it comes to discussing sexual matters."

"Well, it can be a problem for a number of people."

"And to make things worse . . . You see, the last psychiatrist I went to tried to . . . well, tried to . . . seduce me. He was not the first to try—"

Cordis raised his hand in the air to stop her. "Here, in this chamber, you have sanctuary," he said solemnly. "This place is holy ground, as sacred as the Cathedral of Notre Dame. No harm can come to you while you are in this place."

On hearing these words, Renata appeared relieved and a look of serenity passed over her face. "This is the second burden you have lifted from me," she said gratefully.

"Those two were easy," he said cordially. "They come with the territory. The rest of the burdens will prove more challenging."

He scheduled her for Tuesday, March 13th, at 8 p.m.

CHAPTER TWELVE

The day after his session with Renata, Celine Delacross telephoned him, inviting him to dinner. During the previous days, the old woman had appeared to Cordis in several of his dreams, in which she spoke Spanish rather than her native French. Both her appearance in his dreams and the change in her native tongue vexed him, and although he had no reason to be recriminative, he had no intention of accepting her invitation.

"I'm sorry," he explained. "I make it a rule never to socialize with my patients and their families."

"Renata does not live here anymore, Doctor," she said defensively. "Nor will she be at this dinner."

"I still cannot accept the invitation," he said firmly. "I believe I can help Renata more if I remain distanced from all parties involved with her."

"Would you reconsider at some later date?"

Why not? Cordis said to himself. There's no telling how much time those old sisters have on God's earth. He cleared his throat. "Of course," he said, "at some later date when such a meeting might be appropriate. Thank you for the call. Good-by for now."

Later that day he received another call, from the other branch of the family—Simone Delacroix. She began her conversation in Spanish, confusing him for the moment.

So there is an Hispanic link, Cordis thought. After several minutes of struggling to keep up a conversation with her, he apologized. "It's been too many years. But I recognize in your speech the accent of Mexico."

"Of course," she said, her tone suddenly playful. "We met in the north of Mexico some twenty-five years ago."

Her English was fluent, although coated with a thick French accent. He tried to visualize her, but no identifiable image formed in his mind.

"I'm sorry. I don't seem to be able to place you."

"No?" Simone laughed. "Well, I remember you well. Tall and skinny. The poor Jewish boy from The Bronx who won the heart of the Spanish beauty—"

"My God!" he cried out, cutting her off before she could proceed further with what was for him a sensitive subject.

"My husband and I represented the Delacross business interests in Mexico then," she added, sensing that she had touched a nerve with her personalized remark.

Although the conversation continued for almost half an hour longer,

Cordis still found himself unable to remember her. After he hung up the phone, his thoughts wavered between a Mexico that hadn't existed for him for a quarter of a century and a strange and fragmented family that hovered like mad angels around his patient.

"Let me try to understand what's going on," he heard himself say half-aloud. "A new patient comes to me under the veil . . . possible veil . . . of the numinous. As it turns out, one of my oldest friends is, of all things, her godfather. Now a cousin of hers from the Maghreb, the good angel, appears on the scene to rescue her from the Wicked Witch of the West and her henchpeople. And this same cousin crossed my path, so she says, a quarter of a century ago in Mexico, when . . . when Ramona died." He paused and after a deep sigh added, "Is all of this coincidence, or is the hand of Providence at work here?"

The following day, Monday evening, the 12th, as soon as he entered the lobby of the building where he had his professional suite, Cordis noticed a middle-aged couple abruptly rise from their table in the coffee shop and move swiftly toward him. Although he didn't recognize either of them, he knew instinctively that they were Simone and Pierre Delacroix.

"Dr. Cordis! It's so nice to see you again!" Simone said effusively while in the act of embracing him. Pierre grasped his hand in both of his, speaking rapidly in French. Cordis was momentarily overwhelmed and embarrassed. To him the two were strangers, yet they had not the slightest doubt as to who he was. He combed through his mind searching for even the slightest glimmer of recognition of either of them, but there was nothing.

Simone was a tall, thin, stately redhead in her fifties. Pierre was a few inches taller, equally trim, gray at the temples and balding, impeccably dressed and about the same age.

"So," Simone said excitedly, "after so many years we finally encounter *el hombre del norte* again!"

Simone prevailed upon him to join them in the coffee shop, and he ordered a *thé citron*. Then, collecting himself, he realized he had ordered in French and asked the waiter for a "tea with lemon."

Apologetically, Cordis confessed his failure to remember the two of them.

"It was at a party given by your in-laws," Simone said. "We met only that once, but friends kept us abreast of the love of the Yankee lad for the Spanish maiden."

"Like a love ballad from another time," Pierre said debonairly. His English was almost accent-free.

67

"Yes, how the poor Jewish boy from The Bronx won the heart—*el corazón*—of the beautiful young lady from Spain," Simone added.

Cordis sipped his tea and smiled. "You may be making more of it than there was," he said, trying to sound impassive. "Mexico was a stopover on a long journey that I myself was—am—caught up in."

"Only a stopover?" Simone asked, her voice pointed but friendly. "Not the critical Mount Zion of your life?"

Cordis smiled. "Perhaps in the beginning."

"But—"Simone started to say.

"My very name, Rex Cordis, is in memory of Ramona. She called me *rey de mi corazón*, king of my heart."

"A beautiful sentiment," Simone said.

"Yes," Cordis said, "but also the devout Catholic's sin. Christ alone is king in the heart of the believing Catholic."

"But it was only a figure of speech," Simone protested. "A lovely figure of speech, nothing more."

Cordis shrugged. "Still a sin, no matter how lovely."

"And you still mourn her?" she asked.

"What? No. That was nearly a quarter of a century ago."

"Then why so sad?" Simone asked, sounding like the stereotypical Jewish mother.

"My mother died last year."

"Yes, that is sad," Pierre said solemnly. "And you still grieve for her."

"I grieve, not for her passing, for she was mortal and has gone the way of all flesh. I grieve, for with her passing has passed a way of life we shall not know again."

"Nothing lasts forever," Pierre intoned resonantly.

"True, even the old New York is gone," the doctor said, "and the new New York is here. Long live New York!" He raised his tea cup in the air in the manner of a toast and took a sip.

Simone brought the conversation back to the past. "Tell me, whatever happened to that friend of yours, the one who looked like your twin brother?"

"Freddie?"

Simone nodded. "Yes, I think that was his name."

Cordis frowned. "He died in the jungles of Brazil in pursuit of the legendary tailed ape."

Pierre muttered something in French and then asked emotionally, "How did such a thing happen?"

Cordis took a deep breath and let it out slowly. "It's a long story," he started to say. "I was a freshman at the University of New Mexico in nineteen forty-seven taking an introductory course in anthropology with Professor Frank C. Hibben. One day he told the class about a huge tailed ape wandering around in the Matto Grosso." He paused to take a sip of his tea, which had gone cold. "The whole thing was a farce, of course."

"Why a farce?" Pierre asked, listening intently.

"Apes don't have tails," Cordis explained. "Monkeys do."

"Perhaps it was a large monkey then," Simone suggested.

"The only evidence available was a photo or two," the psychiatrist said. "Someone had glued a tail onto an ape and had made it look credible. God, how I tried to explain that to Freddie, but he let his imagination get the better of him. 'Where there's smoke, there's fire,' he said. So off he went in search of this ape, and diamonds, too, I believe. He perished in a jungle that even Tarzan of the Apes would have found inhospitable."

"Horrible!" Simone gasped.

Cordis nodded. "I think it was about nineteen forty-nine or fifty when I saw him last and told him about the tailed ape."

"Just before Kubitschek began tearing down the jungle to build his city of Brazilia in the interior," Pierre noted.

"Right," Cordis responded. He lifted his tea cup in the air. "To Freddie and the Matto Grosso that is no more."

Simone seemed deep in thought. "Is this a tale which is supposed to have a moral?" she asked, looking at the doctor out of the corner of an eye.

"Fables carry a moral," Cordis responded.

"Tell me," Simone pressed, "what was the moral in that story?"

"Don't believe every tale you hear," Cordis answered without a moment's hesitation.

Simone and Pierre looked at each other, and then Pierre broke out in a broad grin. "I understand," he said. "In English, tale, a story, is spelled t-a-l-e, and the posterior appendage, t-a-i-l. Very good, Doctor!" He applauded by tapping on the table English style.

"But it is a true story, isn't it?" Simone asked, doubt filling her voice.

"I wouldn't make a monkey out of you," Cordis replied with a twinkle in his eye.

"Aha," Simone said, slapping him gently on the back of his hand. "*Mon cher Docteur*, you are not so sad as not to be able to make a joke."

The conversation continued along in a light-hearted vein for a little longer, and sensing that Simone wanted to get around to the subject of her cousin, Cordis looked at his watch and said he had to dash off to attend to patients.

On the way up in the elevator, he broke out in a smile thinking about the Delacroix meeting, which he saw as a friendly waylaying by the over-

69

anxious Simone.

CHAPTER THIRTEEN

Renata phoned him the following afternoon, March 13th, to report that she had a touch of the flu.

"Should I keep tonight's appointment?" she asked. "I'd hate to spread my germs to you."

"You do what you have to do," the doctor answered. "Don't you worry about me. Besides, as I told you the last time, the office is holy ground, protecting me as much as you."

"I'll try to be there," she said, making her determination clear.

She arrived fifteen minutes late that evening, looking wan and weary.

"Are you sure you're up to it? Cordis asked solicitously.

Renata nodded. "I'll be fine. I wanted to come." She settled back in her chair, grateful to be off her feet. "What is it that you're reading now?" she asked, pointing to the open book on his desk.

"Audrey Lindrop's *The Singer Not the Song*—a gift from your Moroccan cousin. It tells a tale of the age-old struggle between good and evil."

"Would it hold any psychotherapeutic value for this session?" she asked, managing a faint smile.

"Possibly," the psychiatrist responded. "In this novel, Father Keogh comes to Quantana to do spiritual battle with Anacleto, *El Malo*, the Bad One, also called Malo-of-the-Cats. These are the combatants: the Lord's servant pitted against the devil's choice."

"Where is this place—Quantana?" Renata asked, curious.

"In the mountains of northern Mexico," the doctor replied. "Purely a fictional place. No word in Spanish takes an *a* after *q-u*. The nearest to it would be something like a *kuh* sound, as in *cantante*, with a *c*, which means singer, as in *The Singer Not the Song*."

He was surprised that such a fine point in Spanish grammar should suddenly come back to him.

"Very interesting," Renata said, her eyes only half open.

Cordis continued, while at the same time monitoring her physical condition out of the corner of an eye. "In Father Keogh we see the noblest spiritual potentiality in man; in Anacleto, the lowest depths of depravity."

"This Anacleto is beyond redemption?" Renata asked, more alert now.

"He's kind to cats."

"And I suppose good triumphs over evil in the end."

"Not quite so simple," Cordis responded. "*Singer* is the classic Christian tale. Remember, man is basically evil in Christian thought. Sin is etched into his bones, into his very being. Without redemption through Christ he is doomed to perdition. Life fluctuates between the bivalency of good and evil—"

"Am I wrong in assuming that the good priest dies in this story?" Renata asked, cutting him off before he could complete his last thought.

"You have a deep intuitive sense," he commented. "Well, actually, the book ends in a Mexican stand-off with neither a clear-cut winner and with both of them dying."

Renata sighed. "I have always felt that the power of evil is greater in the world than the power of good."

In Christian theology they appear at least to be on an equal footing."

"Equal? Really?" she said, sounding surprised.

"Yes. The force of Christ is balanced by Satan, the Evil One—at least for now."

"Ah, yes, the Dark Angel, always ready to insinuate himself into the scene. He is everywhere in the world."

"Yes, he can be found lurking everywhere beyond the boundaries of the Holy Trinity—"

"He doesn't sneak in there sometimes?" Renata interjected.

"The Trinity is symbolic of the good in life, so the devil must always lie outside it."

"But he's part of the greater whole," Renata reasoned.

"Well, we're being led into the concept of the quaternity, the major symbol of totality in some systems. Like Jung's, for instance."

"Does Jung suggest we need evil in the world?"

Cordis frowned. "I can't speak for Jung on that point, but for myself, yes. I think so. Evil with all its allies—sloth, mendacity and so on. We would accomplish nothing if evil didn't exist. Just vegetate like Adam and Eve in the Garden before the dawn."

"My, my," she uttered, with a quizzical smile.

"What?" he asked. "Something about evil?"

She shook her head. "No, no, I was . . . you certainly do take an active part . . . really get involved in the therapy."

Cordis smiled. "I'm hardly a benign Buddha taking serene refuge

71

behind my desk, true."

"So many of your colleagues do little more than stroke their beards," she commented with amused irony. "And you . . . you are so involved. And you read. Literature, not just your own medical literature. For this country, you're something of a rara avis."

"I will take that as a compliment," Cordis said. Her flattering observations made him blush a little, but he was more concerned about observations of his own. Although she was trying to sound cheerful, it was clear she wasn't feeling well. "Are you all right, Renata?"

"A slight fever, that's all," she said. "A touch of the flu."

"Why guess about it?" he offered, searching through the top drawer of his desk for a thermometer he kept there.

"No, please. I'll be all right. Let's continue."

Hesitatingly, he closed the drawer. "Okay, but try to take it easy."

Renata was silent for a few moments and then said softly, "Something from long, long ago just crossed my mind. Flashed across it for no more than a second, but so vividly." She paused, and Cordis waited quietly for her to continue.

Finally, he prompted her, "Something from the distant past. Childhood?"

Renata nodded. "Yes," she said slowly.

When she did not go on, Cordis filled the void. "Buried memories often surface in the course of the type of therapy we're doing," he said. Renata remained silent, so he continued. "Like Heinrich Schliemann uncovering the lost city of Troy. As a boy his father had told him stories about the Trojan War and the destruction of Troy by fire some time after the war. A city vanished completely. Obliterated from history and reduced to legend. But Heinrich figured that lost cities must leave some trace . . . just as old forgotten memories still leave their trace."

"I know all about Schliemann," Renata snapped. "And his children, Andromache and Agamemnon."

Cordis had mentioned what he was able to recall about the 19th century German archeologist from Frank C. Hibben's introductory course in anthropology he had taken at New Mexico in 1947. Hibben had never mentioned the Schliemann children bearing classic Greek names, as far as his memory served him. All he could manage to say was, "That's pretty good."

The exchange had served its purpose, for now Renata opened up.

"We, uh, we—my father and I—were in Riyadh, Saudi Arabia, driving slowly in his *americaine* through the main square where there was to be a public execution. My father stopped the car and rolled the window down to say something to a passerby. I could feel the chill in the air outside and smell the aroma of lamb being cooked in duhn, the butter they make from sheep's milk. I saw several women a short distance away, covered from head to foot in their black cloaks with their faces veiled, wailing and beating their breasts. The man by the car, a tall and rugged-looking Arab, had on his *bisht*, the cloak men wear over their *thaub*, a long-sleeved, ankle-length garment. I remember the *ghutra* covering his head—it's a kerchief made of cotton—and the way he stared at me, a four-year-old child—it sent a chill down my spine. I thought he was the bogeyman. I turned away and hid my face on the seat near the door on my side of the car.''

Renata stopped at that point and stared ahead blankly past Cordis. The psychiatrist finally said, "So you didn't actually witness the execution or executions.''

"The man went away, and when I looked up the crown's swordsman was in the act of beheading . . . a criminal. Maybe he had been a drug smuggler or a murderer or a rapist.'' After another pause she added, "What I have related to you I have never revealed before to anyone, and it may be the earliest memory I have.''

Cordis was deep in thought, and then he asked, "Which was he—drug smuggler, murderer or rapist?''

Renata had a ready reply. "Years later, my father mentioned to some guests at our home how he had witnessed a sharia execution. The Arab he had stopped the car to talk to that day had told him that the condemned man was a Shiite from Abu Hadriyah on the Persian Gulf across from Iran.''

She said no more about the matter, letting it dangle like that, and Cordis did not pursue it further. He reflected that a child of that age would understand what murder meant, but would probably have had no idea, in 1953 at the age of four, of what was meant by drug smuggling or rape. Thus, he deduced she had presented him with a screen-memory, a real memory, to be sure, employed by the ego as a shield to hide or cover over another related and important memory. He did smile to himself thinking about her reference to her father's automobile as an *americaine*, a colloquialism used to refer to the big American cars so popular with Europeans at that time.

Renata sat quietly for a while. Then, barely above a whisper, she said, "No one speaks in iambic pentameter anymore." She let out a deep sigh.

"And no one writes iambs like Emily Dickinson anymore, either.''

She didn't speak for half a minute, and then she said, in a weak voice, "Ah, Dickinson, the poetess in the attic." She began to recite:

73

"Because I could not stop for Death,
He kindly stopped for me;
The carriage held but just ourselves
And immortality."

"I believe that's from her poem 'The Chariot,'" Cordis said. "Do you know 'In Winter'?"

Without a pause, Renata recited:

"I died for beauty, but was scarce
Adjusted to the tomb,
When one who died for truth was lain
In an adjoining room."

There was a silence. Finally Cordis spoke. "She echoes Keats."

"So she does," Renata whispered dreamily. "So she does."

Cordis was concerned about his patient's state of health and considered terminating the session at this point.

Just then Renata said, "Poetry is the best tonic, Dr. Cordis." She suddenly stood up, adding, "I'm sorry to have to shorten this hour, this interesting and informative hour, but I think I should get to bed with a hot toddy."

Cordis accompanied her downstairs and hailed a cab for her. "Please call me tomorrow and let me know how you're doing," he said, helping her into the taxi.

He stood at the curbside watching her cab disappear into the evening traffic.

Intelligent and beautiful, with a touch of regality, he said to himself.

The early childhood memory of the public decapitation she had witnessed suddenly stirred a recollection in his own mind. His father had related to him in the 1940's how as a boy in Poland in the last century he had been witness to what was not an unrelated experience. Cossacks on horseback had swept through his *shtetl*, their swords flailing wildly in the air. People were running in all directions to escape the swift-moving, silent horsemen. His father saw one of them swing his sword and sever the head from the neck of a fleeing Jew and heard the man's wife screaming in despair.

Jacob the Good, as Cordis referred to his father, would never leave New York, not even when an opportunity came along in 1937 to take his wife and young children and flee the frosty weather of the East and the Great Depression for a ready-made job in sunny Arizona.

"Chmielnicki, you bastard!" Cordis muttered aloud, still standing at the curbside. "You and your damned Cossacks!"

74

In 1648, Bogdan Chmielnicki, the Cossack hero of the Ukranian Orthodox peasants, launched his attacks against their Polish Catholic landlords, his people's oppressors, but at the same time and extending over the next ten years, he slaughtered Jews—"that accursed breed of Jews," as he referred to them—by the thousands, an estimated hundred thousand in all, the greatest slaughter of Jews between the fall of the Temple in Jerusalem and the Holocaust. To this day every Jew with ancestors from the Pale knows his name.

"Well, Pop, with a childhood memory like that, who could blame you for fearing there might be Cossacks lurking beyond the reaches of the Hudson River," he said half-aloud.

Cordis turned and walked back to the building's entrance. "Chmielnicki, the bogeyman of my childhood . . . Seems as though we have something in common, young lady. Maybe more than just something."

CHAPTER FOURTEEN

Josephine Bondaz, Cordis' fiancee, arrived from Paris on Thursday of that week, and he took several hours off in the afternoon to go out to Idlewild to meet her. Although the name of the airport had been changed to Kennedy International following the president's assassination ten years earlier, he still called it Idlewild. There was airport bus service to LaGuardia and Kennedy, but he took a cab. The last two times he had been on the bus, he had had to put up with marijuana smokers secreting themselves in the rear, but the distinctive aroma floating down the length of the bus was something they couldn't hide. Cordis had gone to the back on each occasion demanding that they "extinguish that rotten weed!" and both times had reported the problem to the driver, who couldn't have cared less.

He brought her back to her apartment on the Upper East Side, and then they went out to an early dinner. Cordis had to be at his office for an

8 o'clock patient, and he arrived a little early, relieved at having an excuse to retreat into a private corner for a few hours.

Well, it's the ides of March—decision-making time, he mused, leaning back in his chair with his feet crossed on top of his desk.

He had met Josie one summer's day in 1971 at Barnes and Noble. He liked to walk over to the bookstore from the clinic during his lunch hour to browse, not only in the medical section but especially through the literature shelves. When he became absorbed in a book, he would note his place on leaving and on his next visit would resume reading where he had left off. Once every two weeks he would buy something. It didn't matter what—he considered it his "rental fee."

Josephine Bondaz just happened to be looking for a book in his vicinity that June day. She dropped a copy of Melville's *Moby Dick* and he picked it up for her, commenting, "That's one whale of a story." She smiled at him and said something pleasant. Once kindled, he kept the conversation going until they were out in the street, when he asked her to lunch—his second of the day.

Josie was thirty-two when he met her. She was tall, with long, dark hair, attractive, but not beautiful by Hollywood standards. It was her clothes and the way she wore them that enhanced her charm and radiance. French was her first language, but she spoke English with equal fluency. She had gone directly from the University of Montpelier to New York in 1968 to work for the French legation to the United Nations as a translator.

The day after he met her, Cordis took her out on a date, and before the evening was out she took him to her church, the focal point of her life.

Now, sitting in his office reviewing his long courtship of Josie, long by modern-day standards, he muttered aloud, "*Muy católica*, just like Ramona. I sure know how to pick 'em." He let out a deep sigh.

Josie wanted to get married, but Cordis was resisting. The religious issue preyed on his mind. She was now thirty-four, and she wanted children. To have her first child at thirty-five would qualify her as an elderly primagravida, so for her the marital issue was a pressing one. Cordis loved her, but he didn't want all of his children raised Catholic. Josie, however, insisted that all of them would have to be baptized in the church.

They were at an impasse, and just before Christmas Josie had announced that she was taking a three-month leave of absence from the United Nations to go back to France. Upon her return, the matter would have to be resolved one way or the other.

Cordis' 8 o'clock appointment was Dr. Howard Bergfeld, a fellow psychiatrist, who had been coming to him for weekly sessions for almost a year. He was about Cordis' age and worked on an inpatient ward at Gotham State Hospital. During his residency training, he met a black nurse, and they had been dating for the past seven years. As long as his widowed Jewish mother remained alive, his marital plans remained on hold. His mother's vehement refusal to allow him to marry Rosa Simsworth was the cause of constant tension among the three of them.

"Divide and conquer," Cordis was saying to him. "It's an effective strategy."

"Rosa doesn't fall into her trap," Dr. Bergfeld responded.

"You're not a little boy anymore, Howard. When you were her little boy, you did what mama said. Now that you are a man—"

"I know! I know!" his patient said loudly.

"We've gone over this again and again," Cordis said. "We've reviewed your life from the day of your circumcision right up until last week. All that needs to be explored has been explored. The time has come for action. Jews believe in action. St. Teresa of Avila believes in action. I believe in action."

Howard could only repeat, "I know! I know!"

"One day you will have to make up your mind," Cordis said, pushing hard.

"It'll kill my mother," Howard responded. "She just won't have Rosa as a daughter-in-law. Even called her 'that black *dreck*.'"

It was the Yiddish word for *dirt*.

"It won't kill her. Rosa isn't thanatogenic." Cordis gave his words a Yiddish singsong inflection, and coined a term in the process.

"My mother is old-fashioned, from the old country. Things like this didn't happen in the Pale."

Most of the million and a half Jews in East Europe at the end of the 18th century lived in Poland, and when Poland was absorbed by Russia a million Jews came under the rule of Catherine II, Empress of Russia. The Jews in the east were then compelled to live in the pales of settlement, much as the Jews of Western Europe had been herded into ghettoes.

"This is America," Cordis said, "the melting pot, a mosaic, the mosaic land of promise, mosaic in lower case, like in a colorful latticework, not like in Moses."

"Rex, you can make light of my situation," Howard said, upset. "What the hell do you know about these problems!"

"Tut, tut, Howard. You're not here to listen to my problems; we're here to discuss yours. You've been crying to me over this marital issue of yours for close to a year. Today is Julius Caesar's day, the ides of March, a day of decision."

77

"How do I decide this?" His patient was agitated. "If I marry Rosa, I gain a wife and lose a mother—kill my mother."

Cordis held his tongue and let Howard calm down over the next half minute.

'I can't tell you what to do, Howard," he finally said. "All I can do is try to help you gain some insight."

"Then please do!"

Cordis stared off into space for a few moments and then looked directly at his patient. "You haven't married Rosa all these years," he said, "but not because of your mother—"

"No?" Howard cut him off, his voice raised. "Then why haven't I? You tell me why." His words were heated.

"Let me finish my train of thought, Howard. It has nothing to do with your mother. The key to the whole issue is your own Jewishness, not your mother."

"Rosa doesn't mind about that," Howard said, calmer now. "That's never been a problem."

"I'm not talking about you and Rosa, I'm talking about you and your mother," Cordis said, with a clever twist. "With you and Rosa the real issue is what will the children be—color-wise and religion-wise. If this were France or one of the Caribbean departments like Martinique, your children would be officially white. But this is America, and here your children would be officially black. Do you want your children to be black? That's the question you need to answer. They will live in a black world, and you yourself will be dragged into that black world. Is that what you want for yourself and for your children? These are the questions you need to address."

The hour with Howard left Cordis drained, and he was relieved when his 9 o'clock, a Medicaid patient, did not show up. His back was aching, and when a hot shower that night and the following morning had brought no relief, he went to see Dr. J. Forseman, a physiatrist, or specialist in physical medicine and rehabilitation, who injected his left scapular area with a large volume of Novacain.

"It all weighs heavily on my shoulders," he said to the physiatrist. "The burdens of this life."

But at least he was pain-free for most of the day and able to concentrate on finding a solution to his own personal dilemma.

That evening he went to services at the synagogue not far from St. Alvin's. A recurrent phrase from the readings was: 'I am the God of your fathers.' Cordis was secure in his faith and he knew he had an obligation to look to the future. There was no way he could pass on the family legacy to someone outside the faith. His nearly two-year romance with Josephine Bondaz would end.

CHAPTER FIFTEEN

Renata was punctual for her appointment the following Tuesday, but she found it difficult to get going. She appeared tired and her complexion was of a sallowish hue.

"You think you're up to it tonight?" Cordis asked her.

She shrugged off his concern and directed attention to a picture on the east wall of the office.

"Is that Samson in chains?" she asked.

He shook his head. "A charcoal by one of my patients of Columbus in chains."

"Columbus?"

"Cristobal Colon himself," the doctor said. "The Genius of the Ocean. The noblest wandering Jew of the fifteenth century."

Renata forced a smile. "Was he that illustrious in Jewdom?" Then she suddenly caught herself. "Wait a minute! Columbus a Jew? Did you say that?"

"Christoforo Colombo. Of the tribe of Levi. Of the family of Santa Maria."

"Are we talking about the same Columbus? The Christopher Columbus of history?"

"The very same," Cordis responded. "Columbus is correct, if you must use the Latinized form of his name."

"I thought he was Italian."

"Well, there are Italian Jews, you know. Like Olivetti, the typewriter manufacturer."

"I know that all Jews aren't named Goldberg or Silverstein," Renata commented cuttingly.

"Well, the Colombo family were Spanish Jews, Sephardim, not Ashkenazim, who moved to Genoa. Colombo is actually Italian for the Hebrew name Jonah. And among French Jews of the time, Colon was a common name, also the equivalent for Jonah."

"I can recall the biblical Jonah," Renata said, "who was swallowed up by a whale." She paused. "I think he was trying to hide from his calling—he didn't want to be a prophet."

"True," Cordis said, nodding. "Well, this latter-day Jonah was a maritime prophet."

"I may have seen his name written as Colon somewhere."

"The Spanish for Colombo is Colom, not Colon," Cordis said, articulating the *m* and *n* clearly. "Colom was too popular a Jewish name in Spain, so Columbus, or Colombo, changed it to Colon, as in the French."

"Such a lot of bother," Renata said. "Why all that fuss over his name?"

"Camouflage, my good patient," the doctor answered. "He wasn't going to get anywhere known as a Jewish explorer."

"I have never heard this theory before," Renata stated forcefully. "I don't know whether to believe it."

"It's not a matter of belief," Cordis responded, with equal forcefulness. "There's a great deal of substantiating historical data behind it. A lot of historians—the Marques de Dosfuentes, Diaz Perez—consider him to have been a Spanish Jew."

"Well, supposing you are correct about his origins—"

"There's more," Cordis interrupted her. "The whole voyage to the New World, its conception and execution, was a Jewish enterprise. Columbus' crew was mainly Jewish and the expedition was Jewish-financed."

"I read that Queen Isabella—"

"That Isabella the Catholic hocked her jewels to raise the money for the ships." The doctor let out a mock laugh. "That's the poppycock they teach schoolchildren here and apparently what you learned, too. No, it was Luis de Santangel, Controller General of Aragon, and Gabriel Sanchez, the Chief Treasurer of Aragon, who put up the cash."

"And you say his crew was also Jewish," Renata stated, sounding dubious.

"Key members were," the psychiatrist responded. "There was the ship's physician, Bernal. The surgeon, Marco. Luis de Torres, who spoke Hebrew, Chaldean and a little Arabic—they needed someone like him in case they met up with the Grand Khan. Remember, Columbus was aiming for Cipangu and Cathay, Marco Polo's names for Japan and China." He paused to let out a breath before continuing. "Let's see," he went on, "there was also Rodrigo Sanchez and Alonso de la Calle. Calle was the fellow who shouted out: 'Land ho!' Torres was the first to actually set foot upon the soil of the New World."

"All these men you named were known to be Jews?" Renata asked, the doubt in her voice still obvious.

"Torres was baptized at the last minute so that he could sail on the Santa Maria," he responded. "All those I've named, including the financiers, were *conversos*, New Christians. The older Christians hated and envied them—many Jews had risen to positions of prominence in Spain, which was then Castile and Aragon. They were called *marranos*, or swine in English translation. Many of them remained crypto-Jews, Christian in public but Jewish in private."

"And why were they converting in such large numbers?" Renata asked. "What was the attraction of the Catholic Church?"

Cordis snickered. "They converted because of Isabella and Ferdinand's Edict of Expulsion, which their Catholic Majesties signed on March thirtieth, fourteen ninety-two. But Jews had already started migrating from Spain in fourteen-eighty with the coming of the Inquisition. By fourteen ninety-two, the law of the land was either convert or get out."

Renata looked at him and smiled. "You make it all sound so . . . timely, as though it happened recently. You make it come alive."

Cordis nodded. "We need to be in touch with the past," he said, looking her squarely in the eye for a moment or two. He then resumed his chronicle. "The Jews of Spain had until July thirty-first to leave the country. And Columbus sailed from Palos on August third, with a great many ships in the same harbor packed with Jews bound for exile in Portugal, France and other countries. They were leaving everything they owned in the world behind or sold for a pittance."

"Would you call that irony—Columbus' ships and ships full of Jewish exiles side by side like that?"

"Quite the case," Cordis replied. "Now, Columbus was ready to sail on August second, the ninth of Ab in the Jewish calendar, a day of fasting in memory of the destruction of Jerusalem by Nebuchadnezzar and again by Titus. But he wouldn't set sail on such an ill-omened day." After a pause the doctor added, "Who but a Jew would act that way?"

"History does rank him high," Renata commented.

"Definitely so," Cordis affirmed. "His place in history is secure."

"Maybe he was one of your Hebrews," Renata affirmed.

Cordis was busy drawing a triangle with three lines across it on a blank sheet of paper.

81

"Columbus signed his name with an acrostic," Cordis said. "On the first line he wrote '.S.', to begin: 'Sanctus, Sanctus, Adonai, Sanctus'— 'Holy, Holy is the Lord of Hosts'. He took it from Isaiah 6:8. On the second line he wrote it out: '.S.A.S.'—the letter A is the Hebrew abbreviation of *Adonai*, the name for God. And on the third line of his signature he had 'XMY'. That line was in deference to the King and Queen. The X was for Christ, as in the Greek *Xristos*, the M for Maria and the Y was to represent the corresponding letter in Greek for *son*. Putting the letters 'XMY' together yielded: 'Christ, son of Mary.'"

Cordis stretched out his arm over his desk and Renata leaned forward to receive the sheet of paper.

She studied it for a few moments and then said, "This is all very deep." She returned the paper to him.

"I know it's heavy stuff," Cordis said. "Even heady stuff. But it's historically accurate."

"Do you think Columbus really believed the earth was round when he started out?" she asked.

"Assuredly," the doctor replied. "The Marranos had read of the earth being round in the Book of Esdras, and Columbus had an obsession about that book."

Cordis continued to relate how, banished from their homeland in 70 A.D., the Jews were scattered to the four corners of the known world. Jewish communities kept in touch with one another via traveling representatives, and as money came into general use in Europe, these Jews became the Church's brokers in its own business transactions. The Church could not lend money to Christians because it would have to charge interest—usury in its original sense—which it was forbidden from doing, so Jews became money lenders. Thus was born the banking business.

Other Jews, as though driven by memories deep within their collective unconscious, took to the sea, first from Portugal and later Spain. It remained for a Portuguese Jew, Levi ben Gershon, to perfect the quadrant, which opened up the seas for Portuguese navigators. Then Abraham Zacuto, astrologer to the Court of Portugal, improved the astrolabe, and Vasco da Gama was able to go on his history-making voyage around the Cape of Good Hope. It was also Zacuto who composed the astronomical tables Columbus would use on his expeditions to the New World."

Renata had listened attentively, and following a short silence asked, "Was da Gama also Jewish?"

"Not to my knowledge."

"How did a little country like Portugal get involved in such an ambitious effort of exploration?" she asked.

"Geogaphically, Portugal stood at the edge of the world," Cordis explained. "Portugal represented the westernmost boundary of the known world."

"So the Portuguese had a national curiosity."

"Yes, a collective curiosity which drove them to discover what was beyond their horizon."

After a pause Renata said, "I've enjoyed the history lesson." Seeing the doctor raise his eyebrows in what she took to be an expression of pique, she quickly added, "Yes, indeed, I have. It has been positively illuminating. But let me ask you this. What does it have to do with me, in particular my psychotherapy? All this talk, does it have anything to do with my purpose in being here?"

The doctor wasn't at all defensive. "I saw at the beginning of the hour that you were still not feeling well, under the weather, so I took over most of the talking for tonight."

"Oh, I see," she said.

"The key word for the hour is the one you just used—illuminating. To illuminate is to brighten with light. Next time we will see how you have been illuminated. Between the time you leave this evening and before you return again in seven days, I believe the material covered in this session will work its way into your unconscious, where it will illuminate you."

"And when it penetrates my subconscious—is that the same as unconscious?—then what?"

"Yes, they're the same, and when it sinks into the depths of your mind where your memory traces are stored, those that you have formed for yourself and those laid down through other means, then . . . well, we'll just have to wait and see, won't we?"

When she left his office that evening Renata was obviously tired, but she looked buoyed up.

Later that evening, before leaving for home, Cordis telephoned Father Dominic.

"I felt it so strongly, so overwhelmingly this evening," he said to the priest, "that with this young woman we are in the Valley of the Numina. I even gave her a little post-hypnotic suggestion without hypnotizing her, that's how sure I am."

"If you are in that mystical valley, it will become apparent soon enough," was Father Dominic's only comment.

CHAPTER SIXTEEN

Madam Bee had phoned him several days in advance to let him know she was going to Wisconsin to visit her nephew for a few weeks, so when Joey Dee wandered into the clinic unscheduled in the afternoon of the 21st, Cordis had her 3:30 slot available for him. Joey, carrying a brown grocery bag as he always did when visiting the clinic, had to wait while Cordis attended to his regularly scheduled patients.

The first was a middle-aged woman, accompanied by her husband, suffering from a depressive illness. Cordis had started her off on an average dose of Tofranil, one of the so-called tricyclic antidepressants, or TCA's for short, and now had her in after two weeks for a check.

"It ain't doin' me no good," she complained to the doctor.

"It takes two to three weeks to start working, if it's going to work," Cordis said, repeating what he had told her when he prescribed the medication for her.

"And supposin' it don't?" she asked.

"Then we increase the dose," he answered. Anticipating her next question, Cordis quickly added, "And if it still doesn't work, then we'll try another antidepressant. Somewhere there's an antidepressant medication that will work for you; but before abandoning Tofranil, let's give it a good trial."

"You know, Doc," her husband volunteered, "it's really her back, low back pain that's the problem. Constant pain like that can make you depressed."

She hadn't mentioned back pain to him when he had seen her initially two weeks earlier, and he spent the next ten minutes obtaining as much medical history as he could obtain about her lumbar pain. The picture Cordis formed in his mind of his patient's pain problem did not add up to a true sciatica, which was the diagnosis she said her family doctor had given her. Cordis had her lean over to her left side in her chair, and he pressed his thumb against a spot on the outer aspect of her thigh near the hip joint.

She immediately yelled out, "Ouch! That hurt!"

"I think you need the bursa right there where I pressed injected with a little steroid or a local anesthetic," Cordis said.

"What's her problem?" her husband asked.

"Bursitis," the doctor replied.

"Can you do that for me?" she asked "Inject it?"

"No, ma'am," Cordis said. "This is a mental health clinic, not a medical office. Get your family doctor to do it for you."

"What about the medication you gave me?"

"Stay on it for a while," he said while writing down her other diagnosis, greater trochanteric bursitis, on a clinic prescription for her to give to her own doctor. "You can have bursitis and depression at the same time—the two aren't mutually exclusive."

A few years later, physicians would learn that TCA's are also useful adjuncts in the management of many forms of musculoskeletal pain.

Before he could call for his next patient, Mrs. Rosenberg asked him to see one from Division II because three of the four doctors on that division were either out ill or off for the day. She presented him with a forty-five year old lady who had been suffering from auditory hallucinations for years and had been hospitalized at Gotham Bedlam, a favorite nickname for the state hospital, half a dozen times.

"Why is her doctor always raising her Mellaril dosage?" her articulate daughter wanted to know right off.

Cordis spent some time reviewing her clinic chart and performed a mental examination in about fifteen minutes. He thought she was functioning rather well and saw no need for her to be on a daily dose of 800 mgs of Mellaril.

"He can't go any higher than what she's on now," he said, responding to the opening comment by the daughter. "Eight hundred a day is what we call our legal limit."

"Every time she complains about hearing noises in her head, he raises her dose a little more."

"Does she ever say she's hearing strange noises?" Cordis asked, stressing the word "strange."

Such a qualifying and loaded word might lend just the necessary reinforcement for an examiner to conclude she was actively hallucinating.

"I hear this grinding noise when I move my neck," the patient said, turning her head from side to side and rotating it. There was discernible anxiety in her voice.

In reading through her chart, Cordis had noticed a reference to spur formation in her cervical spine.

"Aha, so it's in your neck," he said.

"Yes, when I turn my head like I'm doing," she averred, still demonstrating for him.

"We have a term for that," the doctor said. "It's called crepitus, meaning a crackling noise due to calcification, which is what you have in

85

the neck region of your spine. It's not the voices coming back. It's just your arthritis."

"Is that what it is?" she asked, her face lighting up.

"I'll tell you what I'll do," Cordis said. "I see where you left the hospital the last time on two hundred milligrams a day of Mellaril, so I'll cut your dosage down to four hundred a day, and when you come back to see your doctor in a month, if all is going well, ask him to cut it back further. That's what I'll do for you. For your neck problem, you'll need to see an orthopedist."

Mrs. Rosenberg cajoled him into seeing another Division II patient, a young woman who also had head symptoms.

"I've had this pressure or heaviness on my head for years," she told Cordis. "Like a band tied around my head. The explanation I keep hearing is that I'm neurotic. So I count my blessings that they don't consider me to be psychotic." She let out a nervous laugh.

Her doctor was treating her for depression, but Cordis thought the dose of her antidepressant was inadequate.

"If you're going to take one of these new marvels of medicine, take a proper dose," he said to her, writing her a prescription at double her current dosage. Then he added, "Do you have a post-nasal drip?"

"Do I!" she exclaimed. "I drip like an icicle in summer."

Cordis palpated her frontal sinuses and then her maxillary sinuses for tenderness.

"That's sore," she said, flinching both times.

"You may have a chronic sinusitis problem which could account for the constant pressure or tightness you feel around your head. It's quite common. Do you suffer from headaches?"

"Yes, I get them often." She pointed to her forehead.

"Well, if you haven't done so already, you should have your sinuses x-rayed."

"No one ever suggested that to me before," she said. "My complaint has always been dismissed as neurosis."

"It could be physical," Cordis said.

There was a technical term doctors used for pressure on the head: carebaria. Cordis was one who liked to find rational, meaning physiological, explanations for symptoms, wherever possible, and he tried to avoid using the label *neurotic*.

"I don't have a family doctor," the patient said.

"Mrs. Rosenberg will refer you to the city hospital nearest your home," Cordis responded. "To their ENT clinic." Then he thought he better add, "That's Ears, Nose and Throat. If your sinus x-rays are all right, then this pressure problem will probably clear up when your depression lifts."

"Which will be when?"

"When you're on an effective antidepressant dose, which I've just prescribed for you."

After seeing two more patients, in for their PD injections, Cordis was free to see Joey Dee. He was out of medication again, about twelve days before he was due for his regularly scheduled appointment.

"Please don't be hostile wit' me, Dr. Cordis," he said pleadingly. The anguish on his face touched the doctor.

Cordis looked at the pathetic hulk seated across the desk from him for a few seconds, then said, "Don't you mean angry instead of hostile?"

He interpreted the intended meaning of the odd word selection as nothing more than a careless semantic shift, but for Joey it had a definite, unambiguous meaning.

I went t' da movies an' saw a double feature, Dr. Cordis," he said. "A twin bill o' westerns. Where da Indians kep' gettin' killed by da white soldiers. Da redskins were called hostiles. One o' dem killed a cavalry lieutenant wit' an arrow right t'rough his t'roat. Gee, Dr. Cordis, it went t'rough his t'roat."

Cordis figured he could be a representation of the cavalry officer, and the arrow through his throat not only killed him but silenced him. Why would Joey want to keep me quiet? Cordis asked himself. To listen to him, he answered. But what is he really saying?

"So you're angry with Lieutenant Cordis, so angry that you even want to kill him with a bow and arrow," the doctor said as good-naturedly as he could manage.

"Oh, no, Dr. Cordis," Joey protested. "Oh, no." The pained expression on his face was pathetic, and he wrung his hands so hard that the brown bag on his lap fell to the floor, spilling its contents around and under Cordis' desk. The doctor helped him retrieve the six oranges and three BIC's, Joey's established offering, which had been disgorged. "Here, I brung ya a gift," he said, after everything was back in the bag.

"Thanks very much," Cordis said. "You know, you shouldn't be spending your money like this, especially since you're short on cash yourself."

The doctor had said much the same thing concerning his gift-giving ritual every time Joey came to the clinic.

"Aw, dey don't cost much," Joey said. "I get 'em on sale."

Cordis suddenly wondered whether he indeed bought them or perhaps stole them. "I appreciate your thoughtfulness and kindness," he said, looking no further for an answer to his unspoken question.

When Joey saw him place the paper bag with its contents in a drawer of his desk, he asked, "Ain't ya gonna use my pens?"

With each and every one of his clinic visits, Cordis had told him that he turns his gifts over to the personnel in the day-care program. Yet Joey would always ask him the same question.

This time Cordis came up with a different answer. "Well, Joey, I write in black," he said, "and these pens of yours are blue. But don't fret. They'll wind up being used where needed and with appreciation."

"Next time I'll bring ya black pens," Joey said, with a serious look. "I didn't know ya don't write wit' blue pens."

The matter of the pens definitely weighed heavily on his mind. So this time Cordis wrote his prescriptions for Thorazine and Stelazine in blue with one of Joey's BIC's. It helped send him on his way smiling.

Shortly after Joey left, Cordis received a phone call from Sgt. O'Meara at the local police precinct.

"My boy's doin' fine," he said, "but yours is in hot water again." He was talking about Pat O'Connell.

"What's he done now?" the doctor asked, sighing deeply.

"A little mayhem down at his favorite tavern. Can't you get the man to go to AA?"

"You can lead a horse to trough, but you can't make an alcoholic ass drink water," Cordis responded, shaking his head in disgust.

"Next time, he's gonna wind up doin' some jail time," the Irishman said. "I'm sendin' him over to your place with a couple o' my men."

He hung up before Cordis had a chance to tell him that Pat was a private, not a clinic, patient.

The doctor sat quietly mulling over his sessions with several of the patients he had had just treated, rather than have to think about Pat. He had extended himself with a few of them, crossing the boundary from psychiatry into general medicine, something the administration strongly resented. Most of his clinic patients couldn't afford adequate medical care, and what the municipal hospitals offered was sub-standard. So he did what he could to help.

He felt compassion for the woman with the low back pain problem. Had she been trying to collect workman's compensation insurance, it would have been a different matter. Low back pain can be more than just an anatomical disorder. It has its behavioral concomittants—patients have been known to whack their injured areas with hammers, monkey wrenches and crowbars prior to showing up for their physical examination to try to improve their case for compensation.

He liked the way the Division II patient had joked about being neurotic, trusting that neurosis was a defense against psychosis. Some experts still adhered to the continuity hypothesis, that schizophrenia is latent in all of us. Cordis thought that some people were neurologically wired for schizophrenia, and under the pressures of everyday living became psychotic casualties.

The police were at the clinic with Pat in less than half an hour. Pat had sobered up, but his clothing was in disarray, his bushy hair uncombed and his breath foul.

"You're a walking wreck," Cordis said. "You know something, pal. You're giving me a bad name."

"I'm sorry, Rex," Pat said mechanically, with no conviction in his voice.

When he was doing his specialty training in psychiatry, one of his professors had sneered at him for carrying an alcoholic as a long-term psychotherapy patient. A thorough-going psychoanalyst, he thought the residents should treat *suitable* candidates, meaning healthy neurotics. There was even a mnemonic for it: YAHWEH patients—young adult, healthy, white, employed and high IQ. Character-disordered people were not deemed worthy for treatment on the couch. That alcoholics were more difficult to treat in individual psychodynamic psychotherapy was indisputable. But Cordis felt it was worth a try. His training patient had gotten some value out of his efforts, but Pat O'Connell was another story altogether.

"I gather you didn't stay long with the Antabuse, if you gave it a try at all."

"The stuff made my breath stink so bad, Rex, I became a social outcast," Pat said laughingly.

Antabuse, or disulfiram, is a sulfur-containing compound, and when exhaled the breath does smell like rotten eggs. It is one of the reasons patients decide to stop taking it.

"Look at the problems you're creating for me," Cordis scolded. "I'm seeing you, a private patient, on clinic time. That's a conflict of interest. I can get hell for it and probably will. But so what. Even if I were to bill you for this, it would only mean you haven't paid me for your last eleven, instead of ten, visits. You might as well be a clinic patient."

"Aw, it can't be all that bad, Rex," Pat said light-heartedly. "Besides, I've figured out how to beat the drinking problem."

"That I'd like to hear," Cordis said.

"I'm gonna get rid of all my whiskey glasses," Pat said and laughed.

"And we can cure bed-wetting by getting rid of all beds," Cordis said

89

harshly. "After a year of therapy, which you've never taken seriously, you still can't acknowledge that you're an alcoholic. That's the first step, and you still resist taking it."

Cordis' method was a fast-paced psychotherapy accomplished in one year with once-a-week sessions. That was becoming his trademark. Pat O'Connell represented a failure.

"I'm serious," Pat said, but not sounding so.

"What's the use!" Cordis mumbled.

"The truth is, I can't keep up with all the pills you sawbones want me to take," he said querulously. "You want me to swallow Antabuse, another doc tells me to take something for high blood pressure, and last year you were browbeating me to try an antidepressant."

"How high is your blood pressure?" Cordis asked.

"The police doc took it before. He said it was elevated."

Cordis sighed and got up. "Stay put," he said. "Don't move from that chair. I'll be right back."

He went to the nursing station and borrowed Miss Jones' blood-pressure cuff and stethoscope and returned to his office with the equipment. Pat sat silently while Cordis took his blood pressure.

"It's one-seventy over a hundred," the doctor said. "If it's been running this high, you should definitely be on something to bring it down."

"Too many pills, Rex," Pat said, shaking his head in a negative gesture. "Too many pills to take."

"This is my last try," the doctor said sternly. "I'm going out on a limb for you this time, the final time. I'm going to try a novel approach. With one medication, only one, I will try to take care of your three health problems: your blood pressure, your alcoholism and your depression."

"One for the price of three," Pat said facetiously, but showing some interest.

"This drug will bring your pressure down, ruin your taste for alcohol, so don't even think of drinking while you're on it, and it's an antidepressant to boot."

"All that, Rex? Really?"

"Scout's honor. You take it once a day only."

"Wow!" Pat let out, showing a degree of enthusiasm he had never displayed in a year of visiting the doctor.

Cordis reached into the bottom drawer of his desk and retrieved several bottles of the medication, Eutonyl. "You don't even have to pay for it," he said. "It's a monomine oxidase inhibitor, which means you'll have to adhere strictly to the diet I've enclosed. The diet sheet also instructs you as to what medications to avoid. Do not, I repeat, do not deviate from these instructions."

"Well, thanks, Rex," Pat said, glancing at the printed material Cordis had handed him and pocketing the medication.

"If you're still alive in three weeks, call me at my private office for an appointment. Do your mother a favor: try to stay alive." Without further ado, Cordis ushered him out of his office.

Cordis stocked up on drug samples furnished him by various pharmaceutical firms. Some of them, especially items not on the clinic's formulary, he would give to carefully selected patients. Every three months he would clean out his drawers so that the medications wouldn't go past their expiration date. There were a number of relief agencies which would send someone over to pick them up. The latest one, the Costa Rican Relief Agency, inventoried his most recent offering at $5,000.

CHAPTER SEVENTEEN

Cordis joined Harris for early dinner that Saturday evening at Michio's, a Japanese restaurant tucked away in a Queens residential neighborhood. They made small talk for half an hour. Harris sipped his rice wine while Cordis slowly drank an Okinawan beer.

Cordis wasn't much of a drinker, but once in a while he would try a beer to test the durability of his stomach. He was accustomed to taking large daily doses of aspirin for his arthritic condition, and alcohol on top of aspirin was a combination not to be recommended. He swallowed three or four of the 325-mg strength enteric-coated aspirin tablets two to four times a day, depending on how much pain he had. Aspirin, with its anti-inflammatory action, was the analgesic of choice in the treatment of the arthritides. He was concerned about the enteric-coated aspirin's coating, shellac, painted onto the tablets. This protective coating allowed the tablets to pass through the stomach untouched into the duodenum's alkaline environment, where they dissolved. He always read the expiration date on the bottles carefully, because the longer the tablets stood on the pharmacy shelf the harder the shellac would become. It could become hard enough to resist dissolution, and the tablets could pass out into the feces intact. (The manufacturers of these pills would subsequently change the coating to phthalate derivatives.)

Harris liked his fish raw, but Cordis insisted his be baked, broiled or steamed. A case of beef tapeworm he acquired in Mexico in 1947 had left him squeamish at the sight of steak even slightly pink on the inside, and he never again ate sliced roast beef, the quintessential American Sunday dinner meat entree, usually cooked rare, at least for the more carnivorous appetite. The thought of raw or undercooked fish was absolutely anathema to him. During his internship he diagnosed a case of *Diphyllobothrium latum* in a patient, an elderly Jewish lady who liked to eat gefilte fish uncooked. This is the fish tapeworm every medical student learns about, and learns to spell correctly. Rarely seen in the United States, it is common in Japanese waters.

Cordis observed Harris blissfully consume his sushi, while he poked a fork at his baked white fish. Sometimes he could tolerate the sight of the raw fish Harris dined on, but this was not one of those times. Watching what his friend was eating that evening ruined his appetite, and he had to force himself to eat, a rare experience for him, for he loved to eat. He would eat his way through a stomachache, something he would never advise a patient to do. Overcoming stomach pain in this manner represented his first triumph of mind over body, of freeing himself of an organ pain by marshalling forces within his brain that could short-circuit a critical pain pathway.

He was probably one of the first middle-aged men in the country to be on daily aspirin. As such, it probably gave him a "cardiac advantage" — protection against heart attack. On the other hand, he thought all the aspirin he took was causing his hair to thin out prematurely.

Harris wanted the doctor to read a document he had brought along to dinner.

Cordis looked at the envelope it was in and said, "It's in Japanese."

"The contents are in English," Harris responded.

Harris was a man of few words, in keeping with an ancient Japanese tradition that stressed introspection. Through introspection a person finds his inner world and its center, *kokoro*, or "heart." The inner self, *jibun*, is symbolized by both heart (*kokoro*) and stomach (*hara*), just as the outer self is localized to the face or mouth. What lies inside the *kokoro* or *hara* is in harmony with the self, but what is written on the face or issues forth from the mouth, that is, words, is not to be trusted. This philosophical attitude is reflected in a number of Japanese proverbs, such as,

'Mouths are to eat with, not to speak with,' and 'Born mouth first, he perishes by his mouth.'

The document Harris showed the psychiatrist was an English translation of a report from a Kyoto hospital where Renata Delacross had been treated for six weeks in 1966 for a condition diagnosed as *shinkeishitsu*, type 1. The diagnosis had been made by a Morita therapist. Symptoms listed for her were dizziness, fatigue, weakness, gastrointestinal complaints, feeling of fullness in the head, menstrual troubles, headache and several others. The report included an explanation that tried to bring the Morita classification into balance with Western psychiatry by equating *shinkeishitsu* with "nervosity." (Nervosity is now an obsolete term for a chronic state of nervousness, a condition halfway between normality and a formal psychiatric diagnosis.)

The other types of *shinkeishitsu* were also explained in the document. Type 2 was equivalent to what American psychiatry was calling obsessional and phobic neurosis. Cordis thought that such personalities as Joan Crawford and Howard Hughes, with their mysophobia, or fear of contamination, could conceivably fall into this category. Type 3 was equivalent to the West's anxiety neurosis.

Cordis felt he was not qualified to comment on any aspect of Morita therapy. His only statement to Harris after studying the document was, "Well, they pinpointed her psychiatric problem as a neurosis. That part fits."

Harris showed himself to be knowledgeable on the subject, explaining its workings to the psychiatrist lucidly and in detail. Essentially, it consists of a period of complete bed rest in total isolation for five to seven days followed by a four to five week gradational period of work activity. As best as Cordis could make out, Morita therapy seemed to be a combination of milieu therapy and behavioral modification so organized as to be tailor-made to the Japanese character and way of life.

"I don't think Morita therapy is exportable," Cordis commented.

"A Japanese learns to accept things as they are, *arugamama* as it is called, the key to Morita therapy. He learns to submit to his symptoms without feeling disgraced. Then he unites with his illness instead of fighting it."

"Unites? How does he do that?"

"I'll give you an example," Harris responded. "Takehisa Kora, a famous Morita therapist, taught that saliva in your mouth is not filthy because it is in unity with yourself; but once it is spit out it cannot be swallowed back because it is now filth."

"So that's *arugamama*?"

"One more thing," Harris said. "As fire begets more fire, so does fire extinguish itself."

"Oriental obfuscation," Cordis said laughingly. To himself he added, Of course, it burns itself out!

Harris continued in his serious tone. "There is a *shinkeishitsu* called *tai jin-kyofu-sho*, meaning the patient has a problem with blushing. I think you doctors have a word for it in English."

"Erythrophobia," Cordis offered.

Harris nodded and continued. "The patient in Morita treatment is taught to confront it by blushing freely until his sensitivity is extinguished."

"Yes," Cordis said, "the behaviorists here do something like that. Behavioral psychology."

"But like a number of things in the East, Morita therapy stems from Buddhism, particularly Zen Buddhism, not psychology."

"I see."

"Union with nature is the starting point," Harris explained. "The acceptance of what is. Dr. Morita taught acceptance. Summer is hot, winter is cold. 'Endure the given temperature,' he wrote. "

"Harris, we now have air conditioning and central heating," the doctor said. "Few people need endure heat and cold nowadays."

"You must not deny to the body what the body is capable of experiencing," the old Japanese responded. "That is part of *arugamama*. So is not thinking about one's past."

"They would deny the past? You mean to say the Morita therapist doesn't explore past experiences?"

"You learn to bury the past," Harris answered. "To cast it aside completely."

"So," Cordis said, stroking his chin, "Morita therapy operates solely at the conscious level, with no contribution from the unconscious."

"Japanese distrust words. *Taitoku* is what counts—to realize and accept what is, what the reality is, on the basis of one's own experience. Words count for nothing—the therapist's presence is enough. What you do, action, counts; what you think or feel is unimportant in Morita therapy."

"A psychoanalyst would starve to death in Japan," Cordis said jocularly.

"There is no need for so much talk," Harris said. "Japanese like to keep a diary—writing is not only a means of communication but also of self-expression."

"I know," Cordis said, " 'Mouths are to eat with, not to speak with.' "

Harris brought the conversation back to his godchild.

94

"Renata lived with the *sensei's* family when she was in Kyoto," he said. "She used to scrub his back—bathing is a serious activity in Japan."

"Well, Harris, such intimacy is not part of the relationship between psychiatrist and patient here," Cordis said.

He didn't think it prudent to mention the Reichian technique of massaging the patient, stretched out nude on a couch or bed, in order to manipulate areas of tension. Forget about Wilhelm Reich, he said to himself. He was just a renegade Freudian who became a pseudo-physiotherapist and a lecher.

"It is in Japan," Harris said, "because the *sensei's* character is as important as his skill and knowledge as a doctor."

"The Japanese world is not the Western world," Cordis said.

"Do you know that the wife of her Morita therapist still writes to her? She is Renata-*chan*, part of the family."

"I'm impressed, Harris," Cordis said. After a short pause he asked, "Does Renata read Japanese?"

"She reads it and writes it. I taught her myself."

Hmm, Cordis said to himself. She never listed Japanese among her languages. I wonder why. "That's interesting," he said aloud.

"She speaks it well, too."

After reading the document a second time, Cordis said to Harris, "There's a lot of information here, but it doesn't say anything about the effectiveness of the treatment."

"The treatment helped her," Harris responded. "It made it possible for her to dare to venture beyond the confines of the Muslim world that kept her imprisoned."

Cordis didn't know what to make of Morita therapy. He was aware that psychoanalysis had found its way to Japan early in the century, only to have been rejected. Now he could understand why the Japanese would cast aside a therapeutic system based on the exploration of past events to explain present symptoms. He could also surmise that the benefits of the six-week reconditioning therapy Renata had undergone in 1966 had weakened with the passage of time.

Harris surprised him when he related how he had tried Morita therapy himself at the Tokyo Jikei Hospital for a depression he suffered following his grandfather's death. It had been more than an uncomplicated grief reaction in the wake of the death of a loved one.

The elderly Japanese described only his treatment at the hospital; Cordis had to figure out for himself what was going on psychodynamically with Harris at the time. Two issues surfaced in his mind. Harris must have experienced a sense of guilt in turning away from Buddhism, forsaking his ancestors to become a Catholic. Second, he probably suffered intense guilt during the War when he spied for the United States—there was little doubt left in Cordis' mind that Harris had been with the OSS—against the country of his birth. Perhaps that guilt also extended to the atomic bombing of Nagasaki, which had left his grandfather maimed and barely clinging to life.

All in all, it was an informative and satisfying evening. He learned a bit more about his patient, saw a layer drop from his reticent friend's shielded past and picked up a rudimentary knowledge of a distinctive Japanese psychotherapy.

CHAPTER EIGHTEEN

Renata was on time for her next session on the 27th of March. She began by asking, "Do you think I need psychoanalysis?"

"You mean the classical Freudian analysis?"

"You know, five days a week, reclining on the couch, staring into my id or whatever it is that drives and terrorizes my subconscious." She looked directly into the doctor's eyes. "Where I grew up, in the Arab and Iranian worlds, such lore didn't exist. Psychologizing seems to be a pecuiarly American activity."

"Pop psychology," the doctor commented. "Everyone supposes to know the language; few master it."

"Whatever," she said disdainfully. "My question is, do I need it?"

"No one needs psychoanalysis, but nearly everyone can benefit from it. That is, if five days every week out of your life for five years and twenty-five thousand dollars a year are part of the price you are prepared to pay for it."

"What is the other part?"

"Looking within can be painful at times," he answered. "It's also a rigid system with institutionalized rules and a language all its own, which you are apparently in the process of discovering for yourself."

"But I am only here one day a week. A single hour—"

He stopped her by saying, "Versus five hours you would have with a Freudian analyst. And perhaps you are thinking achieve results five times faster for your personal investment."

With his crowded schedule, his time for conducting his private practice was limited, and he preferred, anyway, to have five patients for one hour a week than one patient five days a week. His philosophy of treatment was built on obtaining results, that is, producing positive change in patients, and this he was determined to accomplish within the time frame of a year. Thus he pushed his patients along, sometimes even leading them into areas he chose for them based on his own intuitive inclination.

"Something like that," Renata said. "I grant you that the Freudians may be one-sided, but at least they're consistent. This way, our way, I don't know if what I say will be interpreted in a Freudian sense, a Jungian manner, according to Adler, or by whatever other way an eclectic chooses at a given moment. Do you understand what I am saying? Am I making sense?"

Cordis nodded. "Yes, my eclecticism is creating anxiety for you." Her rapidly expanding grasp of psychology impressed him.

"Precisely," Renata said. "With you moving from Freud to Jung to whoever, I don't know which way I am to go."

"You go forward. Always forward, regardless of the direction I may appear to you to be taking."

Renata sighed deeply. "Let me give you an example," she said. "I have a dream I want you to interpret for me. Now, maybe this dream is important, perhaps even crucial. But a Freudian psychoanalyst will give it one meaning and a Jungian, I suspect, another. And you being so eclectic, how do I know which of many schools of psychotherapy you will use to unravel, you know, to decipher my dream, a dream which may hold great importance."

Cordis looked directly at Renata. "You have a dream you consider important?"

"Freudians are sexual creatures of the mind," she went on, ignoring his question. "Jungians almost theologians. Then these existentialists, well, they're really philosophers. You see, I've been swotting," she added laughingly, using the British student's term for cramming for examinations. "I'm determined to master what you have labeled pop psychology."

"Good for you," Cordis said enthusiastically.

"So now, let me hear how you can approach a dream from more than

97

one school's perspective . . . or bias."

He waited for Renata to continue, but she sat in her chair expecting him to speak. "Okay," he finally said, "tell me your dream, and I'll try to interpret it for you from several different perspectives."

"No, I want an illustration."

"You want me to make up a dream?" he said. "Is that it?"

"Yes."

"Let me think then," the psychiatrist said. He knotted his hands and rested his chin on them for a few moments. "All right, I think I can create an example for you. Suppose you dream you are in a lifeboat, without a life jacket, on a choppy sea with only one oar—"

"An intriguing position to be in," Renata interjected.

"To be sure," Cordis said, smiling. "Well, anyway, you are at liberty to say that the lifeboat is a vessel and thus a female symbol, while the oar represents a penis symbol. The great waves heaving upon the vessel can be waves of sexual energy. And the oar—it takes two to row a boat—symbolizes the dreamer's impotence. Now, this might be a way to begin interpreting the dream from a Freudian perspective—"

"But women do not suffer from impotence," Renata interrupted.

"I should have said frigidity," Cordis corrected himself. "But as I said, that could represent a Freudian approach. A Jungian approach would find the dreamer at sea literally, terribly insecure—no life jacket—and ill-prepared to conquer her dilemma—only one oar against an angry sea."

"So, either sexuality or insecurity can be the essence of the dream," Renata said.

Cordis nodded. "There are other perspectives, too," he said, "but what we need to do is put the dreamer into the dream. We're just waffling through the theoretical. Let's get down to your dream, your important dream."

"Yes, my dream," Renata said, sighing. "I dreamt, and this was last week after my session with you, I dreamt I was a school teacher with a classroom full of little children. A little boy came up to me with a crayon drawing of a canary, a yellow canary. The bird occupied the center of the drawing. The remainder was mainly blue—ocean waves. Off to the side was a round, reddish sun."

Cordis had her retell the dream in an attempt to elicit additional details, but none were forthcoming.

"Where was the sun—to the right or to the left?"

"The left," Renata said, after a moment's thought. "Beginning to set."

98

"And the water?"

"There was lots of it, probably because it was the easiest part for my little artist to do. Just simple blue ocean waves."

"There's nothing else you can recall?" he pressed her.

"Just how I felt in the dream. I actually clutched that drawing to my heart and felt an inexplicable joy. Then the little boy said, 'It's yours forever.'"

"He said that?"

"Yes. I left that out before."

"Anything else you can recall?"

"The intensity of my joy. It was as though I was clutching the whole world to me. When I awoke—the excitement of that moment woke me up and I couldn't get back to sleep." Renata leaned forward. "Do you think motherhood is in my future?"

"It's your birthright as a woman, if you choose."

"Is that what I'm choosing?"

Cordis shrugged. "The choice is yours."

"But what about my dream?" Renata asked, a bit impatient. "What does it tell me?"

"That you have hope and great expectations."

"A palm reader could have told me as much," she said scornfully.

"Perhaps. But don't forget, your dream came following our last session together. The major theme of that hour was Columbus' journey to the New World."

"How can I forget!"

"Well, your dream is linked to that."

"I am linked to the great Jewish enterprise of the fifteenth century?" she asked sarcastically.

"The dream is, yes. And maybe you, too."

"This I have to hear!"

"Sure," Cordis said, pausing to organize his thoughts. "Choose a letter from A to Z," he continued. "Any letter in the alphabet."

"Any letter from A to Zed that pops into my head?"

That's right. You have twenty-six choices in English."

"All right, I choose H," Renata said, smiling at him enigmatically.

He waited a few seconds and then asked, "Why did you choose H?"

"You told me to choose. I could just as easily have chosen D for my name, but I chose H for 'heart,' Cordis rendered into English from the Latin, just to keep this little exercise of yours honest—I do not choose to fall victim to any psychological legerdemain."

"Okay," Cordis said and smiled. "H instead of C. Now, let's look at it carefully." He was deep in thought for several seconds. "Does the name *Hierro* mean anything to you?" He gave it the Spanish pronunciation, with the H silent.

Renata thought for a moment. "No, I don't think so."

"*Hierro* is the westernmost island of the Canaries. The Canary Islands."

"Um, I know. Yes, the Canary Islands. They lie off the coast of Cape Juby."

"Ptolemy, the Alexandrian astronomer of the second century, chose it for the prime meridian of longitude because it was the most westerly place known at the time."

"And?"

"And Columbus used the Canaries as a stop-over on his first voyage in fourteen ninety-two after his ships left Palos."

"So you believe that the canary in the drawing depicts, through the process of symbolization, the Canary Islands."

"Don't forget, this is your dream, not the little boy's. You, not he, created the canary. You also had your sun setting on the left, or in the west. If you were to look out from the Canaries to the west, on a clear day, the New World might be visible to you—adjusting for the curvature of the earth and using a powerful telescope. The world Columbus risked everything to discover for his and mankind's glory."

"Hurrah for Columbus! But where does all of this leave me in the great scheme of things?"

"On a journey of discovery of your own."

"To where?" Renata asked. "Am I to become the first female astronaut to land on Jupiter?" She sounded piqued.

"Outer space exploration may be the more glamorous, but the exploration of the inner realm of the unconscious mind produces rewards of its own." Cordis stopped at that point.

"I'm listening," Renata said, an encouragement for him to go on.

"Perhaps yours is to be a journey to yourself. A voyage to your inner center, where you will encounter the living mystery of the unconscious. On such a journey you go alone. Such a journey—and I stress this—requires the heart and mind of a true adventurer."

"What else do you see in my dream?" Renata asked.

"The sun, was it drawn in full?"

She considered the question for a moment. "Yes, it was round. A setting sun just above the horizon."

"A full circle can symbolize healing," he told her.

"And the water? You asked me to describe the water."

"Water is a common symbol for the unconscious."

"Since there was so much water in the drawing, I conclude that there is a lot of terrain in my subconscious, what you keep referring to as the unconscious—"

"That needs to be made conscious," Cordis said, completing the thought for her.

"Through therapy."

"A lot of what is necessary will be uncovered here."

"I see. Now, let me try to pull all this together. In essence, what you're saying is that I am to heal myself and then go on a personal journey."

"A far journey."

"To a far land?"

"Who knows where the journey courses. But in the end it will lead you to possession of what you have never thought to search for until now."

"Myself."

"You journey to yourself," Cordis answered, nodding.

"And somewhere in that journey to myself is to be found . . . what? Fulfillment?"

"That is it."

"For what I have always sought but never knew, which I can now begin to sense."

"We will consider this your dawning."

"Yes, I think I have it now! You know, I feel like Eliza Doolittle in My Fair Lady."

"Yes, I think you've got it."

Renata paused, and then with a frown said, "But suppose I hadn't chosen the letter H?"

The doctor smiled. "Pick another letter," he instructed her.

"Do I dare?"

"You want to know if this is manipulation or the unconscious at work, don't you?"

She gulped and said, "T."

Cordis responded instantly. "Tenerife, one of the main islands comprising the Canaries. You see, you still landed in the Canary Islands. Nothing has changed."

"Amazing!" Renata gasped.

"The power of the unconscious in the service of the ego."

Then something unusual happened. Renata fixed her gaze on the charcoal drawing of Columbus and for some time remained transfixed.

"I . . . I saw for a moment," she began when she came out of her trance-like state, "instead of seeing Columbus bound, I saw Jesus on his

101

cross." There followed a lengthy silence. "What strange power transformed one image into another?" she whispered dramatically.

"It is for you to tell me," Cordis said calmly, trying to control his own emotional excitement.

Renata took several deep breaths. "I think that will be all for today, Dr. Cordis."

"You still have time remaining," he said.

Renata shook her head. "No, I think that's more than enough for one day."

In the quiet of his office, Cordis pondered the session's dramatic conclusion. The historical Columbus, never a legendary hero and certainly never a demi-god, had nevertheless been elevated in his patient's unconscious to the Great Man level, an archetypal figure, where he could be transformed into a Christ image. There was also the possibility that Renata, raised in Egypt, had encountered the Egyptian sun-god, Ra, during her brief altered state of consciousness, for the sun had been a focus of attention during the session; and Ra, another archetype, could symbolize, through a mental crossover, the most important of the archetypal figures within Christianity: Christ himself.

Whatever had triggered the theophanic experience, what struck Cordis then and there was that the religious compartment, or dimension, of Renata's psyche was the key to her personality . . . and its malfunctioning.

Renata phoned him at The Adams late that night.

"I've been going over this evening's session in my mind," she said. "I don't want to end up wandering around aimlessly all over the five continents in search of God knows what, like kids are doing today. I hope that's not what I'm in for."

Cordis tried to set her mind at ease. "The journey of the soul traveler is different from that of the wanderer. When God said to Abraham, 'Get thee out!' he meant out of Ur and into the world, but also 'Go to your own self,' that is, find your personal destiny."

His words were reassuring to her, and she thanked him for taking the time to talk to her so late at night.

CHAPTER NINETEEN

There were repercussions from Pat O'Connell's visit to Cordis at the clinic. Mansoni confronted him about seeing an unregistered patient on state time, and then sent a memo to Alfonzo Gomez, M.D., the deputy director at Gotham State Hospital about it. Cordis had to take the subway up to Harlem again to explain in person what had happened that afternoon when the police brought Pat to the clinic instead of to his private office uptown. Gomez was understanding and accepted his explanation. In addition to his own well-paid position at the hospital, he conducted a lucrative ECT practice on the side, operating what the psychiatrists facetiously called a "shock palace." He was not about to make trouble for Cordis, given his own circumstances.

Even Miss Jones managed to take a whack at him. She filled out a form to Mansoni complaining that Dr. Cordis had written a prescription in blue ink when regulations required that all notes had to be written in black ink. Cordis explained to the administrator that a prescription was not a note and that all his chart entries were written in black. Apparently, notes written in blue didn't xerox well, and from time to time copies of entries, even entire charts, had to be made for legal purposes.

Cordis kept his progress notes as brief as possible, following the "SOAP" outline: Subjective, meaning the patient's complaint or complaints; Objective, or what the psychiatrist observed, that is, his findings; Assessment of the problem or problems; and Plan, the proposed action to be taken. Some progress notes could be accomplished in a minimum of four lines, one for each of the SOAP categories. Patients seen for the first time warranted a complete psychiatric history and mental status examination, which he would write up in one page. During his initial months at the clinic he had gone by the book, dictating detailed workups and progress notes, which were then sent for typing. The dictation equipment was antiquated, utilizing worn-out belts, and all too often these were misplaced by the secretarial corps. Soon he had learned that the typists didn't like typing up lengthy dictation. They had been hired through the new Comprehensive Employment Training Act, CETA, a help-the-poor-to-work program, and most of them typed at 30-35 words a minute. Belts containing lengthy dictation would conveniently disappear, so now he wrote all his notes and kept them short.

Thursday morning, the 29th, Cordis, along with other staff, was upset to find that Mansoni had drawn a red line across the morning sign-in sheet at 9:15. It was bad enough the professional staff had to sign in. On top of it, Mansoni posted the daily sheet near the main entrance where all the early arrived patients could see them registering for the day like white-or blue-collar workers. The fact that each staff member submitted a summary sheet detailing how every minute of the day was spent seemed sufficient. They grumbled at first, but went along with the signing in when they realized they couldn't overcome the administrator's persistence.

The red line, however, was too much. All the clinic personnel were members of the Civil Service Employees Association, and the rules and regulations contained a clause, clearly worded, prohibiting the state from acting as a timekeeper. Cordis was elected to see their CSEA representative at Gotham State Hospital, and so in the afternoon he took the subway once again to Harlem. The union delegate, a young black, rubbed his hands together gleefully when he heard the problem, confident that this was one case he was going to win. To date, he had lost all his CSEA-backed challenges to Albany.

At their bimonthly Friday morning divisional meeting the next day, Mansoni paraded into the clinic conference room to announce that the administration was close to a decision on renaming the clinic.

"What have your Madison Avenue geniuses come up with now?" the plump Dr. Arnold Grossman asked. He was one of the psychoanalysts and worked quarter-time.

"We kinda like Harbor House," Mansoni answered.

"Whatever happened to The Refuge?" Cordis asked derisively.

"There's something comforting and reassuring about Harbor House," the administrator said.

Grossman had demolished the idea of The Refuge the last time Mansoni had brought up the matter of a name change. Now he challenged him with his new proposal.

"Harbor House?" Grossman said. "That's like saying Mother House. You don't want a safe harbor—you seem to want a uterus."

"The clinic isn't a house, anyway," Cordis quipped in. "We don't have beds to accommodate patients overnight. You're confusing us with the YMCA or the Salvation Army."

"Our facility is so huge, so cavernous," Grossman said, "it's more like a mausoleum or catacomb. Why not name it Charnel House?"

His touch of gallows humor sailed past the administrator.

Cordis had little use for the twice monthly gatherings, attended by the entire divisional staff from doctors all the way to the CETA workers.

Administrative issues were always at the top of the list of matters discussed, but Mansoni liked to introduce patient management problems into the meetings. The two full-time and two part-time psychiatrists present were concerned about issues of confidentiality, but Mansoni stressed the need for a "team" approach to patient care. To that end, he had even recently begun inviting the clinic's scrub woman to their assembly with the words, "She's part of our team."

"This is looking more and more like Communist China," Cordis muttered to Grossman on the way out of the meeting.

"The Chinese dispatched the professors to the countryside to do the farming, and the peasants were brought in to run the people's universities," Grossman muttered back. "And we now have janitors and semi-literate secretarial workers participating in patient care. That's what's known as progress. See you later, comrade."

"And a happy new world order to you, too, comrade," Cordis said.

Cordis was occupied the rest of the morning with a problem that was disturbing a number of clinic personnel from all three divisions. One of his patients had just come back from Metropolitan Hospital where she had been treated with radioactive iodine, I-131, for an overactive thyroid gland. Several of the staff voiced their fear that she posed a health risk to others.

Mansoni usually came to Cordis with the difficult medical issues.

"I think it's much ado about nothing," Cordis told him. "Just keep her away from young children and pregnant staff workers for eight days."

"She should have been sent home after her treatment," Mansoni said, "for those eight days."

"Well, she's here," Cordis responded. "That's the existential reality—she is occupying our space. You're not going to improve her mental health by treating her as a pariah."

"They should have kept her in the hospital for eight days," one of the young female social workers, standing in Cordis' doorway, said.

"She's not sick enough, medically, to be hospitalized," the doctor retorted. "Where do you want them to put her? On a psych ward?"

"There are several women of child-bearing age working here," she said. "More than several. And some of the patients bring small children into the waiting room with them."

"Look, I'm not King Solomon," Cordis said testily. "I can't solve all of your problems."

The patient in question was a thirty-year-old black woman whose hyperthyroidism couldn't be controlled adequately with anti-thyroid medication. As a result the neuroleptics Cordis had tried her on couldn't stabilize her psychotic condition.

"She's crazy enough to be at Gotham State," the social worker pressed.

"I tried to arrange for that last week," Cordis said, "but they were not willing to admit her. Dr. Jaimie Gonzales said she wasn't psychotic enough for them."

"Does she pose a health risk? Mansoni asked impatiently. "That's all I want to know."

"My gosh," Cordis responded, "they only gave her twelve millicuries of I-131. It's not like treating a cancer patient who gets a couple of hundred millicuries. Just make sure that she flushes the toilet immediately after urinating or a bowel movement and that no one comes in contact with her perspiration."

Mrs. White, the clinic's bookkeeper and notary public, was also listening at the door. She was an elderly black, the mothering kind, and she saved the day.

"I'll take her home," she volunteered. "My car's downstairs in Dr. Altman's parking space. I'll instruct her not to piss, poop or perspire on anyone."

"You see," Cordis said laughingly, "and you thought the English lit course I pushed you into taking would be a waste of time."

"Now I'm literate and I alliterate," she said suavely.

"Tell her to stay home for eight days," the social worker said uneasily.

"Can I tell her it's all right for her to breathe for the next eight days?" Mrs. White asked coolly.

It was a rough day for Cordis right up until 5 p.m. As he left the clinic after another week, he made the decision to cut down to half time.

CHAPTER TWENTY

Renata had time on her hands, and she was using it to read American literature as well as psychology. She plunged into the works of Thornton Wilder as soon as she took her seat at 8 o'clock sharp on April 3rd.

She was surprised that her psychiatrist was familiar with *The Bridge of San Luis Rey*, a work well dissected by the noted psychoanalyst Dorothy Burlingham, and an earlier novel, *The Cabala*, about a hopeless love affair between an American in Italy and a woman of Rome.

She then went on to discuss Eugene O'Neill's *Beyond the Horizon*.

"America's greatest dramatist," she said, singing his praises.

"The man who walked on tragic waters and left his characters to drown in grief," the doctor commented.

"The protagonist, Robert Mayo, is certainly a tragic figure," Renata said, smiling over Cordis' metaphoric response. "He wanted to go to sea, but . . ."

Here she blocked, unable to complete her thought. This was the third time he observed her to stop suddenly in the middle of a sentence as though she had difficulty with concentration or memory.

'(?) Aposiopetic—something neurological!'—he wrote in her chart.

"But he never got off the ground," Cordis ventured softly and reassuringly, noting also that she had lost her poise for the moment.

"Yes, true," Renata continued, regaining her composure. "He wanted to keep on traveling so that he wouldn't have to take root in any one place." She paused.

"The restlessness of youth," Cordis commented after a brief silence.

Psychiatrists of the early years of the 20th century explained the Ishmaels of this world—those who had to throw off the restraints of society and wander far from home—under the label of planomania. The Freudians fared little better by making wanderlust part of the unresolved oedipal dilemma.

Renata asked him how the psychoanalyst would interpret the character of Robert Mayo.

"You'll learn more about *Beyond the Horizon* by concentrating on O'Neill rather than on Freud," he responded.

"*Magnifique!*" she exclaimed. "Seek out the author, not the critic from psychology." She laughed as an expression of her excitement. "But how does my Dr. Cordis see Robert Mayo?"

"The way I see him," the psychiatrist started to say, noting how she had personalized her reference to him, "he had the chance to see beyond the horizon by going to sea. He didn't go, however, but remained at home to till the soil, toil that would kill him in the end. His brother, the natural farmer, the homebody, went to sea but never saw what was to be seen beyond the horizon."

"*Très bien!*" she uttered, again in what was her maternal language. "I see the eclectic Dr. Cordis at work." Then she added challengingly, "But how would a Jungian see him?"

He paused to organize his thoughts, but his mind kept coming back to her previous session. Well, we're on the high seas again, he said to himself. That's linkage enough.

Finally, he said to Renata, "*Beyond the Horizon* pits the life of the soil against that of the sea, the male principle versus the female. The fact that Mayo couldn't come to terms with his own animus-anima projection—Jungian talk—spelled his doom."

"Proving?" she asked, looking him in the eye inquisitively.

"That you must rise to meet opportunity when you sense its presence upon your horizon."

"And if you don't?"

"Life offers us chances—but the number is not inexhaustible."

"You must accept the challenge to explore beyond the horizon when it comes your way," Renata said, nodding her head slowly a number of times.

Bravo, he said to himself. You are forging a chain out of these sessional linkages. Aloud he said, "I think you get the gist of it. You now see the sea O'Neill saw. But I wonder if O'Neill is good reading for a young lady with the future in her eye. He dwells compulsively on the theme of failure."

Renata spent the next fifteen minutes on the writings of other literary figures, but the psychiatrist found little or no psychotherapeutic substance in any of it. He finally brought the literature dialogue to an end by saying, "Bibliotherapy is one thing, but literary criticism only for its own sake has no value for us." Here Cordis felt the first twinges of *resistance*, as she took to intellectualization to avoid dealing with personal issues. "It is your story we are here to read, not the works of the great authors."

"Umm," Renata murmured defensively, blushing at the same time.

The doctor became solemn as he said, "I am no more than a mirror held up before you. When you look at me, you are looking into your own reflection. If you fear to gaze upon me, it is because you are afraid to look within yourself." Cordis paused to smile reassuringly to her, a smile designed to dispel any self-reproach she might be feeling for holding back. "I am but a guide on this journey to the far and inner reaches of one named Renata Delacross," he continued. "This is your journey to yourself—your far journey. I am here, but in reality I am not here. For you I am only as real as an image seen in a mirror, and such an image is called unreal by the physicists. So I am not there, not here, not real. You must use me well and use me wisely for what I am if you are to work out your salvation."

The language Cordis used was intense, but for this particular patient

108

he felt it appropriate.

From the littoral North African world to the banks of the Hudson River, he mused when she was gone. She has come a long way in order to journey far.

CHAPTER TWENTY-ONE

Josephine Bondaz had anticipated Cordis' action. Within a week of receiving his decision, she left New York for French Canada, having prepared the way for a transfer to another governmental agency during her stay in France.

Cordis anguished over the breakup. There was no doubting that he loved her, but he would not forsake a religious ancestry that he traced back through the centuries. Life calls for compromise, at least at the diplomatic level. Love, however, is not diplomacy, but a state of neurochemical fastness loculated somewhere within the tangled nerve network of the limbic brain. It was Josie's inflexibility, not any intransigence on his part, that brought the love affair to an end. Time has its own way of healing wounds of the heart, as he had learned—by weakening and eventually abolishing that very neurochemical adhesiveness which has taken hold.

Cordis explained his breakup to Father Dominic, who sympathized, "We are always at crossroads, where we must go in one direction or the other—the idea is not to get hung up in inaction."

Cordis spent Saturday morning, the 7th, at a Jewish bookshop on the Lower East Side, where he liked to go to listen to recordings of the old cantors, or *hazzans*, the solo singers or chanters of Jewish prayer. He browsed through volumes of Jewish history and spent some time reading in Josephus' *Against Aprion*. On leaving, he bought a Mogen David tie clasp and *another* calendar for the year 5733, his fourth.

In the afternoon, he took the subway to The Bronx, on a sentimental journey to his past. On the way, he thought how much he would miss going to the opera with Josie. Dr. Edna Paxton had season tickets to the Metropolitan which she gave him regularly. An elderly dowager type now, she was originally from the hill country of Kentucky and had succeeded in carving out a successful career for herself in psychiatry in New York. Prior to that, she had worked for the CIA in Buenos Aires as a translator, where she taught the great Bernardo Houssay English and had undergone an analysis with the renowned Angel Garma. After her Argentinian experience, she had gone to Italy to study medicine, and subsequently had set up practice in Manhattan. "I'm so tired of that um-pah-pah music, Rex," she had said. "Here, take my tickets." Cordis grew up listening to opera; in fact, it was the first music he heard. His father had sung in the chorus of the old Metropolitan in the 1920's, and every Saturday at home the radio had been tuned in to the opera.

He couldn't find 1833 Clinton Avenue in the East Bronx. Much of the neighborhood of his childhood had been torn down to make room for a thruway. He walked all the way to the Grand Concourse, the great boulevard dividing The Bronx into east and west. Puerto Ricans and blacks had taken over the area he had called home during his high school years. Once a thriving middle-class community, it was rundown now.

Cordis walked up to William Howard Taft High School on 172nd Street, which he attended during the War years, a citadel of learning where election to Arista, the honor society, was the priority prized most by the student body. The city-wide school system was so academically solid and so well recognized throughout the country that college applications needed only to be accompanied by the students' New York State Regents Examination scores. A 90% average on the Regents would earn graduates admission to any university in the country. Every college-bound student took three years of a foreign language and usually two years of another. In his Spanish courses, he read Cervantes' *Don Quixote* in medieval Spanish and even knew the imperfect subjunctive. Cordis thought his high school physics course was better than the same college course he took as a premedical student. Stanley Kubrick, of *Dr. Strangelove* and *Space Odyssey: 2001* fame, had been a classmate of his. Edyie Gorme, the singer, had been a couple of years behind him. And countless scholars . . . Those were the glory years, he mused, standing outside the Taft schoolyard. Now the school has become an oversized day-care center for wayward and maladjusted youths who act out their domestic dramas in the schoolroom.

He took the Jerome Avenue line back to Manhattan, realizing a part of his past was gone forever. He shook his head in disgust and vowed he would never again visit The Bronx. With the memory of his earlier years wiped away by demolition, at that moment he wondered why he remained in New York at all. Even The Adams, as venerable as it was, was decaying. New York itself he considered to be in a progressive state of rot, both in its

110.

physical and moral structure.

At seven o'clock he walked over to 88th Street to attend a party at Dr. Salvatore Romanetti's apartment. Naomi Rothstein, one of the clinic social workers, was showing slides of her recent trip to Israel when he arrived. The place was crowded and there was plenty to eat and drink. It was a happy throng, a mixed group of professionals—black, white, Jewish, Italian, South American.

Dominating Dr. Romanetti's living room was a large painting of Giuseppi Garibaldi, the hero in the struggle for Italian unification. Whether true or not, Salvatore liked to let people think he was distantly related to the "lion of Italy."

Newcomers to his frequent parties would learn how Garibaldi, born on the fourth of July, had been offered a Union command by Abraham Lincoln in 1861. The celebrated general, an expert in guerrilla warfare which he had perfected while commanding armies in Brazil and Uruguay, had refused Lincoln's offer because Lincoln would not openly condemn slavery. Besides, the president had balked at naming him supreme commander of all Union troops.

"Just think," Salvatore was saying, "Garibaldi could have won the Civil War for the North by eighteen sixty-two."

Salvatore Romanetti was in his late fifties and had been living in the United States for fifteen years. He cut an imposing figure with his long gray hair and natty suits, to go with his Italian accent and flamboyance. He was a Division I psychiatrist at Gotham Psychiatric Clinic, and his chief claim to fame was that he had been there at Val-de-Grace Hospital in Paris when Hamon, Paraire and Velluz first tried chlorpromazine, trade-named as Thorazine in the United States, on a psychotic patient in January 1952. It was a turning point in the history of psychiatry, ushering in the modern era of psychopharmacology.

The psychiatrists who came to Salvatore's parties liked to huddle in a corner to talk shop, especially to expound and expand on their own past glories. Dr. Marshall Greenberg had been at Brooklyn's Maimonides Hospital in the early fifties when a call came from the Vatican.

"The pontiff, that was Pope Pius the Twelfth," he was saying, "had a case of intractable hiccups, and we, the Jewish doctors, had to instruct his doctors on how to administer Thorazine i.v. to stop it."

"Did it work?" Naomi Rothstein asked.

"But of course," the doctor replied.

"We were in Rome on vacation in October, nineteen fifty-eight, when he died," Salvatore's wife Rita said. She was an attractive Hungarian, about her husband's age.

That got Salvatore started, uncharacteristically, on religion and Pope John XXIII.

"A great man," Salvatore, known for his drinking, said sottishly. "A good man and a great man."

"Sure, sure, Sal," Dr. Al Tate said patronizingly.

Dr. Tate was the youngest of the psychiatrists present and the only genuine WASP at the party. Born into wealth, he had never had to struggle in life like the other doctors present, most of whom had had to go abroad to be accepted into medical school. He was generally disliked, with two strikes already against him whenever he got into delicate discussions with his immediate colleagues.

"Pope John gave true meaning to the word 'worth,'" Salvatore said, rising to a challenge. "Here in America the measure of a man's worth is how much money he has—Joe Smith is worth five million dollars or ten million or thirty million. When Pope John died, he left his family less than twenty dollars. So by American standards he was worth about nothing. But to me, to us, to men and women of faith, he was worth the world."

Rita caressed his head and tried to hush him, for Salvatore appeared on the brink of getting carried away.

"I remember him," Cordis said, placing himself physically as well as verbally between Tate and Salvatore. "The roly-poly pope."

"Yes!" Salvatore said loudly. "A great friend to the Jewish people, as he was to everyone, great or small."

"You're right," Cordis said. "I was living in Europe in those years, and I remember a Shinto priest, I think it was, came to see him. And the Archbishop of Canterbury."

"And he even visited the criminals in jail at Christmas time," Rita said, still clinging to her husband.

"Just before he died," Salvatore started to say, in full control of himself, "he composed a prayer he wanted read from every pulpit. About the Jews, the chosen people. He said, 'Forgive us the curse we falsely attached to their name as Jews. Forgive us for crucifying Thee a second time in their flesh. For we knew not what we did.'"

"I'll drink to that," Dr. Tate said semi-humorously, raising his glass of beer in the air.

Cordis lifted a glass and said, "Pacem in terris. Peace on earth."

Pacem in terris was Pope John XXIII's encyclical that set the stage for Vatican II's—the second Vatican Council—new thinking of the Church toward non-Christian religions.

The party helped cheer up Cordis, but when he got home to The Adams after midnight, he couldn't get to sleep. He played Edith Piaf records, which he loved to listen to with Josie, until he finally dozed off sometime around 4 a.m.

CHAPTER TWENTY-TWO

Renata Delacross had never developed an interest in the subject of psychology until coming to Dr. Cordis, but she had been to enough psychiatrists to be familiar with the general procedure they followed.

As soon as she settled in for her next session she asked, "Aren't you supposed to test me on proverbs and word pairs? You know, you say a word and I respond with the first word that pops into my head."

"Jung's word association test?"

"Yes," she answered.

"How about if I substitute it with Cordis' association test?"

She looked at him curiously. "What's that?"

"Pick a letter of the alphabet—"

"That again?" Renata said, her voice noticeably wary.

"A variation," he conceded. "Choose your letter and then, using that letter, give me a word that describes men to you and a word that describes women."

She thought for a moment. "R. Men are rapacious; women, relationship-oriented."

"How are men rapacious?" he asked.

"They ravage and they plunder whenever given the opportunity. Men are naturally aggressive beings. Creatures would be a more appropriate label for them."

"All men?" the doctor asked, hoping to tap into a mother lode of beneath-the-surface material.

"There are some unassuming, submissive and unoffending ones," she stated.

Cordis waited for her to elaborate, but she remained silent.

113

"And women?" he asked. "You say they are relationship-oriented."

"They keep the world going. They civilize the male and maintain his home, freeing him to channel his aggression outside the hearth."

"Such as?"

"Um, making war."

"Anything else? Anything closer to home?"

"They vent their natural aggression into the dog-eat-dog business world. Then there's this American football—a form of recreational warfare. If you give me another letter, I would pick H—men are hell-raisers and women are hearth-minders." She swallowed hard, trying to slow the breakneck speed of her words, but the tactic didn't work. "A third letter would be B—men are boisterous boys and women, breeding machines."

Cordis waited, hoping this breakaway train of thought would continue, but she managed to rein herself in and returned to an issue she had raised in a previous session.

"I asked you once if you thought I needed psychoanalysis. Your answer was that no one needed analysis but everyone could benefit from it— "

"Nearly everyone," he interjected. "I don't think the mentally retarded would get much out of it."

"Yes, yes, of course. But tell me, what do you think I really need?"

"I think a modified analysis—what is generally referred to now as psychodynamic psychotherapy—would benefit you," he replied, studiously avoiding the word "need."

"I've already been to four psychoanalysts—"

"But you've never been to me before."

"That's true. Maybe you will succeed where the others have failed."

"Why not?"

"I'm glad you're able to sound so optimistic," Renata said. "But have you lived well enough to attempt to cure me?"

A very mature question, he thought. *Cure* may be too strong a word. We physicians seldom cure, but I like to think we always help.

"I don't pretend mine is among the ten thousand greatest lives ever lived," he replied. "However, I have experienced quite a bit and I have trained sufficiently in my specialty to believe that, if you are willing, our time together can be very therapeutic for you."

He felt a sense of satisfaction in having answered her without reference to cure.

Renata nodded. "You are reassuring."

"Good."

After a prolonged silence, Renata resumed. Looking in the direction of his book cases she said, "I recall seeing a book by someone named Marquez on one of the shelves the first day I was here."

"Gabriel Garcia Marquez."

"Yes," she said. "I am not familiar with his work."

"He's a Latin-American writer who spent the first eight years of his life in a steamy banana village called Aracateca. He has said, on more than one occasion, 'Nothing interesting has happened to me since.' "

Renata burst out in laughter. "Why did he say such a thing?"

"He was raised by his grandparents, and when he was eight, his grandfather died."

Silence ensued. Finally, Renata asked softly, "And what happened to his grandmother?"

Cordis saw the tears welling up in her eyes and he understood that she was thinking of her own grandmother.

"Of her he has said that the rich, fluent, magnificent Spanish for which he is so famous was 'in the style of my grandmother.' "

Renata heaved a deep sigh. "He is that famous?"

"Yes," he replied. "Not only in the Spanish-speaking world, but everywhere people read books."

She shook her head and said, "I find it hard to believe that all my problems stem from what did or didn't happen during my early years of life—if that's the point. If you are trying to associate something I am saying now to an incident or event which occurred when I was four or five, well, please don't. I can't accept it. I cannot see it."

"It is for me to try to see these things," the doctor responded, "and then help you to see them. We are each of us linked, which is not, however, to say inescapably, to everything that has happened to us. When Tennyson says, 'I am a part of all that I have met,' he is not excluding childhood experiences. The psychoanalysts tend to stress that particular part of one's life, childhood, the formative years, for it is the imprint upon which everything else in the ever unfolding drama of the subsequent years is superimposed."

Cordis was stating the Freudian concept of psychic determinism—ontogenetic cause and effect—which links adult behavior to what occurred in infancy and early childhood. As a computer is programmed by the data fed into it, so is the adult emotional and behavioral mind programmed by the input of the early formative years. Once the networks of the earliest memory traces have been laid down, the initial etchings into the mind's tabula rasa, they persist unless powerfully challenged by forces bent on re-routing parts of the memory circuitry.

"But doesn't yesterday or last month count for anything in my life insofar as how I am feeling today?" Renata asked testily.

"Of course," he answered. "It's all grist for the mind's mill."

After another pause Renata said, "I understand that this is not psychoanalysis but a therapy based on principles derived from psychoanalysis, and I would like to know if what's going on in my subconscious is really the key to the restoration of my health. I hate to sound like a bore by repeatedly voicing my doubts, but as you see, I do have my doubts."

"Because the therapists or the treatment method itself failed you in the past? Was it the singer or the song?"

"I do fault the other therapists," she stated clearly. "They made their own identity an issue. They violated what is, after all, a sacred trust—they did not honor the Hippocratic patient-physician relationship. They debased only themselves."

The trauma of the seductions by her earlier therapists obviously was weighing heavily upon her. "What about those therapists?" Cordis inquired. "Do you want to talk about it?"

"Boys will be boys," she stated blithely. "I'd prefer not to dwell on the subject."

"As you wish," Cordis said sympathetically.

After a brief pause Renata said, "I wish . . . I wish I could straighten out my life. Really straighten out my life."

"What you wish for will come about when you have learned to do as well as to wish," the psychiatrist responded. "But patience, patience."

"I can be a patient patient," she said and smiled.

"Good," the doctor said, returning her smile. "Humor is a lubricant of the ego. It assists in diminishing inner friction and the tensions of the psychic apparatus."

"Yes, light oil for the machinery of the mind," Renata added, with a twinkle in her eye.

After Renata was gone and he had brought her chart up to date, Cordis turned to reading one of anthropologist Frank C. Hibben's works on early man in the New World. He broke off his reading—thinking about Renata—to muse, Psychodynamic therapy is like an archeological dig through the psyche. You grub and spade your way through layer after layer of repressed material, much like digging through so many strata of dirt or rock. And down there, in the depths, in all its pristine nakedness, is *the reality . . .*

CHAPTER TWENTY-THREE

The vernal season was in full stride. April 15 was Palm Sunday, commemorating the Galilean's triumphal entry into Jerusalem. Tuesday, the 17th, marked the first day of Passover, or Pesach, in remembrance of Yahweh's "passing over" the households of the Hebrews in Egypt, while the first born throughout Pharaoh's land fell victim to an unknown pestilence, the culmination in a series of efforts by Moses to effect the deliverance of the Israelites.

Cordis had rearranged his Tuesday schedule so that he could attend a seder. Renata would be his last patient for the day, at six o'clock. At five-fifty the phone rang.

"I know this is short notice," Pierre Delacroix was saying, "but Renata will not be able to keep her appointment with you. She's just been hospitalized."

"What's happened?" Cordis asked solicitously.

"Pneumonia," Pierre responded. "She hadn't been feeling well since Sunday, and we finally managed to convince her today to let us take her to the doctor. I'm telephoning from the lobby in St. Mark's Hospital."

"Does her grandmother know?" Cordis asked. "And her aunts?"

"I've already spoken with Celine, and I will keep her informed."

"Is there anything I can do?"

"You have been very kind," Pierre answered. "We all appreciate everything you've been doing for Renata. When she is able, she will telephone you for another appointment."

After he hung up, Cordis sat thinking about his patient. Pneumonia? Hmm. She seemed recovered from her flu these last two sessions. Maybe all her marijuana smoking has finally caught up with her.

The subject of marijuana had come up several times in her sessions. Renata tended to downplay it. "A matter of minor concern," "a trivial habit acquired during my collegiate career," and other such statements was the way she minimized the issue. With each of her expressions of denial, the doctor had punctuated the margin of his notes with an exclamation point within parentheses.

He heard nothing more of his patient's condition until Easter Sunday, when Renata herself phoned him a few minutes before midnight.

"I'm out of the hospital and at home with Simone and Pierre," she said in a soft voice.

117

"I'm glad to hear you're well."

There was a pause. "I'm . . . I'm really down in the dumps. I . . . I hope this isn't inconvenient for you."

"Not at all," he responded, conveying encouragement. "I'm glad you called."

His *contract* with all his depressed patients called for them to telephone him, day or night, if they had any suicidal thoughts.

"I feel drained," Renata confided. "Washed out."

"That's not so unusual following a debilitating illness like the one you had."

"Perhaps that's it then, a post-illness letdown."

"Renata, are you feeling depressed?" Cordis asked, stating the matter bluntly. "Some people develop a clinical depression following a bout of influenza, and—"

"Really?" she said, interrupting him.

"Yes."

"I had pneumonia, not influenza," she reminded him.

"Perhaps the flu you had several weeks ago smoldered into pneumonia," the doctor commented. "You like to smoke the nasty weed, and I keep telling you that inhaled marijuana smoke yields ten times the tars and resins of tobacco. You're corrupting your lungs with that foul stuff." He paused for a response, but Renata remained silent. "And, you know, some people even get depressed smoking that garbage."

Renata still didn't respond, and then he heard her sigh deeply. "So I may be compounding my own problem," she admitted, her voice quavering.

"You're certainly not making it any easier on yourself," the psychiatrist said calmly. Again silence. "Renata?"

"I'm still here," she said. "I'm . . . I'm just feeling so . . . so down . . . This is Easter Sunday. Well, it was—now it's Monday after Easter." He could hear a few sobs. "I don't like being estranged from Grandmama like this." Then he heard her blow her nose a couple of times.

"That's the hardest part of it, isn't it?"

"Yes," she responded softly, sucking up her tears. After a pause she said, "I can't get to sleep. It's past midnight, and I can't fall asleep."

"Have you tried the glass of warm milk routine?"

"Warm milk makes me puke," Renata said, still sniffling. But then she laughed, as though she had shaken off her somber mood. "I do have some Valium."

"Not a bad idea," he said. "Take, well, let's see . . . take five milligrams with a glass of cold milk."

118

Renata laughed again. "I'd prefer to swallow it with water. But isn't five milligrams too much?"

"Nah."

"Supposing I can't get up in the morning," Renata said worriedly.

"You'll get up all right."

"I'll probably be groggy."

"If so, then you'll take a hot shower."

"Hot?" she questioned. "Not cold?"

"Yes, hot," Cordis said. "And while you're in the shower, you are to whisper three times: 'Morpheus be gone!' "

"Dr. Cordis' own paternoster," she said laughingly.

"Yes, but remember, you may not take the Valium for more than two nights."

"I'll remember."

"Good."

"Dr. Cordis, I still have my appointment with you for tommorow evening, Tuesday, don't I?"

"Absolutely," he answered. "Tuesday, eight o'clock is your hour."

"Thank you, Doctor. Let me not keep you any longer. And I want to apologize for calling you at such a late hour."

"No apology needed," he responded. "You call me anytime you're feeling troubled, even if it's three in the morning."

"Thank you again, Doctor."

Actually, hers had been the second call he had received that night. At about ten, an ex-Catholic priest, referred by Fr. Dominic, had called for an appointment. Since there was no urgency involved, Cordis had put him down for May 14th, his first available opening.

Interesting, Cordis had thought, that an ex-priest should call on Easter Sunday. Then he had let out a laugh, as he recalled how Freud had snubbed his nose at Catholic Vienna by beginning his private practice on Easter Sunday, April 25, 1886.

CHAPTER TWENTY-FOUR

By 1973 psychiatry was poised for a leap into the future, a future already foreseen by the German psychiatrist Wilhelm Griesinger in 1845 with his prophetic phrase: "*Geisteskrankheiten sind Gehirnkrankheiten*"—"Diseases of the mind are diseases of the brain." On its way to the future, turn-of-the-century psychiatry got itself sidetracked by psychoanalysis.

Ironically, Griesinger was a firm believer as well in the role of unconscious processes in mental events, a favorite topic among early 19th century metaphysical thinkers of the *Naturphilosophie* school. The historian Otto Marx referred to these German Romantic psychiatrists as *Psychiker*, or mentalists, as opposed to the *Somatiker*, the somaticists. The first half of the 19th century witnessed an energetic debate between those supporting somatic versus those favoring mental explanations of mental illness. The mentalists' views were extraordinarily modern: dammed up emotions—the "passions"—deprived of a proper outlet would lead to personality malfunctioning; ideas could be transformed into symbols finding expression as physical symptoms; people had a psychological development which when it went awry led to mental problems; the unconscious was the hidden dimension of one's personality; et cetera.

After 1850 the influence of the mentalists declined rapidly. Late 19th century psychiatrists drifted away from mental processes and into the area of classifying mental illnesses and trying to localize specific symptoms to sites in the brain. By the time Freud, the proto-psychoanalyst, not the already well-known neurohistologist, began his pioneering work into the sexual origins of hysteria, the rich psychodynamic heritage of the Romantic psychiatrists had been buried. Freudian thought would expand spectacularly during the first half of the 20th century, dominating psychiatry so completely that investigators seeking grant aid to do brain research would find all doors shut tight for them.

With the introduction of drugs to combat psychosis, the neuroleptics, in the early 1950's, followed immediately by the first antidepressants and antianxiety agents, psychiatry picked up where it had left off before the psychoanalytic revolution. The somaticists, now the organic psychiatrists, were back in the driver's seat. Psychiatry, no longer limited to hydrotherapy, electro-convulsive treatment (ECT), old-fashioned sedatives, straitjackets and psychoanalysis, was turning to psychotropic agents, working out the role of neurotransmitters in mental illness, and entering upon the revolutionary era of neuro-imaging—the CT scan of the brain, MRI, PET and SPECT. The specialty's main interest was no longer on the disordered mind linked to the individual's psychic development but was now focused on finding organic lesions in the brain, anything from lesions at the biochemical level to what the new, powerful neuroimaging techniques would be able to discern.

Cordis swam in both streams, the psychoanalytic and the organic. Years of reading the psychoanalytic literature as it pertained to the analysis of art and literature—beginning in 1950 with such works as Daniel Schneider's *The Psychoanalyst and the Artist*—had prepared him for the former, and his undergraduate degree in chemistry had provided him a background for the latter. He was comfortable in both the domain of the modern *Psychiker* and the *Somatiker*.

He was well read in the history of psychiatry, and from among all the legions of psychiatrists who had practiced the specialty, his role model remained Freud. Cordis even had a miniature bust of the founder of psychoanalysis on his desk. Perhaps it was because Freud was a great writer— he was awarded the Goethe Prize for literature in 1930, an honor which nevertheless could not conceal his disappointment over not winning a Nobel Prize for his discovery of psychoanalysis.

Nobels in medicine are awarded to pioneers, researchers who open up whole new areas or frontiers, where others then follow in significant numbers. Freud had achieved this with psychoanalysis—there is hardly a field of human endeavor which psychoanalysis has not touched. Egas Moniz won a Nobel in 1949 for the psychosurgical procedure of lobotomy that he developed in 1935 (a generation before the birth of psychopharmacology). Prefrontal lobotomy was refined into anterior cingulotomy, but psychosurgery became a last-resort therapy. In 1973 less than 200 psychosurgical procedures were performed in the United States, and the numbers have continued to dwindle annually since. Freud, it would seem, had cause to be disappointed over not receiving a Nobel in medicine.

Perhaps it was Freud's Jewishness that had led to Cordis' interest in psychoanalysis. Freud has been depicted as a non-believing Jew, when in fact he was deeply involved in humanistic Judaism. David Bakan, in *Sigmund Freud and the Jewish Mystical Tradition*, portrays Freud as a closet Kabbalist. Freud's library contained a section devoted to Judaica, with some writings on the Kabbalists, but that alone does not make a case for him having been involved in Jewish mysticism.

121

Freud may not have been a practicing Jew, but his Jewish conscious-ness was evident all his life. Between 1897 and 1902 he was deeply involved in the activities of the fraternal organization B'nai B'rith (Sons of the Covenant), delivering numerous lectures, including lectures on the psychoanalysis he was in the process of developing.

His Wednesday evening psychoanalytic circle meetings were exclu-sively Jewish until Carl Jung and Ludwig Binswanger visited the group in March, 1907. As with B'nai B'rith, Freud preferred to surround himself with fellow Jews, in whose company he was at ease. Dealing with the non-Jews who were entering the movement caused him discomfort. After meeting Ernest Jones the following year, Freud wrote to Karl Abraham in Berlin on May 3rd that the Welchman left him with the feeling of "racial strangeness." He wrote to Jung the same day to let him know how he felt about Jones—which was the way he felt about Jung also.

Psychoanalysis was begun by Jews, but from the start it was never intended to be a Jewish enterprise, a crypto-Jewish science. It was the Enlightenment which had led to the Jews' emancipation from the ghetto, and the early psychoanalysts were clearly children of the Enlightenment, with its faith in reason to overcome prejudice, blind faith in authority and the oppressive forces of church and state.

The years following the revolutions of 1848 were exhilarating for Jews, who looked forward to a society in which they would enjoy equal status with non-Jews. Their goal was *Zielbewusstsein*, or complete social integration. By the 1870's, German liberalism gave way to intense nation-alism, as Bismarck completed Germany's unification and established the German Empire (*Deutsches Reich*) early in 1871. When Freud entered the Vienna Medical School in the fall of 1873, anti-Semitism was in full bloom again throughout Austria and Germany. The Jews' desire for social acceptance and integration into the German mainstream now gave way to Jewish pride and a need to find something uniquely their own. In 1895-96, Theodor Herzl wrote the political manifesto of Zionism, *The Jewish State* (*Der Judenstaat*), and Zionism became the ultimate declaration of Jewish national pride.

On another front, those who joined Freud at the beginning formed an intellectual elite imbued with a sense of moral superiority. They believed in the power of Jews to effect reform, and like their political brethren in the Zionist movement, believed in the ultimate perfection of humanity. Otto Rank (ne Rosenfeld), an early follower of Freud, saw in psycho-analysis a Jewish mission of redemption. Fritz Wittels, another early member of Freud's circle, believed "that psychoanalysis would change the surface of the earth . . . [and bring about] a golden age in which there

122

would be no room for neuroses any more . . . " They were the new philosopher-kings, and their goal was to lift mankind to the level of the philosopher-genius, the Nietzschean "overman" or superman.

CHAPTER TWENTY-FIVE

Joey Dee was in the waiting room at 9 o'clock the day after Easter. His appointment had been for the previous Thursday, but missing it by only four days was as close to showing up on the right day as he had ever come. He waited patiently for two hours while Cordis saw his scheduled patients.

His jacket and trousers had tears in several places and his shirt, originally white, was dirty yellowish from accumulated food stains and lack of laundering, but otherwise he looked presentable. His hair was combed, he smelled of eau de cologne, and he appeared to have had a shave within the past two or three days.

He handed Cordis his customary offering, a grocery bag with oranges and BIC's, and right off said, "Please, Dr. Cordis, gimme da Tractan an' Hadall. Dey're da red pills an' green pills."

"I know what their colors are, Joey, but we don't dispense medication by color. Just stay with the Thorazine and Stelazine as prescribed. You have been taking them, haven't you?"

"Sure, Dr. Cordis. I take 'em."

"As prescribed?"

"Sure, Dr. Cordis."

"I hope your *sure* is an honest-to-goodness yes."

Cordis doubted whether Joey ever took his medication as he was supposed to, but he apparently was getting enough of it into his system to remain reasonably compensated. The doctor was content as long as he could keep Joey from relapsing into florid psychosis—decompensating—and having to be rehospitalized, the ultimate failure of community psychiatry. That was about all he thought he could offer Joey.

While Cordis was in the process of writing his prescriptions, Joey said sheepishly, "Please, Dr. Cordis, I need da Hadall an' Tractan."

The doctor eyed his patient for a moment and took a deep breath, exhaling heavily. "You're doing just fine on the Thorazine and Stelazine, our super polypharmacy specialty," he said, handing him his scripts. To himself he added, He keeps reminding me of Lenny in *Of Mice and Men*, beseeching George: 'Tell me again how it's gonna be, George. Huh?'

"T'orazine an' Stel'zine," Joey repeated.

"That's right, pal. They were designed with you in mind."

Joey picked the scripts up gingerly by his fingertips and, mumbling something about "Hadall an' Tractan," left Cordis' office headed slowly for the pharmacy.

In the afternoon Cordis saw Madam Bee, who had phoned him from Milwaukee a week earlier asking him to write her into his schedule for the 23rd. She arrived back in New York in the morning and was at the clinic for her 3:30 appointment, appearing fresh and in good health.

The Supreme Court's decision in January legalizing abortion—*Roe v. Wade*—was very much in the air, and Madam Bee had her own insight into the issue.

"There are some cultures that credit the newborn with one year of life at birth," she said.

"True," Cordis averred. "The uterus is forced to release the fetus at the end of nine calendar months because its rapidly growing head wouldn't be able to exit the pelvic outlet if it stayed any longer."

"But for that the fetus would remain in the womb to allow its brain to mature further," she said. "So the anatomy of the human pelvis determines the time of birth. Intra-uterine and extra-uterine existence are part of a continuum."

"Correct."

"Life is life from the moment the sperm unites with the ovum," Madame Bee added solemnly.

"Some would say that," Cordis commented. The fertilized ovum is what is referred to in biology as a totipotential cell—it's destined to become a human being if uninterfered with."

"When the world was young," his patient continued thoughtfully, "it was a sin for a man to spill his seed upon the ground, so says the Bible. Sexuality was focused on procreation."

"Rephrased, when the world was underpopulated, every human life was precious."

"Exactly," Madam Bee said emphatically. "And in an overpopulated world, is every life now less precious?" She did not wait for him to comment, but continued, "For America, a Judeo-Christian society, to sanction the mass killing of fetuses marks a turning point in her moral

124

development."

"We are into a time of moral laxity," Cordis said flatly.

"This is where Freud's revolution has taken us," she said.

As a young woman, Madam Bee had spent nine months in Zurich being treated by one of Jung's proteges, and she carried a staunch anti-Freudian bias ever since.

"You're confusing Freud's psychoanalysis with the sexual revolution, made possible by penicillin and the oral contraceptive."

Cordis avoided reference to Kinsey's data, that the sexual revolution had its roots in the twenties with the automobile—the "portable bedroom"—and key social changes, such as the movement of large numbers of women into the workplace and the decline of the patriarchal order.

"But it was Freud's pansexualism," she pressed on, "that sex is the cause of all neuroses, which has led to the devaluation of human life and has shrunk the dimensions of our humanity."

"It was some of Freud's followers—Otto Rank, Wittels, Wilhelm Reich—who were the pansexualists. Freud's goal was to liberate humankind from repression and neurotic anxiety. He was the new Moses, preaching a secular message of personal psychological liberty."

Madam Bee would not give ground. "That dreadful man with that lighted penis symbol forever in his mouth—"

"Freud reminded those critical of his stogie habit that sometimes a cigar is just a cigar," Cordis interrupted her.

Madam Bee continued to press her point effectively, and finally Cordis yielded by switching to a different theme.

"If Freud had built his psychoanalysis upon a foundation of shame instead of sexuality," he said, "creating an affective psychology, perhaps we'd all be better off for it."

"Why didn't he?" she asked coolly.

Her question made him ponder why Freud chose to devote so little reflection and energy to shame, especially in view of Wilhelm Fliess' influence on him during the second lustrum of the 1890's. Fliess' monograph of 1897, which Freud read thoroughly, contained critical passages devoted to the psychological origins of shame in childhood. Also, despite the obvious link in German between shame (*Scham*) and the genital organs—*Schamteile*, genitals; *Schamglied*, penis; *Schamgang*, vagina; et cetera—Freud turned a deaf ear to shame theory as he went about laying the groundwork for psychoanalysis.

"Freud, the assimilated Jew, had a need to escape from his own shame culture," Cordis said simply.

Madam Bee did not respond to that, but instead said sarcastically, "There is irony in the Freudian legacy. The man who saw religion as a neurosis could never have dreamt that his psychoanalysis would become today's religion of intellectual salvation."

Cordis could only nod and manage a faint smile.

As Madam Bee was leaving, she turned back to face Cordis and asked, "Did you reread Chaucer?"

Cordis was prepared with his response. "What does woman desire most?"

"Yes, that's the quintessential question."

"Power over men," Cordis said.

"How very true!" she said, smiling. "The conflict of our time is now clearly out in the open."

"In the sixties the key societal issue was the alienation of the young from their elders, and now in the seventies, it's the alienation of women from men."

When he was alone again, he reflected, Well, Sigismund, they're coming at you from all sides, tearing down your psychic world for God only knows what. Whatever comes, it looks like it's going to be a fatherless one . . .

Instead of referring to him as Sigmund, Cordis in private moments such as this occasion, called him by the name given him at birth, Sigismund, honoring the first, second and third Sigismunds, Judaphilic kings of Poland. For Cordis it represented a special, intimate way of expressing the deep affection he had for him. Freud had lived for many years in pain, suffering till his death from cancer of the mouth and enduring more than a dozen operations. Cordis, with his own chronic pain problem, drew added inspiration from Freud's remarkable ability to carry on despite the constant pain that plagued him.

CHAPTER TWENTY-SIX

Renata arrived some ten minutes late for her April 24th session looking tired and thinner. As always, she was elegantly dressed. At a time

126

when young women were turning to jeans and men's shirts, Renata continued to clothe herself in raiments.

She spent fifteen minutes going over her recent illness, and then she described her homecoming from the hospital on Easter Sunday. She ended her recapitulation of events since last seeing her doctor with another lamentation on how much she missed her grandmother and aunts.

"I sent a bouquet of flowers from the hospital," she added as a postscript, "but not a word from them in return." She reached over to his desk for a tissue and dabbed at her eyes.

"It will come," Cordis said sympathetically. "Matters like this take time to sort themselves out." Since she didn't say anything in response to his statement, he continued, "Now you've got to take care of your health. That marijuana *hazzarai* you use is not only bad for your pulmonary function, it's poison to your brain cells."

Renata chuckled. She had heard him use that Yiddish word—meaning junk—before.

"Are you suggesting that it can damage brain cells?" she asked, now serious.

"Well, there are forty or fifty cannabinoids in cannabis and they all cross the blood-brain barrier, which means they gain access to the brain proper."

Cordis used the generic term, cannabis, for all the concoctions—marijuana, hashish, bhang, ganja, et cetera—prepared from *Cannabis sativa*, the hemp plant.

"So these . . . whatever they are . . . cross the barrier. So what?"

"Well, these cannabinoids, all of them, not just the psychoactive THC, inhibit DNA, RNA and protein synthesis within cells. And all cells have to constantly replenish their insides. In short, it's not good having these grotesque molecules inside your neurons."

He felt she wasn't ready yet to hear that the occasional mental blocking she exhibited might be due to cannabinoids in her brain.

Renata remained silent for a while. When she spoke again it was to say, "I was reading about a famous American surgeon, a Dr. William Halsted, who was a drug addict for most of his successful career." She was deliberate with her delivery. "He had a very successful career, I understand."

She's dodging the issue, Cordis said to himself. Marijuana is bad for her nerves, but talking about it gets on her nerves. So we'll let it go for now.

"You're right," he said to her. "He was an opium addict."

Halsted, along with Sir William Osler, Howard A. Kelly and William

127

Welch, were immortalized in a John Sargent painting, *The Four Horsemen*. These men of science came together at Johns Hopkins University after World War I to help establish the first truly modern medical school in the United States.

"In fact, he had a magnificent career despite his addiction, didn't he?" Renata said, trying to seize the offensive.

"But he took the cure," Cordis said. And then he decided to add, "Much like the poet Francis Thompson."

Renata's eyes opened wide at the mention of the name and her jaw dropped. "You know of Francis Thompson?" she gasped.

"The Catholic poet? Of course I do." He was surprised she would find it necessary to ask him that.

Thompson was a 19th century mystical poet who started out for the priesthood only to discover he wasn't suited to it. He tried medicine, but after failing his exams several times, gave up on that as well. At the age of twenty-one he arrived in London, where he became addicted to opium and lived the life of a vagrant until he was rescued by a benefactor, in true dickensian fashion. He then spent a year in a private sanitarium undergoing a drug cure.

"Francis Thompson!" Renata whispered, dragging out the name.

" '*You who belong to me, I will always find you,* said the Lord,' " Cordis recited softly.

"Ohh, my God! My God! 'The Hound of Heaven,' " Renata said, still whispering, as she recognized the quote from Thompson's most famous poem. Tears began to flow, and she reached for another tissue, avoiding eye contact with the doctor. When she finally spoke to him, it was to turn biblical. "Like Jonah in the belly of the whale, there was no place to hide from the Lord." She looked at Cordis and forced a smile.

"Thompson rounded out his life by serving the Creator through his poetry and writings for the Church," Cordis said. "But the earlier abuses he had inflicted on his body led to his untimely death . . . from TB . . . corruption of the lungs."

Renata heaved a heavy sigh. "His death reminds me of another's . . . Someone possessed of great strength, it seems to me. But I don't know who."

"Christ perhaps?"

"No. Christ possessed inner strength. I have someone in the back of my mind . . . possessing great physical strength."

"You once mistook the Columbus-in-chains charcoal for Samson," he said by way of a suggestion.

"Samson?"

"Samson the Nazarite."

"I thought Jesus was the Nazarene," Renata said, squinting momentarily.

Cordis nodded. "Jesus was called the Nazarene. Samson was a Nazarite, one consecrated to Yahweh—"

"And his enemies took out his eyes," Renata inserted.

"True," the doctor averred. "But though blinded by his enemies and forced to grind the grain like a beast of burden at the mill in Gaza, in the darkness of his night he found his God, the God who had never forsaken him."

Renata leaned forward in her seat. "You're saying he might have forsaken his God, but God never abandoned him?"

"In the end, God restored his great strength and—so the Bible tells us—Samson destroyed the Phillistine temple to the god Dagon with his dying act. What better death could heaven bestow upon him!"

There was a prolonged silence, which Cordis allowed to go on. Finally Renata spoke. "Thompson died of tuberculosis you said."

"In the end, and a premature end at that, he succumbed to TB."

Renata was deep in thought, drumming two fingers of her left hand against her chin. "Tuberculosis was the insignia of the nineteenth century," she said smugly, now leaning back confidently in her chair. "Who didn't have it? Keats, Chopin, Chekhov and countless others, great and small, died from it in those days."

"Quite so," he conceded.

"A hundred years ago no sensible man would be found marrying a skinny woman for fear of tuberculosis. If they had held beauty contests then, Olga from Leningrad, fat Olga, would have been crowned Miss Europe. And today's toothpick-shaped fashion models would have been carted off to a health farm for fattening up." She let out a laugh. When Cordis remained silent, she looked him in the eye challengingly.

"True, true," he said defensively.

Rubbing it in, she went a step further.

"At college the students parodied Hamlet's famous soliloquy in a way appropriate to this occasion: 'TB or not TB—that is the congestion. Consumption be done about it? A cough! A cough!'"

Renata laughed, the loudest and longest he had heard her laugh. The doctor smiled good-naturedly over the familiar Shakespearean burlesque.

So, she avoids the confrontation over marijuana as though it were the plague, Cordis mused. Even enlists humor in her cause. This cannabis business runs deep, and its wellspring needs to be searched for in some obscure recess of her psyche. That is going to take time.

129

The session continued a little longer, with Renata exploiting her new-found audacity. But in the end the doctor had the final word.

"Who knows what further poetic *inspiration* Thompson might have had had his lungs delivered purer air to his fertile brain," Cordis said. Polyglot that she was, he knew his tactic would not be wasted on her

Actually, he knew his statement didn't hold together well physiologically speaking, but psychologically it had the impact he was after: she left his office nodding to herself and seemed deeply immersed in thought.

CHAPTER TWENTY-SEVEN

Edna Paxton, with her Latin-American ties, enjoyed the luxury of an overflow of Spanish-speaking patients and recently had referred several of them to Cordis.

Rosa de la Luz Cordero Sanchez was a 21-year-old from Vera Cruz studying political science at New York University. Translated into English, her name literally means "of the light," a common designation of "Our Lady" in Mexico. She looked like a younger version of the famous Mexican actress Dolores del Rio, whom Cordis had seen in a number of Spanish-speaking and English roles and whom he greatly admired.

Señorita Sanchez was a sophomore, and had spent the greater part of her freshman year in psychoanalytic treatment for a supposed depression. Her analyst repeatedly insisted to her that she must make an accommodation to the New York scene and interpreted her failure to do so as "resistance."

Cordis spent the first three sessions in getting to know his patient, and now on her fourth visit he said to her, "You're unhappy here, and there's no overriding imperative, psychological or pragmatic, dictating that you should force yourself to fit into this local mold for which you have not been shaped."

At first she thought he was hinting at having her return to Mexico, but gradually she came to realize what he had in mind was a transfer to another university closer to her roots.

"Texas?" she said, pronouncing the name in Spanish.

Cordis nodded. "San Antonio, for instance, is a city with a large Mexican-American community," he said. "You want to pick a town with a major airport so that you can fly home conveniently whenever you feel the need."

"Is it actually possible to do such a thing?" she asked, eyeing him carefully.

"Positively," Cordis responded. "It's done all the time. By the end of this term you will have two years of college credits, which I expect you should have no difficulty transferring elsewhere in toto."

"¡Ójala que sea!" [May God grant it!] she exclaimed, kissing a cross dangling from her neck.

"It's to your credit, your character and fortitude, that you have lasted out two years at a place like NYU, an academic pressure cooker if ever there was one."

"Did you go to NYU?" she asked ingenuously.

"No," Cordis answered simply.

He had gone to college in New Mexico, which turned out to be the gateway to Old Mexico for him, where the most tumultuous events of his own life would take place.

"You really believe I can transfer to another university?" she said, still not sure of her ground.

"This place is not for you," Cordis responded. "If you were *puertorriqueña*, you would have a chance here, but as a wealthy *mejicana* you're just another *extranjera*. You might as well be a WASP." His last statement failed to register with her.

In a society that had become minority conscious, she did not fit into the scheme of things because she was excluded from the privileged Puerto Rican grouping and was not dark-skinned enough to make it into the Negro, now the black, category. She was the quintessential outsider in the new ordering.

"I will have to think about this," she said at the end of her session.

"By all means," Cordis said. "You now have another choice in your life. Ponder where you are, and then choose wisely."

Edna Paxton had also sent him Zelda Amado, a middle-aged Turkish Jewess, who had come to New York via Israel. Her maternal language was Ladino, or Judeo-Spanish, and that fact alone had immediately endeared her to him, for his own maternal grandfather in Bulgaria had spoken Ladino.

"Was he Sephardic?" she had asked during her first session.

"No, Ashkenazi."

131

When Queen Isabella expelled the Jews of Spain—the Sephardim—in 1492, the Ottoman sultan, mindful of their contributions to Spanish civilization, opened his doors to them. Ladino, a medieval Spanish, continued to be spoken among the Jews in the Ottoman empire, surviving into the modern period in Greece, Turkey and Bulgaria. Even Ashkenazi Jews, like his grandfather, acquired a knowledge of Judeo-Spanish from daily contact with their co-religionists.

Zelda Amado spoke Turkish, Hebrew and Ladino as well as a broken English. When she did say something in Ladino, Cordis had little difficulty understanding her. For instance, when she said, "*Se lo dishe*," for "I told you so," it sounded very much like contemporary Spanish.

On her second visit to Cordis, she had brought along several recordings of *romanceros*, Ladino folksongs, which she had insisted he play during the session. The music had delighted him, but in order that it not monopolize the hour, he had had to force her to focus on the task of the session.

She had come to him with symptoms of constant fatigue, anorexia, weight loss, vomiting and constipation alternating with diarrhea, a serious constellation of symptoms dismissed by a non-medical psychotherapist as psychosomatic complaints related to "acculturation difficulties." Cordis had insisted that she have a thorough medical examination, and now, in her third session, she had the results for him.

She had uterine cancer which had spread to the large bowel, and her condition was inoperable. The surgeon her family doctor referred her to estimated she had only a few months to live.

"Finito," she said calmly to Cordis.

After a long pause, he responded, "I'm so sorry to hear your news." The pain he felt was clearly evident in his eyes and wrinkled brow. "Is there anything I can do?"

She shook her head and in modern Spanish said, "I will return to Israel, where the patriarchs are buried." She paused for more than a minute, during which time Cordis sat motionless, and then she added, "Eretz Ysrael . . . where I will dwell in the house of the Lord forever."

With that she rose to her feet and hugged Cordis good-by.

Somehow, fighting back tears that threatened to choke off his words, he managed to say, "*Vaya con el Dios de nuestros antepasados.*" [Go with the God of our ancestors.]

He kept his next patient waiting while he tried to regain his composure. After some five minutes with him, it was obvious to Claire Esse that Cordis' mind was elsewhere, and she turned the tables on him by asking him if he was troubled.

132

Cordis forced a weak smile and responded softly, "I just learned that one of my patients is dying of cancer."

He had decided that the question put to him deserved to be answered with candor. After all, his patient was paying for him to concentrate on what she was saying, and he always strove to give value. Responding to her the way he did had the effect of producing a catharsis, and he was now able to focus on the patient seated before him.

Dr. James Henry of New Orleans, an old friend, had given Claire Esse his name in the event she found New York overwhelming. She was from St. Francisville, Louisiana, the old capital of the Republic of West Florida in the early 1800's, before President James Madison agreed to incorporate it into the rapidly growing United States. She was working toward a master's degree in social work at Columbia University, and this was her first experience in the North. For six months she had tearfully threatened to give it up and return to the South, describing New York as a "monstrosity, an ill-conceived patchwork of humanity"; but Cordis had nursed her along to the point where she was at least willing to finish out the first year of her two-year M.S.W. program.

Now, suddenly, she talked more optimistically about remaining at Columbia to complete the entire course. She had organizational talent, and she told him how she had just managed to obtain tickets to a Broadway show at half price for the graduate students living in her off-campus housing unit.

"I found out I can get tickets like this for nearly every Broadway show," she said cheerfully. "Some I can even get free. I plan now to take New York by storm, like Lee took Richmond."

Cordis thought it was Grant who had taken Richmond but he smiled benevolently, anyway. The Civil War remained a touchy subject among many Southerners with antebellum roots, who still called it "The War Between the States" and even "The Late Unpleasantness."

Claire, at 35, was the oldest in her class and had taught grammar school for ten years before deciding to change careers. Widowed for five years, now she casually mentioned that she had recently found a boyfriend, a Fordham University professor, with whom she was "very comfortable."

Cordis was pleased to see her new-found enthusiasm, and was not at all surprised when she informed him that she felt she could manage her life on her own "from now on."

"Ol' Fulwar would be proud of you at this moment," he said to her. The reference was to Fulwar Skipwith, president of the short-lived Republic of West Florida, an ancestor of hers.

"When she was gone, Cordis, sipping a cup of coffee, reflected on how he had just lost two patients, one to death, the other to triumph. Raising his cup in the air as a toast, he said aloud, "To both of you. May God's light shine on you through darkness and despair, triumph and tragedy, good times and bad." In a whisper he added, "In the end is the beginning.""

CHAPTER TWENTY-EIGHT

Renata Delacross' next scheduled session was for May 1st. Cordis took the time while waiting for his patient to arrive to read over her chart.

Intelligent, beautiful, with savoir faire, speaks French, Italian, English, Arabic, Parsee, Latin, Greek, even Japanese, he mused. Doesn't smoke cigarettes, no alcohol, never a vulgar word passes from her lips. But she smokes reefers! Marijuana is a drug which wipes out one's sense of time, imprisoning the user in the present dimension, where past and future do not exist. What is it that is sucking her out of the three-dimensioned world and into the one-dimensional realm of cannabis?

Renata came in on time, looking healthier and stronger than she had appeared the previous Tuesday. She shied away from the topic of cannabis, spending some time on how she was actually feeling physically, and then rambled on for a while about May Day parades around the world. Cordis nodded in agreement with her when she mentioned that the Soviets possessed a formidable war machine, but commented that they didn't know how to grow crops and trade the ruble internationally.

After a silence, she said to him, "How come you've never asked me to interpret proverbs for you? That's a standard part of the procedure."

"Is it now?"

"Yes, of course. My other therapists always tested me on proverbs," she stated challengingly.

"You mean like, 'Don't look a gift horse in the mouth.'"

"Exactly. And that's a good one."

"Well, you're probably so efficient at the task by now, what purpose would it serve to go over such familiar ground?"

Generally, an introductory session like the one he had conducted with Renata in January would be divided into two phases: history taking and a mental status examination. All physicians, regardless of their specialty, take a history. The psychiatrist adds a detailed assessment of the patient's on-going mental functioning. In the course of Renata's initial session, Cordis had failed to cover a number of items due to his patient's late arrival.

Proverbs are employed during the mental status examination as part of a testing sequence designed to gauge a patient's ability at abstraction and informational processing. A mentally retarded patient will give literal and concrete—oversimplified and insubstantial—interpretations. A patient with schizophrenia or an organic brain syndrome might also respond with concreteness.

"Well, try me, anyway," Renata said in response to his question.

"If you insist. Try this one. 'Shall I beat the bush and another take the bird?' "

"Hmm," Renata muttered. "No one has ever asked me that before."

"Good," the doctor said. "What we're looking for is spontaneity."

"It doesn't sound like a proverb," she complained.

Cordis shrugged. "Well, whatever it is, tell me what it means."

Renata seemed suddenly irritated. "Oh, I don't know . . . something like, I'm to do all the work and someone else will get the prize."

The psychiatrist smiled. "Right on! That's about what Henry the Fifth said at the siege of Orleans."

"Hah!" Renata cried out, straightening up in her chair. "I said it wasn't a proverb! Try me on another, but a genuine proverb this time. Something like 'A bird in the hand is worth two in the bush,' or 'People in glass houses shouldn't throw stones.' Something along those lines. You know, the classical proverb."

"Something classical," Cordis said, resting his chin on his clasped hands. "But not something for which you already have a well-rehearsed response."

He was going to say something else but Renata quickly stuck in, "Sure, sure."

"Try this Spanish proverb: 'Shrouds have no pockets.' "

Renata promptly responded, "You can't take it with you."

"Well done!" Cordis said enthusiastically, impressed by the quickness of her mind. "Here, tackle one a little more demanding: 'What is bred in the bone will never come out of the flesh.' "

Renata narrowed her eyes. "That's a proverb? It sounds more like a

135

riddle than a proverb."

"I grant you it's one of the less frequently used test proverbs, but it is on the list," the doctor responded.

She closed her eyes. "It makes me think of maggots coming out of stale rags."

"Good, good," Cordis said, impressed.

"Good? Good for what?"

"It shows that you are imaginative. How about one from Plutarch? 'When the candles are out, all women are fair.'"

Without pausing a moment Renata responded, "Under the cloak of darkness a lady must be discreet."

Cordis raised his eyebrows. "Witticism in the service of discretion." To himself he added, Ah, she finessed that sexually-laden trap nicely— she's not as fragile as she lets on.

"So, what does all this tell you about me?" Renata asked.

"Simply that there's nothing wrong with your abstract thinking ability and that you possess a sense of humor."

"Well, thank you for that, Dr. Cordis," she said warmly. "And then don't forget, there are questions to test my general fund of knowledge. Like, who is the governor of New York or the name of the congressman from my district."

Cordis made a face. "That's current events. Civics, we used to call it in high school. It's a waste of your time and mine. You have more important things to discuss during these sessions."

It was at this point that Renata began telling him about her gastrointestinal complaints: recurring abdominal pain, diarrhea, mucus in her stools, gas, nausea, belching, and on and on.

She had been x-rayed repeatedly from top to bottom—barium swallows and barium enemas—without any significant findings. She carried a small bottle of atropine in her purse, and she would measure out six to ten drops, depending upon how she felt, into a little water before meals. "It's for stomach catarrh," she said to Cordis.

"Stomach catarrh?" he repeated questioningly. "I doubt if that's in the World Health Organization's 'International Classification of Diseases.'"

It was the sort of diagnosis he could have expected from Father Dominic, not from a Park Avenue internist.

"I have to take other medications, too, besides atropine, like antacids."

No wonder her pupils are always dilated, Cordis mused. She takes extract of belladonna.

"You know," he began to say, "what you have kind of adds up to a clinical picture of what is termed nervous indigestion, also called spastic colon, functional colitis and irritable bowel syndrome."

"I left out sour stomach."

"Anyone can have dyspepsia," he said. "But for your bowel problem, I would think proper nutritional intake—a high-residue diet—might do you more good than all the pills in the kingdom."

"I've read all the nutritionists," Renata said, waving her hand in a gesture of dismissal. "Fredricks, Adele Davis—"

"That's pop nutrition," Cordis stopped her. "You should be reading the real experts, like Roger Williams, a member of the medical profession."

"I thought he was the founder of the Massachusetts Bay Colony," Renata sniped.

"Rhode Island colony," Cordis corrected her. "This one is a contemporary."

"What about enemas?" Renata asked, ignoring his comment.

Cordis came back with, "What about them?"

"Grandmama believes in cleansing the bowels every night to get rid of the poisons."

She's back to referring to her grandmother as "Grandmama," Cordis mused. That represents some degree of progress on the home front. "Ah, the fabled toxic waste products of digestion," he said aloud, "supposedly lurking in the muddy depths of the bowel like so much decaying slime in the city's sewage system."

"Yes," she said, missing his sarcasm.

"What toxins?" he asked. "What poisons?"

"Oh, I don't know their names," Renata answered, flustered. "But they cause much of the illness mankind suffers."

"Is that so?" he said, humoring her. "Let me tell you, there's no archeological evidence to suggest that enemas played any role in man's evolution—"

"You're teasing me," she said, blushing a bit.

Cordis shook his head. "No, I'm making a point. If enemas were a physiological necessity, then even primitive man would have used some kind of enema, something consistent with the technology, if you can call it that, of his time."

"Well, of course," she snapped back, "he didn't go to his local cave store and plop down three glittering pebbles to buy an enema bag."

The psychiatrist smiled. "The nightly enema routine enjoyed a vogue in the twenties and thirties and, it seems, still lingers on in some house-

137

holds. Your grandmother and apparently you, too, need to know something about how the lower part of the digestive tract functions." He opened the lower drawer of his desk and removed a multi-colored chart illustrating the gastrointestinal system.

"You're the all-purpose doctor," Renata said facetiously.

"I'm here to serve," he said with mock seriousness. "Now, here," he continued, pointing with the tip of his pen and with Renata leaning forward in her chair, "in the small intestine, most nutrients after being broken down, that is, digested, are absorbed into the blood stream. The small intestine is, by and large, sterile. However, the large intestine, or bowel," he added, tracing its outline on the chart, "is heavily populated with bacteria—hundreds of billions, trillions upon trillions—all constituting the normal bacterial flora."

"That's normal?" she said, making a face.

"Yes," he replied. "It's nothing to fret about, though. Thanks to these friendly bacteria, your bowel stays in tiptop shape."

"Uggh!" Renata feigned disgust.

"Growl if you must," Cordis said, "but don't knock 'em. Rather, say, 'Bless you, little beasties, for a job well done.' The bacteria in your bowel are making some of your vitamins for you, you know. As long as you don't upset the normal bacterial flora of the bowel, life in your lower depths goes on tranquilly."

"What upsets the bacterial flora? What disturbs the little beasties, the little darlings?" Renata asked drolly.

"Now that's showing the proper respect," the doctor responded. "A number of things both in or outside the bowel, such as a viral or bacterial gastroenteritis."

"Bad beasties mixing with the good beasties."

"Yes, that's the idea," Cordis said jocularly. "I can see that you have a natural flair for this sort of thing."

"I have had considerable practice," Renata said, sighing. "Is there anything else that upsets the gutty little vitamin makers in our lower regions?"

"Changes in locale—ingesting food or water with different strains of microorganisms—"

"Montezuma's revenge?"

The doctor smiled. "Regardless of the name, we all dance to the Aztec two-step at some point in our travels. In fact, it even happened to Freud on his famous visit to Clark University early this century. Come to think of it, all three of them—Freud, Jung and Ferenczi—were plagued by diarrhea while here on their lecture tour."

"They probably never dared come back after that," Renata opined.

Cordis frowned and then let out a laugh. "You know, Freud never did come back, but Jung was of a tougher constitution."

"What else upsets the flora of the bowel?" Renata asked, trying to hold back a giggle. "I can't help it," she added, bursting out in laughter. "Flora? Flora was the Roman goddess of flowers! She would bust a gut— I think that's the expression—if she knew her name was being so misapplied."

Cordis felt her verbal ridicule was a defense against her rising anxiety level: bowel talk was a sensitive internal barometer for her.

"Well, to answer your question," Cordis started to say, "there is the darling of the naturopaths: the enema. The enema, let me point out, is the enemy of the enteron."

"Why do you say that?" Renata asked coolly, as though sensing that a part of her built-in security system was about to come under attack.

"The enema creates an artificially induced diarrhea, which alters the bowel's bacterial population. You don't want to keep doing that. Its immediate effect, especially with plain water enemas, is to suck electrolytes—salt ions—out from the blood stream across the bowel wall. Water from the enema crosses into the blood stream, further diluting concentrations of nearly everything in the blood, upsetting the normal biochemical balance of things."

"Hmm," Renata murmured. "So much for enemas."

Cordis entered a note in her chart: "Enemas—bowel. Important issue!"

For the remainder of the hour Renata mentioned a host of remedies she had employed for one thing or another, remedies prescribed by her physician and remedies concocted by her grandmother and aunts. Her vocabulary included a number of seldom heard terms, at least on this side of the Atlantic, such as theriacs, electuaries, carminatives and emmemagogues, words well within the reach of someone of her intelligence, but also indicative of an undue concern with bodily function. In the *Diagnostic and Statistical Manual of Mental Disorders* of the day, she fulfilled the criteria for an additional diagnosis of Hypochondriacal neurosis, her major diagnosis being Depressive neurosis.

CHAPTER TWENTY-NINE

Cordis had jarred his neck the previous day on his way to work when the subway train he was riding had suddenly lurched forward after apparently coming to a stop. For the rest of the week he wore his hard collar while traveling around the city by any means of conveyance, subway, bus or taxicab.

Thursday, the 3rd, started off on an upbeat note at the clinic with the arrival of a letter from Dr. Irvine Page, a senior cardiologist with the Cleveland Clinic in Ohio.

Dr. Page, as a young researcher in the late '20's, had set up a department to study the chemistry of the brain at the Kaiser Wilhelm Institute for Psychiatry in Munich, Germany, only to find on returning to the United States that there were no funds available for him to continue his work: the psychoanalysts controlled the purse strings. He switched fields at that point in his career and went on to become one of the leading hypertension researchers in the country.

Cordis had written a biographical sketch of Sir James Mackenzie, a pioneer in the field of cardiology, for *The New England Journal of Medicine* in 1968, which was how he had come to know Irvine Page. Mackenzie won fame for his Ink Polygraph and a number of other inventions, instruments crafted for him by a watchmaker named Shaw. Cordis' own grandfather, a watchmaker, had met Shaw in England before World War I on a trip from his home in Mannheim, Germany. In 1919 Mackenzie founded the St. Andrews Institute for Clinical Research, and forty years later, in 1959, Cordis arrived at the University of St. Andrews.

As he sat rereading Dr. Page's letter, all these intriguing events passed through his mind. He smiled to himself and thought: Not by chance alone.

Edna Paxton came into his office to chat. Only two out of four scheduled Medicaid patients had showed up the previous evening, and she told Cordis she was tempted to start billing Medicaid for no-shows. He didn't know what to advise her. Compounding the issue was a sense of guilt he felt over accepting patient referrals from his *patrona*, whose own income was being compromised by her generosity.

"I'd be ashamed of myself to bill them for patients I don't actually see," she said with her characteristic probity.

"I feel guilty taking your cash-paying patients," Cordis confessed.

They overcame their mea culpa self-examination by switching to an intellectual device: spelling out the difference between shame and guilt from a psychoanalytic perspective. The best they could do was to say that shame, which was pre-oedipal, arose from tension between the ego and the ego ideal, whereas guilt followed from the ego's transgression of a superego boundary.

A little before noon, Cordis' Puerto Rican social worker led a patient he had not seen before into his office. She was visibly ill at ease standing next to the gaunt-looking young man, also Puerto Rican, and ever so slowly eased herself to the door while engaged in a rapid-fire dialogue in Spanish with him which Cordis had difficulty following. As soon as she crossed the threshold, the patient kicked the door shut behind her.

It was official policy for the staff to see patients with their door kept open, and Cordis adhered faithfully to the regulation, except for a few select patients such as Joey Dee and Madam Bee, considered "safe."

The patient spoke too rapidly in Spanish for Cordis to pick up what he was saying, but what he did fathom was the young man's frenzied emotional state. Each office desk was equipped with an alarm button so positioned as to be readily activated by a lateral movement of the knee, sending its signal to the security officer's station. Just as Cordis was making contact with the button, the patient lunged at him with a hunting knife. Instantaneously, Cordis grabbed his hard collar lying on the desktop while at the same time standing up and sliding his body laterally. The knife plunged into the collar, and Cordis, taking advantage of the man's forward momentum, hurled him over the desk landing him on his back behind his chair, where he shrieked and pounded the floor with his fists but made no attempt to get up. Pete arrived at the moment of impact, and for security's sake handcuffed him.

The patient's social worker was summoned and she lamely explained that Armando Tee, the patient, told her he had a gun and would shoot her unless she took him immediately to see the doctor.

"Well, he had a knife, not a gun," Cordis said staring at her angrily.

At the same time he realized the fear she must have felt on being threatened by the intruder, who was not a registered patient. The security system had been set up some years earlier following the killing of four social workers in a Queens clinic by a deranged patient. The possibility of violent attacks from patients was an occupational hazard all the staff had to live with in New York's various outpatient clinics. By 1973, Pete had amassed quite a collection of guns, knives, razors, clubs and other weapons he had confiscated from patients.

"I . . . I think he wanted you to prescribe Valium for him," his social worker said feebly.

"Is he a drug addict?"

"I think so," she replied nervously. "He came in here high on something and threatened me. I was scared and didn't know what to do."

Pete had propped the patient—or intruder—up in a chair. Armando, looking none the worse for his ordeal, sat silently, breathing heavily.

"I'm gonna run this guy over to Bellevue," the security guard suggested. "Is that all right with you, Doc?"

"Yeah," Cordis responded. "Take Charlie with you," he added, referring to a burly social worker who was standing in the doorway observing the proceedings. "And don't take the cuffs off until you deliver him there."

Alone in his office, Cordis muttered, "This job is getting to be too much."

In the afternoon, the clinic was visited by Mansoni's administrative assistant in charge of patient management, as the director titled him, a young black psychiatric aide from the hospital who had been dropping in one day a month since the beginning of the year. No one knew exactly what he was supposed to be doing. "He's an efficiency expert," Mansoni had explained. "He's gonna make you people do your work more efficiently."

What he had succeeded in doing was to make himself generally disliked among the doctors, like his boss, and he in turn had developed a particular dislike for Dr. Schlosberg. He would taunt him, always managing to stay within the bounds of propriety, but on this occasion, as he was walking past Schlosberg's office, he was overheard by Cordis next door saying, "Hymie, *du bist a Yid?*" [You're a Jew?].

Schlosberg's first name was Hyman, and Hymie was how his friends referred to him. But Hymie was also employed by non-Jews as a term of insult, and his "Du bist a Yid?" comment was an out-and-out insult as well.

"You're a foul-mouthed, uneducated barbarian!" came Schlosberg's loud voice from within his office.

Cordis was drawn to his doorway by the verbal exchange, which had also attracted several other staff members. Mansoni's man noticed that he was attracting attention and started to walk away, delivering one more uncensored verbal assault, clearly overheard, "I'm gonna fix that mother-fuckin' Jew."

The elderly Dr. Schlosberg was a mild-mannered individual, not known for emotional outbursts or fluency of speech. But he stormed after the efficiency expert, who was retreating to Mansoni's office, where he verbally blasted him for his blatant racism and Mansoni for his "stupidity in hiring such a fool." With that he made a phone call from his office, gathered up his briefcase and stormed out of the clinic.

As 5 o'clock rolled around, Cordis said to himself, "Two more months of this and then I'll be half-time at this crazy place."

CHAPTER THIRTY

When she returned the following Tuesday, Renata continued on the subject of her digestive-tract ailments and added another dimension to her medical history: difficulties associated with her menstrual cycle— dysmenorrhea, or period pain, and irregular menstruation. As she had with her gastrointestinal problems, Renata had tried a vast array of pills in her attempts to find relief. It didn't end there. Her doctor had resorted to cervical dilatation and the insertion of a stem pessary, an introduced foreign body designed to produce strong contractions of the uterus so as to increase the vascularity of the uterine musculature. This procedure had led to a severe cervicitis, landing her in the hospital for a week. She had gone along with all of these treatment approaches, balking finally at the suggestion of a presacral neurectomy, a surgical cutting of some nerves in the pelvis.

Sounds like 1950's medicine to me, Cordis said to himself. Stem pessaries? Isn't that what they call IUD's nowadays? You'd think she'd get better medical advice than that in 1973.

"My menstrual problems began when I was seventeen," Renata said.

"No menstrual problems until then?" the doctor asked.

"None," she affirmed.

Cordis couldn't get her to discuss the circumstances surrounding the onset of her dysmenorrhea. "Well, how's the problem now?" he asked, hoping he hadn't run into a dead end.

"I've been through the whole bit as I've indicated—I've been probed and tested for everything known to medical science, swallowing every conceivable type of pill and getting all sorts of injections and . . . well, my problem . . . isn't organic in nature."

"And just what does that mean?" he asked, probing her.

143

"I am led to believe it's psychosomatic—originating in my mind," Renata answered and smiled weakly.

"You have some understanding of the issue, it would seem," Cordis commented.

"Oh, yes, I understand the issue. My mind is exercising control over my body."

A silence settled over the room and Cordis then decided on a bold move—to use her menstrual problems to try to pry open the door to her sexual history.

"How does sexual activity affect your menstrual-cycle problems?" he asked.

"I think very little of men," she responded enigmatically.

"Can you amplify on that?" he asked, wondering if she meant that she held men in low esteem or if she just paid little attention to them, or both.

"Elephants do it in thirty seconds, rodents in only a few seconds and whales in less than a second while leaping together out of the water. Kinsey's research indicates that three-quarters of all men ejaculate within two minutes, no longer than it takes to boil an egg. With so little time involved, why all the fuss about sex?"

"An interesting perspective," Cordis commented.

"While men busy themselves with the rise and fall of empires, women are supposed to concentrate on fulfilling the sacred offices of love," she said sharply.

The statement struck Cordis as a more forceful rewording of a comment she had made on the status of the sexes during an earlier session.

"It seems as though you have gone from sex as a topic to love," he commented.

"*For love is of man's life a thing apart;*
'*Tis woman's whole existence,*" she said, quoting Byron.

"Do you believe either half of that to be accurate?"

"Women in this age of ours are self-divided," she announced.

"Self-divided you say."

"Self-conscious, and suddenly the rivals of men for economic equality. They have become independent of the family, individualized entities floating on the sea of life. Women are at war with their own sex, so why shouldn't I flee from my own sexuality?"

"Is that what you're doing?"

"Apparently," she answered. "And as for men, they have become the subjects of women, developing only a pseudo-masculinity." She paused and remained silent.

144

"Tell me more," Cordis encouraged.

"Men fear the domination of women and the new sisterhood being forged in the feminist cause. The new creations of American history are the hapless male and the aggressive female."

"All that?"

She ignored his comment. "He has become the single male whose father vanished from the historical scene decades ago, perhaps at the time of the American Civil War, an early period in the evolution of this country. That would leave him mired at the adolescent level of historical development, to draw a comparison to Freud's system of marking personal development."

"That's the male then," Cordis said. "What about the female?"

"She's the woman who thinks she can be a man."

"Yes?" he said after a short silence.

Renata blushed and smiling weakly said, "Don't take me too seriously on everything I'm saying."

"Why not?" Cordis asked, surprised at her retreat from her strongly worded position. "It all sounds genuine."

"Oh, I read something like that somewhere. I can't recall where." She was still blushing.

"Whether these views originated with you or elsewhere, they seem to reflect your own thinking and feelings."

"Yes, that's the case," Renata affirmed. "It fits me to a tee. But now I have to ask myself where do I fit into all of this."

"And what answer do you come up with?"

"I feel like Artemis, the goddess of wild animals and the hunt, but also of chastity and childbirth." Again she stopped abruptly.

Hmm, Cordis was thinking to himself. Artemis, the Greek goddess of the wilderness, was also depicted in antiquity as being free of sexual desire. Atalanta, the beautiful and belligerent virgin huntress, the fleet-footed man-slayer running away from her femininity, is generally recognized to be a by-form of Artemis. It was Atalanta who speared to death all potential suitors who could not beat her in a foot race, until Hippomenes dropped the three golden apples which she stopped to pick up, and so defeated her.

She's got a high 'Atalanta count,' Cordis said to himself.

Cordis had heard Desmond O'Neill, psychiatrist at Chelsea Hospital for Women in London, lecture on the "Atalanta syndrome" in the early '60's. The syndrome—painful intercourse, frigidity, vomiting in pregnancy (past the third month), post-partum depression, failure of lactation and the disorders of the menstrual cycle (period pain, irregular men-

145

ses, loss of periods and excessive bleeding)—occurs, according to O'Neill, more often in women who repudiate or have difficulty accepting their role as wives and mothers.

"So," Cordis said, "you feel like Artemis."

Whatever information he was hoping to elicit from her was not forthcoming at this point, for Renata now maneuvered herself into other psychological waters.

"I've been reading Victor Hugo's *Les Miserables*," she said.

So we're back to bibliotherapy, Cordis said to himself, and then quickly added, I hope it's not just literary criticism.

"Basically, *Les Miserables* is nothing more than a detective novel with hundreds of pages of nonessential material padded in on the Battle of Waterloo, life in a French convent and a history of the Paris sewer system."

"What was that? Did you say the Paris sewer system?"

"Yes," Renata answered laughingly. "I'll have you know that sewers have played an important role in my life. My father was a sanitary engineer and traveled the world over building sewer systems. He died when I was ten."

"I know."

"You do?"

"You mentioned it in January."

"Did I say what the cause of his death was?"

Cordis shook his head. "No, you did not."

Renata lowered her eyes. "He died in Bolivia of hemorrhagic fever while on a project there. He was only forty-five."

"Oh, I'm sorry to hear that," the doctor said.

Strange, he thought, most of my patients' fathers will die of a heart attack or from a stroke or maybe get killed in an automobile accident. But her father had to die of Bolivian hemorrhagic fever. I'd better look that up later.

"When we were in Rome the year before he died . . . I told you my mother was Italian?"

"Yes, you did."

"We used to spend some time in Italy . . . well, that last visit, my father showed me the old Cloaca Maxima, the ancient Roman sewer. It's still in use, you know."

"No, I didn't know," Cordis responded. To himself he said, We've got a sewers-on-the-mind syndrome here.

"Did you say something else?"

"No, not yet. I was about to ask if you have ever seen a duckbill platypus?"

146

"A what?" Renata looked at him, perplexed.

"The platypus of Australia."

"Oh, I know what you mean. Well, maybe in the movies. Never in the flesh. Why?"

"The duckbill platypus and the spring anteater are the only mammals with a cloaca. In the adult stage, I should say. Most mammals have a cloaca during their embryonic development."

"Cloaca?" she voiced loudly. "What . . . ?" Renata was momentarily befuddled. Then she saw what he was getting at. "Oh, a sewer. Of course, sewer. "I'm supposed to be the Latin scholar!"

"Right. Sewer."

"But what has that to do with me? I don't have a cloaca, do I?"

Cordis smiled. "We all do at about the fifth week during our embryological days in utero. During those golden days, before we are thrust out into the world, there is a cloaca, a common chamber into which the intestinal, urinary and genital tracts open."

"I'm fascinated," Renata said with a touch of sarcasm, wondering where her doctor was going with his embryological discourse.

"Then a urorectal septum forms," he continued, "to subdivide the cloaca, so that the lower parts of the digestive and urinary systems become separate. That way, everything doesn't mix and come out the same opening. Get the picture?"

"Sort of," she said, sounding tentative.

Cordis drew her a diagram to clarify the anatomical structures discussed.

"And supposing something goes amiss during those golden days in the uterus?" Renata asked, nodding to indicate that she now had a clear picture in her mind of the pertinent anatomy.

"If the urorectal septum should fail to grow properly, you wind up with what is known as a persistent cloaca, an anatomical anomaly in which the bladder and rectum remain in continuity and the rectal and urogenital openings stay merged."

"Which is, I believe, the way birds do it," Renata said, an indication that she understood what he was saying.

"Exactly."

"With . . . droppings."

"Correct. A uro-digestive mix that exits as a plopping."

"Not at all the way we do it," Renata commented.

"You really do get the picture," Cordis said and smiled.

"Yes, I've learned a little embryology. But tell me, Dr. Cordis, what has all this talk about cloacas have to do with me?" Renata asked, convey-

147

ing some anxiety. "And why do you retain all that medical school stuff, anyway? You're not a prenatal psychiatrist, if there is such a thing, are you?" At that point she laughed.

Cordis grinned. "I had to review some human embryology because I have several young women coming to treatment who don't know where their digestive tract ends and their genital system begins."

"I don't either. Well, I didn't before this hour, but I do now."

"And they developed what I might call a cloaca syndrome as a consequence," Cordis continued, "with all sorts of lower abdominal and/or pelvic pain and discomfort as a result. All born of anatomical ignorance or confusion."

"Aha, I begin to understand."

"Think about it when you get home. I don't say this explains your particular pains, but it may be a contributory cause. There are other factors involved, of course, some of which we will uncover as we go along, maybe even the most important ones."

"There's relief in sight for the lower depths," Renata said, tittering.

"You see, there's more than one way to treat a sewer."

"If the shoe fits, I'll wear it," Renata said, shifting the metaphor.

"Search through the box it comes wrapped in also," the doctor added.

"My subconscious?"

Cordis nodded. "Subconscious pertains to what is to be found under the conscious. That, too, is a sewer of sorts—at least in the Freudian persuasion."

"And in the Jungian?"

"An underground realm containing the priceless treasures of man's heritage, as well as a few dark alley ways."

Renata smiled. "I'm beginning to like this Jung of yours."

"You will encounter him again and again as you continue your personal exploration."

CHAPTER THIRTY-ONE

Ruby Lokko, from Accra in Ghana, was visiting New York, and Cordis squired her around town for a week. She was the younger sister of a St. Andrews classmate, Nini Lokko, one of a number of British Commonwealth students who had been in his class. Ruby was in the country attending a United Nations conference, and Monday, the 14th, was her final day. Before leaving for Kennedy International, she stopped by Cordis' office late in the afternoon to say good-by. He was booked from 6:00 through 10:00, and regretted being unable to see her off at the airport.

His 6 o'clock was late, which gave Cordis a little extra time to spend with her. They were chatting in the waiting room when his patient arrived at 6:15. Ruby took that as her cue to leave and she hugged and kissed Cordis, switching from English to French to deliver her parting words. His patient took in the scene with more than passing curiosity.

She was a 19-year-old with a marijuana addiction whom Cordis had been treating for several months. What she brought to therapy was a great deal of anger . . . and a vocabulary to rival any truck driver's.

"Very charming African," she said smugly for an opening statement, once seated in Cordis' office. "I could tell she's no Harlem broad—not with that fancy native costume she was sporting and her highfalutin' French. You have good taste in women, Dr. Cordis."

"Thanks," he said, "but you haven't come all this way to discuss what I do in my private life."

She stared silently but angrily at him for a few moments and then said, "I had to get out of this fuckin' city for a breath of fresh air. My carburetor was about to flood, so I drove across the GWB [George Washington Bridge] to New Jersey."

"Your carburetor was about to flood," Cordis repeated.

"Yeah, that's right. Or my radiator was about to boil over. It's the same fuckin' thing."

Interesting metaphors to start off the evening, Cordis thought. It seems we're going to be using the language of the machine this hour.

"Something's knawing away at the anger center in your brain," Cordis said to her.

"You! Dammit, you! Trying to get me to stop smoking weed. You just hate anyone with a joint in their hand. Why don't you admit it?"

"I don't hate," Cordis responded. "Period. I'm opposed to the use of drugs as recreational playthings. That's all. The concept, not the individuals involved, is what produces displeasure in me."

"You hate the idea of people having a little fun because at heart you're a goddamn Mormon."

Cordis wondered where that one came from. It seemed to him that she was confusing Mormons with the Puritans of New England.

"In my heart of hearts, all the way up to my Semitic nose, I'm a Jew, not a Latter-Day Saint nor a tribal relation to Hester Prang. Your ascription to me of so much hating is beyond my affective capacity. Or to rephrase what I've just said, I don't squander energy from my emotional reservoir in hating, a useless, wasteful and unchristian activity. Your engine is running on high-octane hate, apparently, and engines fueled on such a hydrocarbon mixture don't run smoothly; furthermore, they're constantly in the shop for repair."

"You think my engine needs repair?" she asked, seething with anger.

"Why else are you here at Ye Olde Dr. Cordis' Repair Shoppe? You certainly haven't come for an oil change or a tune-up. Those are minor things. Your needs run to an overhaul, a thorough overhauling. And the sooner you get down to the business of the shop, the sooner you'll be on the road again, only this time purring along like the Cadillac you can be."

"What the fuck do you know!" she yelled. "If I stick with you, I'll be running on low-octane boredom."

But a clean engine will run a long time—"

She didn't allow him to finish. "You stick to your nigger ass," she screamed at him, "and I'll stick to what I like." She stood up and went on, "I'm finished with this shit." The last words he heard her yelling as she stormed out of the office and made her way to the corridor door were, "Rex! Rex? What kind of name is that? It's a dog's name. Here, Rex! Here, boy!" And she was gone.

"Good grief, Charlie Brown!" Cordis muttered half-aloud. You win some and you lose some, he added to himself as he wrote the words "Engine Dead" in her chart.

He had another young woman with a marijuana addiction for his next hour. Her dialogue lacked the scatological fire of her predecessor, but she had been proving equally difficult in her own way.

"I don't see where you earn your fifty bucks an hour," she said to him. "All you really do is just listen."

"Listening is an art," Cordis responded. "Only by listening can you hear."

"Hear what? What do you hear when I accuse you of only listening?"

"Someone who is weak challenging someone who is stronger."

"Well, sure," she said, smiling nervously. "I mean, sure, you're a good hundred pounds heavier than me."

"I'm talking about inner strength, not avoirdupois. You're draining off your vitality with marijuana. When are you going to come out from behind that foul smokescreen and face the world?"

"You tell me," she said challengingly.

"When you have first learned to face yourself. You're the one with the problem, after all."

"The world's screwed up."

"Everyone lives in that same screwed up world. Try reordering yourself before you blame the world for all your problems. That's the purpose in your coming here—to undertake the process of self-reordering."

So it went for the entire session, although she mellowed near the end of the hour, leading Cordis to think that she might yet make some progress.

Monday at his office was turning into pot night, for the next patient, Sonja Olamstein, a 20-year-old from one of the colleges now comprising the City University of New York, was another troubled young woman with a marijuana problem. She had the advantage over the previous two in that she was insightful and motivated to change. But it had been a struggle, like pulling teeth, Cordis had told her more than once, to convince her of the harmfulness to health of marijuana.

"You know a great deal about cannabis," she said, using the generic term she had learned from him. "You're about the most knowledgeable person on this subject I know."

While leisurely leafing through a medical journal one day in 1969 in the library of the Medical College of Charleston, South Carolina, where he was in his second year of residency training in psychiatry, he came across the formula for delta-9-tetrahydrocannabinol, worked out only a few years earlier. He was surprised that the active ingredient in cannabis was not an alkaloid but a complex steroid-looking molecule like cholesterol, whose very structure suggested it was fat soluble. How will the body detoxify—get rid of—such an unusual looking molecule? he had asked himself. And that was how he, a former chemist, had become intrigued and then caught up in the cannabis issue.

"I spent some time down Mexico way, when maraguango was still a novelty," Cordis said to Sonja.

"I never heard it referred to as that."

"Down there it's a term for any substance producing an intoxication.

Marijuana itself, as you know, goes under many names. Mary Jane and also Mary Weaver and Mary Warner. Doña Juanita, or simply Juanita. And Rosa Maria. And that strange crone who sold Timothy Leary his first batch of magic mushrooms—her name was Juanita Loca, or Crazy Jane."

Sonja managed a smile and then said, "You know, I'm really gonna give it up."

"That would be an important step toward your future," Cordis responded.

"How long do you think it will take to get all those cannabis chemicals—what do you call them—?"

"Cannabinoids."

"Yes, cannabinoids, out of my body?"

"Well, the historian az-Zarkashi mentions that the Shaykh Ali al-Hariri, a thirteenth century Sufi—the Sufis were a Muslim mystical sect—who, unlike his brethren, was against the practice of using hashish, advised abstaining from the stuff for forty days to allow the body to be rid of it and then forty days more of rest before tackling serious matters."

"About six weeks to excrete it all?"

"No one can say for sure as yet," Cordis answered. "But given a half-life of about a week, half the THC, the psychoactive component in cannabis, in your body stores will be gone a week from today, and half of what remains will be removed in another week, and so on. Certainly, after six weeks, you may very well be cleared of it all, as al-Hariri seemed to know."

"It will be out of my body?"

"Yes, and that means your brain as well."

After half a year of talking about the dangers of pot, she seemed genuinely ready to give it up.

Nine o'clock found him tired, with one more patient to go, but his apparent success with Sonja Olamstein buoyed him up.

His final patient of the day was the priest referred by Father Dominic, who had phoned him Easter Sunday night. Cordis no longer spent 90 minutes on Saturday mornings working up new patients. He restricted all his sessions to 50 minutes and had cut out working altogether on Saturdays.

Johann Klinger turned out to be an Austrian priest who had left the priesthood to marry a parishioner in Germany. After six years of marriage and two children, they divorced, and the ex-priest came to the United States in 1960, where he eventually became a high school history teacher.

He was in his sixties, tall with blond hair and blue eyes, and he spoke softly and unhurriedly, with only a faint German accent.

Cordis had German-speaking patients and he came into contact from

152

time to time with German-speaking psychoanalysts, but they were all Jewish. His encountering a German Catholic as a patient was a new experience for him.

They talked at length, with Cordis gathering up personal data, but most of it was talk. At one point the former priest mentioned that while still a student he had met Benito Mussolini in Rome before the War broke out.

"I was doing some research on the Jews of Rome, and Mussolini said he was fond of the Jews," the ex-priest said.

"Did you believe him?"

"He was all bombast; Americans would have called him a blowhard."

He went on to add that he had also researched the life and work of Alexander Haindorf, the first German-Jewish psychiatrist, who had written an important work on psychiatry the year before our War of 1812 began—the word "psychiatry" had been coined by the German physician Johann Christian Reil during that period.

It was obvious to Cordis that Fr. Dominic had made his patient aware of the fact that he was Jewish. After this informative exchange, he felt comfortable with him, confident that he could handle countertransference issues—German gentiles as a whole represented a group he continued to dislike.

Near the end of the hour, Cordis asked him, "And what, since all I find in this preliminary examination is a non-life-threatening existential depression, did Fr. Dominic have in mind in referring you to me?"

Johann Klinger flashed an uneasy smile. "He wants you to determine if I am fit and ready to return to the priesthood."

Cordis took that as a singular honor, since he assumed that such an evaluation would have to come from a Catholic psychiatrist or special tribunal.

"Is that what you want to do?" he asked.

"I have been giving it considerable thought of late. I'm sixty-four, and next year I will have to retire from teaching. I won't have enough to live on after that."

"So that's your situation."

"Either I return to the Church or I will have to find a rich widow," Cordis' patient said laughingly.

"We shall talk again," Cordis said, rubbing his chin thoughtfully. Then he added, "How do you want to be called? Father Klinger?"

"*Dumbkopf*," he answered jokingly. "Seriously, just Johann. I haven't said mass in more years than I can remember."

Cordis retorted, "They say once a priest always a priest."

Johann smiled weakly and in his calm voice said, "Time will only tell."

"Time usually does just that," Cordis said, shaking hands with his patient and wishing him good night.

Fr. Dominic called a little past 10 o'clock while Cordis was drinking a cup of Sanka.

"What do you think of my lost sheep?" he asked.

"Lost indeed," the doctor responded.

"Any thoughts?"

"He's thinking about his sixty-fifth birthday and he's scared."

"Yes, I know."

"I guess he's not too old to be a priest again."

"Oh, he's a special case," Fr. Dominic said.

"You know—did you know?—that he waited five years before marrying that woman while he was still a priest. He shacked up with her all that time he was still saying mass."

"Yes, I knew about that. Now you know what sinners even priests can be. But Christ didn't come to save the saintly among us."

"I'll be seeing him once every two weeks, and when I've found out if he really belongs to Christ, you'll be the third to know—after Johann Klinger and myself."

CHAPTER THIRTY-TWO

When Renata Delacross arrived for her next session the following evening, she was in a pensive mood. The previous Sunday had been Mother's Day, and that subject was very much on her mind.

"There seems to be no end to the battling between the Catholics and the Protestants in my family's private civil war," she complained, starting the session. "Simone has been calling Grandmama occasionally, but their conversation invariably turns into a shouting match with one or the other, sometimes I think both, slamming down the receiver. It's not good for Simone, or me, or Grandmama. Especially Grandmama. I don't want

154

her blood pressure going up, not at her age. You probably know, she's already had one stroke—last year." The doctor nodded his assent. "I don't know what to do," she added.

"What can you do?" he asked softly.

"I sent her a gift for Mother's Day, but she hasn't acknowledged receipt of it."

"That must be difficult," Cordis commented when she grew silent.

She dabbed at her eyes with a tissue drawn from the box on his desk. "Well, back to the cloaca," she said, forcing a smile. She continued while blowing her nose, "Last week I was telling you about my father's death."

"You did mention that he died of hemorrhagic fever in Bolivia."

"Yes. Fourteen years ago. I was ten."

"Tell me, what do you recall about his illness?" the doctor asked.

Renata took a little time to collect her thoughts. "I was with him at the time," she began slowly. "I remember that his skin had taken on a terrible discoloration and that he ran a high fever. And he bled a lot." The information came forth slowly, as if being dredged up from some dark part of her memory. "They kept him in isolation because the disease is so contagious."

"You didn't contract it?"

"I was spared."

He noted the word "spared," from the religious vocabulary. She was still a practicing Catholic at the time of her father's illness, Cordis recalled.

"Can you remember where he bled from?" he asked.

Machupo hemorrhagic fever of Bolivia, like yellow fever, another of the hemorrhagic fevers, is a mosquito-borne viral disease characterized by high fever, purpura, or purple skin blotches, and bleeding from the nose and gastrointestinal and genitourinary tracts.

"Everywhere," Renata answered. "He was bleeding from every opening of his body." She reached for a fresh tissue to dab her teary eyes.

"Perhaps, just perhaps," Cordis began after several moments of silence, "your cloaca syndrome has its origins in the memory of your father's suffering, especially the memory of bloody bowel and bladder discharges."

Renata blew her nose several times before she was able to respond. "Maybe," she finally uttered between sobs. "You could be right. In any event, I will probably relive the Bolivian tragedy tonight and find out for sure." She looked up at the doctor, and regaining some of her composure, said, "We were there only a few weeks in the summer of fifty-nine, and that brief spell changed my life unalterably. Poor Daddy. He lived for his little girl. How I loved that gentle man." She paused again before adding,

155

"His was not a good death."

Ah, she understands what is meant by a good death, Cordis thought. She has something of the wisdom that may come, for some, in later years.

"That event may have left its mark on you," he said, "may have, as you say, changed your life unalterably, but only to this moment. From this day forward you have it within your own power to alter your life in a direction of your choosing."

Renata stared at him. "Do you really believe that?"

"If I didn't, I wouldn't have said it."

After a brief silence, she whispered almost like a prayer, "Mine own destiny."

"In this life, we are each entitled to try to find our destiny," Cordis added.

Renata remained silent for half a minute, and when she spoke again it was to focus on a skin condition that plagued her, a long-standing atopic dermatitis, with its intense itchiness. "I have all the health problems I can live with and on top of those I have this skin ailment to contend with. Any worry and I start itching. I need a whole new outer covering to my body."

"Rub your psyche the wrong way, and what happens?"

"I itch."

"Precisely."

"But why? It can't be because of something that happened to me when I was three or five or seven, now buried in my subconscious. You would have me believe that, I know."

Cordis shrugged. "You never know. But the answer might be more accessible than that."

"What do you mean?"

"The nervous system is linked to the skin system—both are derived from ectoderm. In other words, the skin is connected to the brain from embryological days. So—"

"What happens to one can affect the other," Renata said, completing the thought.

"That's it. You get it—even without a lecture on the ectoderm, mesoderm and entoderm."

She beamed, "Yes, I do see it."

"Great," Cordis said enthusastically. "Now tell me this. How old were you when you developed this skin problem of yours. Did you have eczema as a baby?"

Renata had to think. "I'm sure I didn't have any severe skin problems as an infant. This particular problem I've had for about a dozen years."

156

"Did it start before or after your father's death?"

She remained silent for several seconds, concentrating. "After his death. Yes, it was after. Perhaps a year after."

"In describing his illness, you mentioned skin discoloration. Now, let me give you the Freudian perspective on the development of your dermatitis—identification, a technical term, with your father's suffering and untimely death."

Renata remained quiet and motionless, her eyes watery. Finally, she nodded several times to indicate her understanding of what the psychiatrist had said.

Following a short pause, she changed the subject. "Do you think I should go back to the university in the fall?"

"It is for you to choose," Cordis answered. "You have now proposed the college option as one of your choices."

"You never tell me what to do, do you?"

"Therapy is not advisory. Its fruits yield a fuller range of choices. In fact, to find the freedom to choose is close to the heart of what therapy is all about."

"So, now I at least know what one of my choices can be. And I have more than one to choose from."

"Choose wisely and do not go in haste, for what you do next will determine the course of your life for years to come."

"You know that for a fact."

"I know it in my bones."

"But supposing you're arthritic like Grandmama?" Renata said in a playful tone. "Do I dare place my trust in someone's aching bones?"

Cordis smiled inwardly, amused that she wasn't aware of how arthritic he himself actually was. "If that were the case," he replied, "I would still know it in my intuitive brain, where gestalts form without the benefit of a summation of constituent parts."

"My, my, but that sounds deep," Renata said facetiously. "Now I may have to go to graduate school in order to figure out what you have just philosophized or psychologized."

"Work on your choices," Cordis said somberly, "and then work out your salvation with diligence."

"You know, there's a familiar ring to that," Renata said scratching her forehead in thought. "As though I have read it somewhere."

"Yes, T.S. Eliot," Cordis said, smiling.

"Of course! Is it from The Cocktail Party?"

"Why, yes! You are indeed well read, young lady."

"The psychiatrist, Sir Henry Harcourt-Reilly, has a line like that in

157

the play."

"Yes, yes, Harcourt-Reilly, Eliot's alter ego," the doctor commented. "You seem to know your Eliot well."

"After Ezra Pound, he's my favorite American poet."

"Well, you've picked two of the best."

"This Henry Harcourt-Reilly, he is purely a fictional character, isn't he?" she asked.

"I don't know if anything is ever pure," Cordis replied. "But if you want some words from a wise nonfictional Reilly, then listen to this stanza from 'The Infinite' by the nineteenth century poet John Boyle O'Reilly:

We may question with wand of science.
Explain, decide and discuss;
But only in meditation
The Mystery speaks to us."

Renata had fixed her eyes on him while he was engaged in the recitation, but as soon as he finished, she turned away. "There's something for you to ponder till we meet again," he added.

CHAPTER THIRTY-THREE

Renata phoned Cordis at the clinic first thing Friday, the 18th. Simone and Pierre were returning to Casablanca for three weeks before coming back to New York. She wanted to know if he thought it would be all right for her to go with them.

"The choice is yours," he said.

"Will it set my therapy back?"

"Life always goes on," Cordis responded cryptically. "It never stops and it never flows in reverse."

"Then you approve?"

"You don't need approval from me."

"Then I choose to go."

"I'm pleased that you have chosen from among your available choices."

The Friday morning staff meeting produced something of a bombshell. Dr. Irving Kissel had come from Gotham State and introduced the clinic's new director, Dr. Troylene Armazón-Goldstein, Ed. D., J.D.. Mansoni, who had maintained a low profile since his encounter with an angry Dr. Schlosberg two weeks earlier, was out, dispatched back to the hospital, and his administrative assistant had been returned to his former duties as a psychiatric aide. Dr. Schlosberg sat quietly, conveying no outward emotion, as Gotham's superintendent made the introduction. It took him less than five minutes to say what he had to say, and then he departed, not stopping to talk to anyone.

"Did he say 'Amazon'?" Dr. Arnold Grossman whispered to Cordis.

"Armazón," Cordis whispered back. "Spanish for skeleton."

"She's built more like the first," Grossman added.

Dr. Armazón-Goldstein was massive, with a husky voice to match her frame.

"That kind of throatiness reminds me of Greta Garbo," Cordis commented, continuing the undertoned dialogue. "' I vant to be alone,' " he said, straining to imitate the great Garbo.

"The silent film star?"

"Yeah, talkies killed her career."

"Our new leader can't be a day over twenty-nine," Grossman continued.

"Just what we need—a doctor of education and a lawyer," Hyman Schlosberg, leaning forward in his seat behind the other two whispered, but with a little more volume.

"Yup, a lawyer," Grossman repeated. "The lowest form of primate life."

"Just above the invertebrates," Dr. Brown, Cordis' biological psychiatry peer, quipped.

With that the three psychiatrists burst out laughing. Dr. Armazón-Goldstein shot them a lingering, cold stare and remained silent for a while until all the commotion in the conference room—whispering, giggling and head turning in the direction of the disruptive clique—died down. She then resumed and rambled on for another twenty minutes, delivering a standard bureaucratic pep talk which consumed a great many words but conveyed little of substance. Near the end of her sermonizing, which was how Cordis viewed her speech, she picked up on what had become Mansoni's favorite topic: a name change for the clinic.

"Something that presents a neutral position," she said. "The concept of a medical facility conveys a threatening image to our clients. They need a sense of security in a serene setting."

"You want to call it 'The Facility' maybe?" Grossman suggested derisively, gesturing with his entire body in a very Jewish manner.

"'The Retreat' is what we have in mind," the director responded.

"She said 'we,'" Grossman whispered to Cordis. "There must be a horde of them working on this particular project up at the hospital."

"That would be copyright infringement," Cordis said in a loud voice. All eyes were now turned in his direction. "A tea and coffee merchant by the name of William Tuke, he of the Quakers, established the original 'Retreat' near York, England, in seventeen ninety-six for mentally ill patients."

"We refer to our clients as MII's, mentally ill individuals, not patients," Dr. Armazón-Goldstein said, trying to hide any emotion in the wake of Cordis' short academic discourse aimed at embarrassing her.

At that point she thanked the staff for their cooperation and suggestions and concluded with how she was looking forward to working closely with each and every one of them to help improve the clinic's delivery of high-quality care to its clients.

As they were filing out of the room, Cordis said to Grossman, "She hasn't learned that doctors and nurses have patients, and social workers have clients."

Grossman nodded and added, "Amazon, I mean, Armazón-Goldstein—what kind of mishmash is that?"

"She heap, powerful woman," Cordis said facetiously. "Troy and the suggestion of Amazon—them's fighting words."

Dr. Schlosberg, never known for off-color jokes, listening in on the exchange, said gravely, "From now on protect your *putz* at all times." It was Yiddish for penis.

"You're all a bunch of little boys," Dr. Paxton chimed in mirthfully.

"This is man talk, madam," Cordis said playfully.

Grossman was still concerned about her name. "I always thought you had to petition parliament or the diet," he said, "to get your name hyphenated."

"Maybe in nineteenth-century Austria," Cordis offered. "But don't forget, this is now that brave new world of ours."

"Enough of this idle chatter," interjected Dr. Brown mockingly. "It's time we got down to seeing our MII's."

Anna Bee was among the patients Cordis saw in the afternoon. He noted a change in her demeanor—a constriction in her affective or emotional range—as well as intensification in her anti-Freudianism.

"Talk—words stacked together," she said petulantly and uncharacteristically. "That's all Freud's therapy ever amounted to. You would think that a neurologist of his stature would have had a few profound insights drawn from medicine to have offered his patients."

Cordis acknowledged that she was correct in her identification of Freud as a neurologist. Freud had never done a residency in psychiatry, that is, had not undergone a specified period of post-graduate training in psychiatry, as her hero, Jung, had done. He had eased into the study of hysteria because the traditional therapeutic approaches of the neurologists to this baffling array of conditions had proved ineffective. His intervention, psychoanalysis, was successful in resolving cases of hysterical paralysis and blindness, functional problems with roots in psychodynamic factors, but was of no utility where patients had organic lesions involving the nervous system.

"Freud went as far as he could with the medicine of his day," Cordis explained. "He knew that a scientific psychiatry would supercede his psychoanalysis. In fact, one of his professors at the University of Vienna, Theodor Meynert, had already defined psychiatry as the study of lesions of the frontal lobe and its connections, a remarkably modern view."

Madam Bee moved on to another peeve, one she had not voiced in previous sessions.

"What I miss here in America," she started to say, "is that sense of community, of communal cohesiveness, of conviviality, bonhomie—call it a highly developed social togetherness. The Germans have a word for it: Gemeinschaft."

"America is still a young country," Cordis responded, "one which has yet to define a national destiny."

"Young is correct," his patient stressed, "with an emphasis on youth and the immaturity which goes with it. The old people dream only of juvenescence, and nowhere is there evidence of what the mature can bring, for there is no maturity here. This is a country destined to grow old without ever having grown up."

Cordis was concerned by what he perceived to be a widening depression underlying Madam Bee's sourish dialogue, although he did agree in principle with what she was saying.

"You know," he said, "I usually refer the clinic's postmenopausal patients to our gynecology consultant for hormonal replacement assessment."

"Why is that?" she asked blandly.

"The estrogen shutdown that follows menopause can affect some women's outlook on life," he answered tactfully. "Dr. Stella Shafer-Epstein is an octogenarian, and all our patients referred to her find her delightful."

"Will I be able to afford her?"

"She takes Medicaid or whatever our patients can pay. At eighty-three she's not in this for the money." Cordis wrote his consultant's name and telephone number on a sheet of the clinic's stationery. "Call Dr. Shafer-Epstein for an appointment, if you're interested," he added, handing her the sheet. "And call me in two weeks to let me know what has transpired."

Madam Bee peered at the paper and forced a smile, fully aware of her doctor's maneuvering. Folding it into her purse, she said, "I will consider it. Thank you."

"Do that," the doctor said. "Estrogen replacement can make a world of difference for some women."

Cordis preferred to have his older female patients try estrogen therapy, usually as Premarin, if there were no contraindications to its use, before proceeding on to a trial with one or another of the antidepressants. In Madam Bee's case, he thought he was on the right track, but he also sensed the presence in her life of an issue that went beyond psychiatric considerations.

CHAPTER THIRTY-FOUR

Chaim Cohen phoned Cordis Sunday night, the 20th, requesting an appointment. Cordis hadn't heard from him in three months—three months to the day—and had finally written him off. Actually, he had sent his bill to Mr. Cohen on the last day of each month since February for his two sessions, adding a note to his April billing that in the event he did not communicate to him in some manner he would be closing his file. It was a legal step to guard against any possible future charge brought against him of abandonment. As far as collecting his fee for services rendered, Cordis would not turn the matter over to a collection agency, as several colleagues were recommending.

Chaim Cohen wanted to see him the following evening, but Cordis' Monday office schedule was booked solid with young adult patients whose problems centered around marijuana use. He could have fitted him into Renata's temporarily vacated Tuesday slot, but decided on Thursday. He felt he needed some time to review the intriguing dream Mr. Cohen had so eloquently related to him and perhaps do a little research on it at Barnes & Noble or at the New School for Social Research library.

On Thursday, as his wall clock was striking 8:00 p.m., Chaim Cohen arrived. Dressed in a gray, light-weight, three-piece business suit with matching silk tie and a neatly arranged four-pointed white handkerchief in his breast pocket, he was the very essence of the well-dressed New York jim-dandy.

For his first session, he had seated himself on the rickety chair Cordis used for the sole purpose of reaching the upper shelving of his bookcases. On his second visit, he had chosen the armchair in front of Cordis' desk, as most of his patients did. This time he sat on the analytic couch, his back as straight as any army sergeant's.

After scrutinizing his surroundings in silence for a good minute, he finally spoke. "I know my ways are not those of most. In spirit I am with the High Lama in Hilton's novel when he says to Conway: 'Forgive my eloquence—I belong to an age and a nation that never considered it bad form to be articulate.' "

How appropriate! Cordis thought. How utterly appropriate for him to quote from *Lost Horizon*!

"I accept the King's English, vulgate English and pidgin English here," a smiling Cordis said.

Chaim Cohen again searched the room with his eyes, obviously ill at ease.

Then he said, "Did you know, Cordis, that Ben-Gurion was at the train depot in Beyrouth when Richard Wagner's coffin arrived home for burial? What do you think of that?"

"No, I didn't know that," Cordis answered.

As best as he could figure, he thought the Israeli statesman would have been born after Wagner's death. Certainly he couldn't have been more than a little boy at the time. Cohen, you old blubber-mouth, Cordis said to himself, you don't quite fit the infallible Mr. Belvedere's shoes. Either that or you're putting me through some kind of test.

"Do you think Jews should patronize the works of such a notorious anti-Semite?"

"Gustav Mahler conducted his music and was his greatest interpreter," Cordis replied. "When I was in college, the Hungarian conductor-composer Ernst von Dohnanyi, a Nazi sympathizer, came to our campus to conduct. It was nineteen fifty, only five years after the War, but a lot of the Jewish students went to his concert, including a concentration-camp survivor."

"Really?" Chaim Cohen looked surprised.

"In art, as in science for that matter, I would think you look at the achievement, not the achiever's politics or morals. Achievements, it would seem, transcend personality. Who thinks about da Vinci's personality profile when viewing the Mona Lisa? Who would turn down an opportunity for a good buy on a van Gogh just because he was thought to have been crazy?"

"Well said, my good doctor," Chaim Cohen commented animatedly, perhaps surprised to discover that his psychiatrist was able to say something that measured up to his standards. "Indeed well said." He even relaxed his rigid posture and flashed a smile.

For Cordis this was the moment to get down to business. Retrieving his tape recorder from the bottom drawer of his desk, he said, "It's been a long time since you presented me with that fascinating dream of yours."

"Ah, yes, my convoluted dream," Chaim Cohen said, stroking his chin and showing another quick smile. He then stood up and transferred to the patient's armchair.

"I'll play it back to you, since it's been—"

"There is no need for that—I remember every last word of it."

"I was listening to it again yesterday," Cordis said, "and let me share a few of my thoughts on it with you."

"Please do."

Cordis leaned back in his chair for a few moments and then sat up straight. "You stated previously when I asked you for your age," he began, "that you are in your late fifties. Now I think I can narrow it down further: you're fifty-nine approaching sixty."

Chaim Cohen's nostril's quivered and the furrows in his forehead deepened. "A good beginning," he said. "Indeed, a good beginning."

The dream and its post-dream material had been presented to Cordis back on February 20th in an unwavering, dramatic tone. Whether it represented an actual dream or something Chaim Cohen had concocted was immaterial, for in its overall effect it represented a production of the unconscious, the realm Cordis was to explore with him.

Cordis had dealt effectively with part of the final segment of his recital. He reasoned that the thought of turning another page in the calendar, of moving up a decade, was depressing for him, which he verbalized in disguise as "the moment when autumn ends and winter comes."

164

Chaim Cohen had presented the dream in three segments, and to find the undercurrent running through all three would establish its unity and in the process reveal its meaning. The key was in the symbolism, essentially Jungian.

Time was the quintessential issue for Chaim Cohen. As he began with a description of a journey, so did his recitation end. Regardless of whether he had a day or a lifetime in mind, at high noon when the sun is at its zenith, that is to say, at the age of thirty-five, half way through the allotted biblical span of three score and ten years, the high point is reached in the path of a parabola, the curve of life, and after that the second law of thermodynamics, with its pronouncement of the inevitability of decay, takes hold. Or as people often say: After that, it's all downhill.

The "mighty warrior" segment required that the dream interpreter be familiar with the Gilgamesh epic account; otherwise, it would have been unintelligible, and the result would be to fall back upon a Freudian approach, not at all applicable in this instance. Thus the "sword of strength" would have been rendered as a phallic symbol, and with the fight he mentioned involving the bull of heaven, castration anxiety would be read into the dream. But what the dreamer was describing from the Akkadian epic was actually straightforward. Gilgamesh, ruler of ancient Uruk, with his faithful companion Enkidu, "had defeated the bull of heaven sent by Ishtar." With the subsequent death of Enkidu, Gilgamesh sets out to find the secret of eternal youth. (Cordis compared this to Chaim Cohen's reference to *Lost Horizon*, as he was going about unraveling the dream to his patient.) For a moment he holds it in his hand—a fruit—but loses it to a serpent of the deep, which promptly sheds its outer skin and is rejuvenated. (The air and water of Shangri-La accomplish much the same thing, he pointed out to his patient.)

That Cordis had touched the very core of the dream was corroborated by Chaim Cohen.

"I was thirty-five," he said somberly, "when I first consulted a psychiatrist, a Freudian analyst, because of a severe problem. My life, with all its hopes and promises, seemed to be dying at that point. Now, with a new decade on the horizon, I fear the vengeance that is to come from above." He raised his eyes heavenwards for a moment.

Thus the opening segment of the dream with its description of the power of Yahweh. Underneath his veneer of sophistication, Chaim Cohen was a traditional—and apparently frightened—Jew.

"And now you again seek out someone to guide you through that darkness you so fear."

"Do you remember anything about Dante's *Commedia*?" Chaim

165

Cohen asked plaintively.

"About Beatrice?" Cordis volunteered. He did remember *something*. "Dante himself."

Cordis thought for a few moments and then grasped the similitude in his patient's mind.

"Dante began his journey through the world that lies beyond the grave at the age of thirty-five," the doctor said softly.

Chaim Cohen smiled and said, "The County Medical Society may have underestimated your talent."

Cordis returned the smile and asked, "Have you ever been treated by a woman psychiatrist?"

In the *Divine Comedy* it is Virgil who guides Dante through the infernal regions to salvation. Beatrice then takes over and leads him up the levels of heaven to a glimpse of the Divine.

"No," he responded. "For seven years I saw a succession of psychoanalysts, but never made any definitive progress. Perhaps it was all my fault. Resistance. I feared the unseen mind—what you would call the subconscious or unconscious. I equated it with the hell I was going through, and failed abysmally with all my analysts."

"There's something there I don't quite follow," Cordis said.

"The nineteen fifties belonged to the Freudian analysts," Chaim Cohen began explaining, "intrepid explorers of the underbelly of the human mind. But for me the unconscious was literally the House of Hades of the mind, equivalent to what I have referred to as the unseen mind. If you are deficient in your knowledge of the classical languages, Hades is from the Greek *Aides*, the Unseen."

"I am deficient in that area," Cordis said, "Thank you for the etymological rundown."

After a brief period of silence, Chaim Cohen asked, "Do you agree with Browning in 'Andrea del Sarto' that 'a man's reach should exceed his grasp, [o]r what's a heaven for?'"

"Youth, which possesses energy and strength for the great tasks of life, must run the risk of reaching beyond what can be safely grasped," Cordis answered, "if anything new is to come into the world."

"Quite so, Cordis," Chaim Cohen said, nodding in approval. "Quite so."

"But you believe that life has passed you by," Cordis commented. "You made mention of the herb of youth now lost forever."

"That is so."

"Your question to the stargazers of Babylon was to find out if you still have time. Time for what?"

"To unleash my own creativity . . . before time has sapped me of it all."

To achieve creatively, whatever it was he had in mind, Cordis was thinking, he would have to liberate his anima, the female component of the male psyche. It was Beatrice, Dante's anima, who had led the poet to his most divine heights.

"And what about your wife Marsha, who in the dream welcomed you, with apparent felicity, to the morning?"

Chaim Cohen sighed deeply. "That is the problem," he said wearily. "She has been the problem for thirty-five years."

Her happy wake-up call was in reality nothing more than a wish projection. He had resorted to reaction formation, saying the opposite of what he felt, when he had presented the dream three months earlier.

Cordis avoided a direct inquiry into the state of their marriage, for he felt Chaim Cohen had already covered an unusual amount of therapeutic ground for one session.

I'm curious," he said. "How do you get from Jericho to Babylon before the sun goes down . . . before the era of modern transportation?"

Cordis wasn't making small talk. He was still searching for hidden clues. In a dream strategically placed towns are usually anima symbols.

"I have two daughters," Chaim Cohen replied. "In the morning we were visiting one in Jericho, and in the afternoon we went to see the other in Babylon. Long Island."

"Ah!" the doctor exclaimed and grinned.

"I have two grown daughters I love dearly," Chaim Cohen said gloomily. "Too bad they cannot reciprocate that affection."

Chaim Cohen was visibly tired, and now when he stated that he wished to terminate the session—at 8:40—Cordis had no reason to comment.

"I do owe you this," the Long Islander said, reaching into his jacket pocket for an envelope, which he placed on Cordis' desk. "Your fee for the previous two sessions."

Cordis gave the envelope a quick glance and said, "Thank you." He viewed his patient's payment as a statement of his willingness to go on with the therapy. "If you wish," he added, "I can schedule you for another session."

"Please do. Two weeks from now at the same hour?"

"So it is entered," Cordis said, writing him into his appointment book.

"So it shall be done," Chaim Cohen said somewhat dramatically as he stood up.

167

It sounded to Cordis like something Yul Brynner, as Pharaoh in *The Ten Commandments*, might say. Was his patient just a ham, or would he now, belatedly, work through to his own salvation?

CHAPTER THIRTY-FIVE

Joey Dee showed up at the clinic Monday afternoon, the 4th of June. He had missed a scheduled appointment for Monday, May 21st, but he was only two weeks late—and he had come in on the right day of the week, a Monday, at what would have been the right hour.

Joey appeared to be a little heavier than when last seen by Cordis. His shirtsleeves were a couple of inches too short and minus their buttons, his socks didn't match and his jeans had a silver-dollar-sized hole in front of his right knee. He could have used a shave, a vigorous brushing of his teeth finished off with a strong mouthwash and a good soaking in the bathtub.

Despite his untidiness and unkempt appearance, he was in good spirits; and from the professional point of view he was still compensated. If the month's supply of medication he had received from the clinic in April represented all the medication he had on hand and if he had taken it as prescribed, he would have run out of pills two weeks earlier. Joey had some insight into his condition and his judgement remained fairly intact, so he always managed to show up at the clinic before he would fall victim to the process of decompensation. His deteriorating physical appearance was evidence the insidious process was starting up, and he knew it was time to replenish his medicine shelf.

Joey handed Cordis his usual offering, the brown bag containing six oranges and three BIC pens.

"Don't go broke on my account," the doctor admonished in a friendly tone.

Joey scoffed at that. "Dey don't cost much," he said, his face reddening.

The ballpoints are still blue," Cordis commented. "I thought you were going to bring me black ones."

"Next time I'll bring ya black pens, Dr. Cordis," Joey responded ruefully.

Holding up one of his own BIC's Cordis said, "See, the clinic requires that I write in black, not blue."

Joey stared at the doctor with his mouth partially open, as though not comprehending why the clinic was so fussy about the color of the pens. He remained silent for a while, and when he did speak again it was to return to his numerology theme.

"Four is a divine number," he monotoned.

Cordis sighed deeply, but went on to listen attentively as Joey rehashed his way through the four humours of the body and the four elements, still pronounced in his inimitable manner. His words were fairly coherent when he spoke of the four winds, and he even quoted passably from several poets who had the winds in their poems. When he referred to addition, subtraction, multiplication and division as the "four mathematical operations," Cordis interrupted him.

"That's arithmetic, not mathematics," the doctor said with measured false sarcasm.

Joey merely ignored his comment and continued on his numerological junket through his world of fours. Much to Cordis' surprise, he knew of Franklin Roosevelt's "Four Freedoms": freedom of speech, freedom of worship, freedom from want and freedom from fear. He was even able to name the Four Horsemen of the Apocalypse, the biblical allegorical figures, but puzzled over the identity of the riders, and wondered if his psychiatrist could help sort them out for him.

The idea that Joey was interested in something that had absorbed his own interest at one time was enough to gain Cordis' full cooperation.

"The rider on the white horse usually represents Christ," Cordis said. "The rider on the red horse is war, on the black horse, famine, and death rides the pale horse."

"I saw da movie *Da Four Horsemen o' da Apocalyp*," Joey uttered.

The fact that he pronounced Apocalypse as Apocalyp was a minor matter, almost predictable in his case.

"Which one?" Cordis asked. "There was the original based on Blasco Ibanez's novel and a modern version."

"Da one wit' Glenn Ford, Charles Boyer, Lee J. Cobb an' Paul Lucas," Joey answered without the slightest hesitation.

Cordis had already learned from his own sessions with Joey and from reading through his old clinic records that he was a movie buff who re-

169

membered everything he had ever seen on film. The manner in which he was able to retrieve information from his movie data bank was reminiscent of the idiot-savant.

"You named all four major players correctly," Cordis said encouragingly, although he really didn't know who had starred in the movie. He felt the movie must have had a female leading role, which would have broken up Joey's cherished pattern of fours, but Cordis was not about to raise the point. Nevertheless, he was intrigued to know how Joey would have rationalized his way around that little obstacle.

"Why isn't black da color o' deat'?" Joey asked. "Deat' is blackness an' blackness is deat'. Why doesn't deat' ride on da black horse?"

Cordis had to mull over Joey's latest question for a while. Finally he responded, "No, not death but famine rides the black horse."

"Black is da opposite o' white," Joey came back with, "an' whiteness, which is light, is da symbol o' life. Deat' must be black."

Christ, of course, is the symbol of life and after death of resurrection, Cordis said to himself. "At one level, I tend to agree with you, Joey," he said, impressed by the consistent and forceful nature of his argument. "But at a deeper level, no. The rider on the pale horse is death."

They had inadvertently stumbled upon the psychological law of the opposite, in which opposites may stand for or replace each other in unconscious productions. Thus, paleness and silence come to signify death. Theodor Reik was the great interpreter of this psychological principle. In *Lear*, Cordelia "loves and is silent." The aged king must choose from among his three daughters, and in the final scene Lear carries the chosen dead Cordelia across the stage. But by the principle of psychological reversal the audience knows it is the shape of death that is actually carrying the body of Lear. Cordelia's silence announces her as the symbol of death.

In *The Merchant of Venice*, Shakespeare has Bassanio choose a lead casket over one of either gold or silver, and has him say, "Thy paleness moves me more than eloquence."

"When the creative artist uses paleness or silence within a dramatic framework, Joey, it usually signifies death," Cordis said aloud.

Joey accepted his doctor's explanation of paleness as the color of death, but he was not about to run out of his fours. Now he gave him the ages of the Ancient World. Much to Cordis' surprise, Joey ticked off the Greek ages with ease: the Golden Age, ruled by Cronus; the Silver Age, ruled by Zeus; the Bronze Age and the Iron Age. His only failing was with the names of the rulers of the latter two ages.

Cordis tried to throw a damper into his Greek world of fours by

170

saying, "I think Ovid wrote of four ages, but Hesiod may have added a fifth, if I'm correct, a Heroic Age just before the Iron Age."

"Four Greek ages," insisted Joey, sounding like Rocky Graziano.

"I believe it was during the Heroic Age that the Trojan War was fought," Cordis added, seeming to ignore Joey's last statement. "Yes, it appears to me that there indeed were five." He paused, feeling as he would had he just made a good move in a chess game.

Joey was not about to be derailed by his doctor's reference to five and continued with his fours. To Cordis' astonishment he unfolded the Hindu cosmogony—built on the concept of the four yugas—with ease and a sense of certainty: the Krita Yuga, a golden age lasting 1,728,000 years, followed by an unrighteous age, the Treta Yuga, of 1,296,000 years, a very dark age of 864,000 years, the Dvapara Yuga, and now the present age, darker than the previous one, the Kali Yuga, which began in 3102 B.C. and is to endure for 432,000 years.

"Da whole cycle is known as a Maha Yuga," Joey said, concluding his recitation.

Cordis had been taking notes all along, and now he questioned him as to how the Hindu sages knew that the Kali Yuga had begun exactly in the year 3102 B.C.. He reminded Joey that the scientist's radioactive C-14 dating technique, the best method for marking time, still had a ten percent error. But Joey was sure that the stated years of the four yugas of the Hindu world cycle were accurate figures.

The psychiatrist brought up the 17th century Bishop Ussher, who decreed that the world had been created in the year 4004 B.C., and even furnished the exact hour, day of the week and month of creation. Cordis also mentioned that 4004 contained his favorite number.

By no means had Cordis succeeded in shaking up Joey, who calmly proceeded to tell him that 3102 B.C. was a holy year.

"If ya add da first an' second numbers," he said, "ya get four, and if ya add da second an' fourt' numbers ya get t'ree. Ya see, Dr. Cordis, any way ya add dem up, ya get four an t'ree, da magic numbers."

Cordis held back from saying that if you add up all the numbers in the date you get 6, for he knew that Joey would turn 6 into another "magic number"—6 is 2 times 3, or a magic number invoked twice.

The psychiatrist had a line of thought of his own. "I believe most anthropologists," he started to say, "estimate that our own species has been around for maybe fifty thousand years. Let's say forty thousand, since you prefer fours to fives. I doubt if there were any truly cerebral hominids around during the Krita Yuga, that splendid golden age you mentioned lasting nearly two million years."

171

"It coulda been a golden age fer da animals," Joey retorted cleverly.

"Touché!" Cordis exclaimed, acknowledging that he had been out-maneuvered. "A double touché!"

Joey flashed a smile of satisfaction and said, "Ya see, da numbers are correct."

Cordis had been adding up on paper all the years Joey mentioned in his Hindu chronology, which came to 4,320,000.

"Your Maha Yuga is only some four million years old, Joey, a number which no doubt pleases you, but geologists estimate the age of the planet at about four billion years, maybe even five billion. But for you we'll allow that the world we know is four billion years old. And life has been going on in one form or another for about half that span."

Cordis was giving him his number, but was trying to demolish it at the same time.

"Four billion—dat's a good number, Dr. Cordis," Joey said enthusiastically.

"How do you reconcile the four million years of the Maha Yuga with the scientist's figure of four billion?"

Joey had a ready answer. "It means ten cycles," he responded easily.

Of course! For the Western mind time is linear; for the Eastern, circular! The Hindu world cycle proceeds over and over again, an active cycle followed by a quiescent cycle of equal duration. And everything happens exactly as it did before, in defiance of the Heisenberg principle, but in support of the notion that we have all been here before.

Cordis found himself reciting from T. S. Eliot: " 'Home is where one starts from . . . In my end is my beginning.' "

"Dat's true, Dr. Cordis," Joey said. "Da endin' o' one Maha Yuga leads into da beginnin' o' anuder."

Cordis hoped that Joey wasn't drifting away from his own religious mooring and into muddied waters. Zen Buddhism and the Hare Krishna movement were popular with the young in the early '70's. But Cordis wondered if Western man can go beyond acquiring the trappings of Eastern philosophy and religion. Eliot, who studied Sanskrit, had been fascinated by Buddhism and Hinduism, whose concepts infuse several of his works, but he remained a devout Christian throughout his life. He never pretended to penetrate the cosmic curtain that separates the two worlds.

His reverie was abruptly ended by Joey, the undaunted one, who had suddenly switched from fours to sevens.

"I'm da sevent' son o' a sevent' son," he intoned.

"O for Krishna's sake!" Cordis exclaimed in Jack Benny style.

172

Earlier, Dr. Paxton had passed Cordis in the corridor, within earshot of the waiting room, and had said to him, "Did you know that Dr. Kissel has seven children, all sons?"

Is he joking, or is he indeed about to embark on a run of sevens? Cordis asked himself. He wanted to keep the session going, but the clinic was getting ready to close.

"We'll continue this dialogue in a month," he said to Joey, writing him into his appointment book. "Your next session with me is scheduled for July third, one day before the Fourth of July, Independence Day, an easy day to remember, and for eleven o'clock, which will be in the morning. Don't drop in unannounced in the afternoon anymore, because beginning with the new fiscal year, July first, I'll be at the clinic only in the morning, Monday through Friday, and never on Saturday or Sunday. Got it?"

"Sure, Dr. Cordis," a smiling Joey said.

"I hope so."

Cordis handed him a slip with his appointment written out for him — which would be reinforced by the clerk at the main desk on his way out — and prescriptions for a month's supply of Thorazine and Stelazine. This time Joey took the scripts without fussing.

"See ya next mont' in da mornin', Dr. Cordis," he said, grinning as he left the psychiatrist's office.

I will have to research sevens in the encyclopedia before he returns, Cordis said to himself.

CHAPTER THIRTY-SIX

Cordis received a phone call from Madam Bee at the clinic on Wednesday, the 6th, as he was getting ready to go out to lunch. She began by thanking him for introducing her to Dr. Shafer-Epstein, whom she described as warm, caring, selfless and a wonderful gynecologist. As a result of the examination, she was now taking Premarin, and already felt

173

better. After only a few days on her new medication, Cordis thought it premature to attribute any pharmacological benefit to it, but there was no discounting the positive placebo effect derived from swallowing a pill that inspired trust and confidence.

Her other news came as something of a surprise to Cordis: she was completing arrangements to return to Kazakhstan and to the city of her birth, Alma-Ata. The visit she had made to her nephew in Wisconsin at the end of the winter had been for the purpose of organizing the trip.

"I miss the old ways," she said plaintively. "In the end one must go back to where one started."

"I hope you will have many years ahead of you," Cordis responded dolefully.

"I plan to live a long time."

"And don't forget to work on your memoirs," Cordis encouraged. "You've got a book there."

"Thanks to you it can become a reality," Madam Bee said, clearly conveying her gratitude. "I don't know how to thank you for all the help you have been to me." She sounded to him to be on the verge of crying.

"It has been my pleasure to know you and to have been able to be of service to you," Cordis said, his voice cracking. "Please drop me a picture postcard now and then, if the commissars will allow it."

"I will," she said softly. "I will . . ." Her voice trailed off and then all he could hear was a dial tone.

He skipped lunch altogether and instead spent an hour wandering through Central Park Zoo. When he returned, there was a message for him that Marsha Cohen had phoned while he was out and would call again later.

Her call came at about 4:30.

"Dr. Cordis?"

"Speaking."

"Chaim and I didn't always get along," she said, beginning in medias res. "In fact, ours had been a stormy marriage." Her voice was steady and strong, with a trace of a Yiddish accent.

Her use of the past tense alarmed Cordis. "Yes?" he said anxiously.

"My husband died over the weekend."

"O my gosh!" Cordis whispered into the phone.

"He had a heart attack. It was quick. He did not suffer."

"I am so sorry!" Cordis said, anguishing. "So sorry!"

"Chaim was an unhappy man all his life," she continued. "He suffered from depressions throughout our married life together, but he could never bring himself to listen to what his psychiatrists had to tell him—he

174

was a know-it-all. I must tell you this: you were the only doctor he admired, and he was looking forward to seeing you regularly. When he came home from his last visit to you, he was a different man. He had hope . . . for the first time since we were married. During his last week, he was a changed man—joking, laughing, playing with our grandchildren. I thought you should know that you helped free him from himself."

"Then I think he had a happy death," Cordis said, trying to sound cheerful. "What more can anyone ask for?"

"Yes. He was always afraid of dying. But in the end he died well."

"Thank you for allowing me to share in your grief and in Chaim's triumph."

"God's blessing be with you," she said concluding the conversation.

Cordis remained at his desk while one by one the other physicians left for the day. Soon he was all alone on Doctors Row; and in the quiet of the early evening, the droning of the cleaning lady's vacuum cleaner and the noise of the traffic outside somehow muffled, he let his mind dwell on that last session with Chaim Cohen.

So, he went away . . . rejuvenated, which was what he always yearned for, Cordis said to himself. In the end, he had one happy week on earth. He reminds me of Hemingway's jaded hero in 'The Short Happy Life of Francis Macomber,' the weakling who found his manhood on safari in Africa . . . and then died. If Hemingway could be here now, we'd drink a toast to you, Bwana Cohen.

He picked up his briefcase and headed dreamily toward the door. Before closing it behind him, he turned around to face his silent and empty office, and forcing a smile said, "*L'hayim*, Chaim Cohen."

Cordis had a sandwich and a cup of tea for supper in the coffee shop of his office building. Afterwards, he sat quietly at his desk on the top floor, reviewing the day's traumatic events.

D-day, he mused. Disaster day. Death and defection day.

Actually, it was the day to mark D-Day—the 29th anniversary of the Allied landing on the beaches of Normandy on June 6, 1944.

Chaim Cohen had a good death, he continued reflecting. No cause to anguish over his crossing the river Styx. But Madam Bee, that's another story. Why am I so upset? She chose. That's what I do: I help people find their choices and then encourage them to act. She did just that. What defection? She didn't defect to the enemy. Kazakhstan, in Central Asia, is light years away from the Bolsheviks in the Kremlin, and she was apolitical, anyway. Who wouldn't want to return to a birthplace bearing a lyrical

175

name like Alma-Ata? It may be her Shangri-La on the Ili.

He went to his mini-refrigerator for a bottle of black cherry soda. Sipping it slowly while leaning back in his swivel chair with his outstretched legs crossed on his desk, he resumed his musing.

Maybe I need to turn the spotlight around. How does her departure impact on me? Well, I'll miss her—I've grown fond of her. It's more than that, though. She has become for me the embodiement of European womanhood, what I came back to New York to find. I came close with Josie, but close has only produced a scrapbook full of memories. Surrounded as I am by 7-million people—12-million in the daytime—and even with my social contacts at the United Nations, I don't believe I will ever find the woman I need here. Deep down, where it matters, I'm an old-fashioned European. Too bad I can't fly off to a place like Alma-Ata myself! Or to Brigadoon, or to High Barbaree . . .

The clock struck seven, rousing him from his reverie. He had a new patient, a 30-year-old woman, who came in accompanied by her 6-year-old boy. She appeared older than her stated age and looked gaunt and ill at ease. Her son chose the davenport to Cordis' right, sitting quietly and saying nothing. He had a cough that emanated from his bronchi.

"Dr. *Albert* Fogelman told me you might be able to help me," she said, pronouncing the doctor's first name in French. Her English bore a distinct French accent.

Cordis had known Dr. Fogelman, then a medical student, during his export-import business days when he had an office in Romandie, the French-speaking region of Switzerland. His old friend was now a neurologist, and had called him the previous week to refer a patient to him—her.

For fifteen minutes she related her story, one of constant struggle to care for her three young children on a meager income following the death of her husband two years earlier. Pulling the information obtained together, including Dr. Fogelman's medical workup, Cordis came to the conclusion the poor woman was suffering from exhaustion, or stress as we now like to call it, and not from a depression, the neurologist's impression.

All the while, her little boy punctuated her conversation with a noisy, productive bronchitic cough, spitting yellowish phlegm into an already stained handkerchief.

"And what about little Francois there?" Cordis asked, pointing to her son.

His patient had deliberately avoided going into his medical history, but now Cordis coaxed it out of her. Francois had been a sickly child all his young life, suffering from frequent colds and episodes of sinusitis and bronchitis, which had progressed to bronchiectasis. It was his health problems more than anything else that was draining his mother's energy and bringing her to the brink of collapse.

"I can't afford the regular gamma globulin injections and the various antibiotics he needs," she said. "I . . . I don't think I can even afford to come to see you; but *Albert*—Dr. Folgelman—said you would be able to help me."

"Don't worry about the bill," Cordis said to her reassuringly. "What we need to do here is to relieve the pressure on you—the burden is too great—the center cannot hold—which we can do by doing something for Francois."

"*Merci, Docteur,*" she whispered, with tears in her eyes.

Cordis flipped through his Rollodex and plucked out a card. "This pediatrician," he said to her while dialing a number, "owes me a favor." A few seconds later, he intoned into the mouthpiece, "Is Jaime there? Please tell him Cordis is on the line." He had to wait half a minute, and then he said loudly, "*¡Ey, hombre! ¿Qué tal?*" Cordis explained his patient's problem—her son's hypogammaglobulinemia—and asked him to see the boy, adding, "*Ella no tiene ningún dinero—su marido está muerto.*"

"Send them right over," came the response.

After hanging up, Cordis wrote his colleague's name and address on the back of his business card and gave her directions to his office three blocks away.

She thanked him profusely, crying all the while.

"It has been my pleasure to have been of some service to you, madame," was all Cordis would say.

Francois stopped momentarily on the way out to wave good-by, coughing but at the same time showing him a smile.

That smile is my payment, Cordis said to himself.

At 8 o'clock Cordis saw a young couple who were in for marital therapy. This was their first session, and he used it to get to know them and for them to become familiar with his style of doing therapy.

They were a professional couple, he an engineer and she a registered nurse. Each tried to outdo the other in claiming to be motivated to save the marriage, this in spite of their three years together of constant bickering and giving one another the silent treatment for days on end when one or the other or both was in an angry mood and didn't know how to make peace.

Cordis was a realist: he had progressed beyond the rescue phantasy stage in his career and, especially in dealing with couples, discouraged his patients from casting him in the savior role.

"The marriage may be salvageable, and then again it may not be," he said soberly near the end of the hour. "If not, you will at least learn why and go your separate ways amicably."

Cordis divided marriages into two kinds: the traditional, or biblical, marriage, the authoritarian type; and the egalitarian marriage, or as he liked to call it, the American type. He thought their marriage, which he placed in the latter category, could be salvaged, and he encouraged them to work at applying the insights they would be gathering from the therapy.

He settled on weekly sessions for the first month, and if there was progress, then he would see them every two weeks afterwards.

"What happens if you don't see progress after four weeks?" the husband asked. "Do we continue to come every week?"

"If it doesn't look promising after four weeks, then forget it," Cordis responded. "Then we work on developing parting skills."

It was a time before modern marital therapy, which would give us a new terminology and sophisticated theories. Most of the time, Cordis was successful in helping his patients resolve their marital discord, but then again some couples would wind up parting, if not amicably, at least with peace of mind.

CHAPTER THIRTY-SEVEN

Each Friday or Saturday, from May 25th through June 16th, Cordis received a beautiful picture postcard from Renata Delacross in Morocco. Simone Delacroix also sent a couple.

They were back in New York on Thursday, the 21st of June, and Renata phoned him immediately. She sounded ebullient.

"I have no need for an emergency Saturday session this time," she said cheerfully.

"That's certainly good news."

"Have you been keeping my eight o'clock Tuesday hour open?"

"It's still yours," Cordis replied, "except this Tuesday only when it's been rented out. After that you can have it back. You're on for this Tuesday at six."

"Thank you, dear Dr. Cordis."

Renata looked healthy, radiant and full of self-confidence when she showed up for her first appointment of the summer on June 26th. She devoted the entire session to a detailed account of events of the past month since seeing her doctor last on May 15th.

Near the end of the hour, she said apologetically, "I haven't done any work of therapy this session. I've wasted the hour with idle chit-chat."

"Not at all," the psychiatrist said. "It was fitting, even necessary."

"But at least I *chose* to go on the trip," she said, stressing the key word in the middle of the sentence. "I weighed the factors and made my own decision."

"That's right," he affirmed for her. "You did just that. And in doing so, you have demonstrated mastery of the Eriksonian third stage of the life cycle: initiative versus guilt."

"What have I done?" Renata asked, not clear as to what he was saying.

"You have achieved purpose," Cordis answered. "First comes hope, then will, and third in the life cycle, purpose."

"I don't think I quite follow all of that . . . just yet."

"Perhaps not now," the doctor said, "but in due time you will."

Cordis had cited the successful outcomes of the first three developmental stages in Erikson's Eight Ages of Man. One progresses in life along an epigenetic pathway, each new epochal stage dependent on what has gone before. Any weakness in an earlier stage, and the next stage will of consequence be weakened or undermined. What Cordis was saying to Renata was that he thought she had handled the third stage of her psychosocial development satisfactorily, which meant that the first two stages had been traversed adequately.

The key issues of the first three stages or ages, oral-sensory, muscular-anal and locomotor-genital—equivalent to Freud's oral, anal and phallic—are basic trust versus mistrust, autonomy versus shame and doubt, and initiative versus guilt. By giving her a clean bill of health for the initial stages of development, he was saying that he thought her difficulties that had brought her to therapy were not pre-oedipal, but rather had their origins in conflicts arising in a subsequent stage of life, which for him meant they would be more accessible to therapeutic exploration and resolution.

Cordis had a new patient, Leah Chomsky, scheduled for seven that evening, referred by Zelda Amado. Zelda was back in Israel and had written him several weeks earlier that her cancer so far was causing her no undue pain and that she was cherishing each and every day that she drew breath. "I thank God," she wrote, "that He chose me to be among those who represent Him by giving me this life in human form."

Leah Chomsky sat in his office together with her mother, Naomi Zeda. They were strikingly beautiful, both dark-haired with olive complexions, and to Cordis they looked like sisters. He had difficulty coming to terms with the ages Leah furnished him: she told him she was twenty-seven, her mother, forty-one, and her three children, thirteen, twelve and ten.

"You must have had your first child at fourteen," Cordis said, sounding a bit incredulous.

The two women smiled at each other and then, despite efforts at suppression, they giggled. Leah explained, "It's not at all unusual for Georgian Jews to marry young. I was married at thirteen."

"Which Georgia are we talking about?" Cordis asked.

"Soviet Georgia," she answered. "We are from Tiflis, Soviet Georgia."

Cordis had heard of the city under both its Russianized name of Tiflis and its more familiar name of Tbilisi. Beyond that he knew almost nothing of it.

"I married at thirteen also," her mother said, still tittering.

"We emigrated to this country ten years ago," Leah said.

"You both have an intriguing accent in English," Cordis commented.

Mother and daughter exchanged a few sentences in Hebrew, and Naomi said, "We spoke Hebrew all our lives until coming to America."

"Well, you both speak English fluently," Cordis said.

"Thank you," each said in turn, with Leah adding, "We studied English in school."

Leah, when calling Cordis for an appointment, had stated her problem to be hair pulling, but now he set aside his plan to proceed with the usual psychiatric workup in order to listen to something of their unusual background.

Much to his surprise, he found out that early marriages were common in the Jewish communities of *Gruzia*, the Hebrew name for Georgia that they used, in order to discourage intermarriage with the dominant Christian population. He thought that they came to the United States to escape anti-Semitism or to seek a better life as so many of the world's poor have always done.

"No," said Naomi emphatically. "We lived very well in Tiflis. In fact, we lived better there than we do in Brooklyn. No violence. No street gangs. No garbage piled up everywhere. We had lots of money, a television and we lived in a nice house. Now we live in a crowded apartment in

180

an old building that deserves to be condemned."

"We were very well off," Leah contributed. "The Jewish community of Tiflis is the wealthiest of all our communities in the Soviet Union."

"The Tiflis subway is finer than New York's," Naomi added.

"What about anti-Semitism then?" Cordis asked.

"There was no anti-Semitism," Leah responded.

"No?" Cordis said, raising his eyebrows.

"No," Leah said forcefully. "You see, Christians in the old country don't like two—" She broke off to confer in Hebrew with her mother to find the appropriate word she was grasping for. "—groups. They despise tax collectors and moneylenders. Matthew, in the Christians' New Testament, was hated because he was a tax collector, but then he became a follower of the man they called the Messiah. Jews, however, don't collect the taxes in *Gruzia*, nor are they the moneylenders—Armenians are in that business."

"Ah," Cordis said.

The two women exchanged smiles. Naomi continued the dialogue.

"We have always lived on good terms with the Christians," she said. "They credit us for the spread of Christianity in *Gruzia*."

"Is that right!" Cordis exclaimed.

"Yes," said Leah. "You see, Doctor, Jews have been living in *Gruzia* since the time the Temple of Solomon was destroyed by the Babylonians twenty-six hundred years ago."

"We are a very old community," Naomi said, leaving Cordis to wonder whether she was identifying with the Jewish community or with *Gruzia*, as he himself was now referring to Soviet Georgia.

"And no run-ins with anti-Semitism in all that time?" Cordis asked, surprised and wondering if they had to say such nice things about Soviet Georgia to protect relatives still back there.

The story which Leah, with an occasional assist from Naomi, related fascinated Cordis. According to legend, two Georgian Jews, Eliyoz of Mtskheta and Longinuz of Karasani, were witness to the crucifixion of Jesus, and it was they who came into possession of Jesus' robe, which they brought back to *Gruzia*. They told Eliyoz's sister that Jesus had been crucified, and the news so overwhelmed her that she soon died of grief. When they buried her there in Mtskheta, the robe was in her hands.

A second legend has it that a saintly woman, Nino, from Cappadocia came to *Gruzia* around 300 A.D. to spread Christianity, starting in Urbnissi. She spoke Hebrew and was a friend to the Jews of Urbnissi all her life, managing to convert a few.

It was only at 7:30 that Cordis got around to Leah's problem of hair

181

pulling. Throughout the session, he kept wondering about this, for she seemed to have a full crop of hair; and thus he underestimated the severity of her "chief complaint," the main issue that brings any patient to see a doctor. Only when she removed a wig she was wearing did Cordis realize what he was up against: she was nearly bald.

"Have you treated anyone with my problem before?" Leah asked worriedly, as she promptly repositioned her wig.

"No, you're my first case of trichitillomania," the doctor replied, resorting to the physician's jargon in the hope that his use of the technical term would instill some confidence in his patient.

"Can you cure me?" she asked beseechingly.

"I can try."

Cordis got a clue from the family history part of the psychiatric inquiry. Like her mother, hers had been an early, arranged marriage back in *Gruzia* to forestall any chance of her becoming involved with a Christian boy. In 1960, the family immigrated to the United States. The women of the family acculturated more readily than the men. Leah's husband, Abishai, in particular, clung to the old ways, and now he wanted to marry off Hannah, their 13-year-old daughter, to a hand-picked 18-year-old. Cordis settled on this issue as the precipitating factor in driving his patient to pluck out her hair — she was doing, literally, what a lot of people intimate when they say, "It's enough to make me pull my hair out."

"I don't think the laws of the State of New York will allow it," Cordis said to the two.

"In our culture, state laws count for little," Leah said, shaking her head. "We lived under a communist regime, and breaking laws was an everyday occurrence."

"The *Gruzinim*," Naomi added, "are known as blackmarketers, bribers, counterfeiters — all that is commonplace back home."

"The religious law comes first," Leah stressed.

"But no Brooklyn rabbi, no matter how ultra-orthodox, would violate the civil law," Cordis countered.

"My husband will take the couple to Tiflis to have the wedding performed," Leah said, breaking into tears. Naomi tried to comfort her, exchanging words in Hebrew. "And I will never see my daughter again," she continued, dabbing at her wet eyes with her mother's handkerchief. "He will even take Sarah, our twelve-year-old, with him back to *Gruzia*.

Cordis now saw the depth of the problem. His suggestion was to have Abishai join Leah in marital therapy.

"He will never come," Leah scoffed, still crying. "He would say, what for, he's not sick in his head."

Leah gave a history of losing weight, eating little of late, and sleeping poorly. Cordis decided on medicating her with amitriptyline, an antidepressant which, because of its sedating effect, he would have her take at night as a single dose. But he knew nothing would improve until the family issue was resolved. In concluding the session, he urged her and Naomi to try to get Abishai to come with her the following week, and if not, for Leah to continue to see him by herself on a weekly basis. Cordis could feel their pessimism as he ended the session at 7:50.

On this occasion, he would not run longer than the fifty-minute hour, for he wanted the waiting room cleared for his 8 o'clock patient, another new one. She was an 18-year-old with a drug problem, referred through Medicaid. When she had not arrived by 8:20, he threw his hands up in disgust and muttered, "The last Medicaid patient I will schedule. And to think I gave her Renata's favorite hour for her introductory session."

CHAPTER THIRTY-EIGHT

Earlier that month, on June 11, *The New York Times* ran an op-ed page article Cordis had written on the health hazards of passive cigarette smoking. The article saw his stock rise with the "Three Sisters" and even their Park Avenue internist, who was suddenly on a first-name basis with him. When the article came to Simone's attention, she started phoning him regularly. In fact, it seemed that hardly a day passed without a telephone call from either a Delacross or a Delacroix.

Simone had been badgering him to come to dinner ever since their meeting three months earlier. Cordis kept refusing. She continued to badger. Finally, he agreed to a dinner engagement on one condition: that both sides of the family, the two Delacroix Huguenots and the three Delacross Catholics, sit down together at the same table with him. To his surprise and satisfaction, both sides agreed, making him believe that a family rapprochment might be possible.

They arranged to meet Saturday evening, the 30th, at a downtown restaurant. Cordis and the two Protestants arrived at about the same time.

Simone and Pierre greeted the doctor effusively, as they had done on that previous occasion in the winter.

A short while later the Delacross sisters arrived — two of them, Celine and Edith. They resembled each other physically — both petite and straight-backed. They were dressed elegantly along the lines of the 1940's and both carried themselves in an imperious manner. Celine walked slowly with the aid of a cane.

The evening went well, with each side acting politely toward the other early on and warmly by dessert time. Afterwards, as they were preparing to leave, they even promised to get together again soon.

Celine Delacross took Cordis aside before they were to go their separate ways, and in a surprising gesture tightly grasped his right hand in both of hers.

"I have enjoyed meeting you," she said, a note of contriteness in her voice.

"It has been a pleasure, madame," he reciprocated. "And give my regards to your other sister."

She nodded in a gesture of appreciation. "Dr. Cordis, I want to tell you this," she said. "I am impressed with all the changes — for the better — which Renata has undergone this year. You have worked wonders for her mind and her body. But I am still concerned, very concerned, about her soul, that immortal part of her which dominates the life of us Catholics." She cracked a faint smile. "Such matters which go beyond the flesh and the psyche become uppermost in the mind of an old woman as she nears her appointed hour with her Maker. So I ask you, Dr. Cordis, can you help her explore the third dimension of human existence, her spiritual life?"

Cordis looked into the elderly woman's searching, beseeching eyes, and placed his left hand over hers gripping his hand so tightly. She had touched him to the core. He had never thought of himself as a soul-doctor — he left such matters to men and women of the cloth. Yet he recognized that the goal of therapy, a sound mind in a sound body, was not necessarily the be-all and end-all — he heard his mind say the alpha and the omega — of therapy. The spiritual was not the exclusive preserve of the priest, minister, or rabbi any more than sound physical health was the private domain of the physician.

"I will try, madame," he said softly and with noticeable compassion. "By the living God who guides me, I will try."

CHAPTER THIRTY-NINE

Cordis had to schedule Renata at an earlier time again for July 3rd to allow him to prepare for the holiday festivities. He was now working part-time, mornings only, at the clinic, and was in the process of re-arranging his schedule so as to treat three patients per afternoon at his private office, which he expected to start doing the second week of the month. Most of his regular patients, however, those who were working, had already confirmed that they preferred to continue with their evening sessions.

Renata was in high spirits from the good news Simone and Pierre had brought back after their Saturday night dinner.

"History is being made," she beamed. "My Protestants and Catholics are going to end their war, I do believe. It's like the Hatfields and the McCoys I have heard so much about."

"The age of miracles may never end," Cordis said, smiling contentedly.

Renata continued discussing the dinner for fifteen minutes. What pleased Cordis most was hearing that she had phoned her grandmother on Sunday.

"Even Simone and Pierre chatted amiably with *les trois soeurs*," she added excitedly, mingling her sentence with some French.

Cordis had been able to confirm, if indirectly, the family thaw: her grandmother had just sent him a check for her June bill. Celine Delacross had stopped paying for her treatment after Renata had moved out of the house, at which time Pierre had assumed responsibility for her account.

Renata's physical health was improving at a remarkable pace, to the extent that it even surprised Cordis.

"I think I am in less turmoil emotionally, so my pruritis problem has diminished dramatically," she said.

"Ah, so you see," the doctor said, "the integumentary system is indeed connected to the nervous system — you have validated that."

"You've made me a believer," Renata affirmed, "and the proof is in my being able to shelve all the lotions, potions and pills I have for my skin."

"Good news like that tickles my hide," Cordis said, buoyed up by her favorable progress report.

"And I have been able to cut back on the medications for my bowel problem. I think going on a high-residue diet, as you suggested, has been of enormous help."

"Any more good news like that and I'll have to raise my fee," he said facetiously.

Renata smiled. "I even use atropine less frequently, and when I do resort to it, I measure out fewer drops. I still carry the bottle in my purse, but I would say more for security than anything else."

In the early '70's, Cordis adhered to the psychoanalyst's distinctive diagnostic approach, since he had been trained primarily by analysts during his residency years. This included a so-called genetic formulation, which had nothing to do with genetics but was rather a psychogenetic formulation pin-pointing the origins of the patient's condition in time according to Freud's timetable of psychosexual development; a psychodynamic formulation, which spelled out the conflict(s) generating the problem; and a diagnostic formulation, or the official diagnosis according to the *Diagnostic and Statistical Manual*, Second Edition.

Renata's problem was not pre-oedipal, as he had already determined, that is, it did not originate in the three earliest stages—oral, anal, phallic—of development. He saw her trouble arising later on, in latency or perhaps in the next stage, adolescence. From a practical point of view, the later the onset of difficulties, the easier the therapeutic solution. Thus, once he had formulated this part of the diagnosis, he had become optimistic about his chances of helping his patient resolve her dilemma.

The psychodynamic formulation pivoted around her relationship with key familial figures and pertinent events associated with them: her father's death in Bolivia; her mother's suicide after a long history of depression, alcoholism and psychiatric hospitalizations; and other possible events occurring later of which he knew nothing as yet.

The diagnostic formulation was the DSM-II disgnosis: depressive neurosis. He also categorized her skin and bowel problems as psychophysiological, or psychosomatic, disorders. Her depression had lifted without recourse to antidepressant medication, and he liked to think that psychotherapy had played a key role in its resolution. Likewise, he felt therapy was helping her with her dermatitis and irritable bowel syndrome.

There remained one thorn in this otherwise rosy picture. Renata Delacross continued to smoke marijuana, but, on the positive side, had at least succeeded, with his constant prodding, in cutting down to two reefers a week, still too much from his point of view. The cannabinoids have a half-life of about a week, meaning that after one week half a given dose remains in the body stores, and a week later one half of that, or a quarter of the original dose, is still in the body, and so on.

"You ought not to have those exogenous neurotoxins in God's temple," he said to her, "which is your brain. And they're hard on your lungs and ovaries, too, which, even though you have two apiece of these organs,

186

they can stand only so much abuse—each of these organs on your left side can blow out as readily as the one on your right side."

"I'm cutting down," Renata said, trying to placate him after listening to his awkwardly phrased criticism, a deliberate bit of syntactical messiness to drive his point home. "I'm getting there. Rome wasn't built in a fortnight. Well-entrenched habits die hard, you know that."

Psychotherapy becomes her, he mused, when she was gone. It was designed for the Renatas of the world. Freud, Jung, Adler and all the other pioneering psychodynamicists bequeathed us something of value, and we are all the better for it.

Leah Chomsky had been scheduled for 7 o'clock, but she failed to show. Cordis wasn't too surprised, given what he perceived was the overwhelming obstacle facing her: a balking husband with an Old World sense of Jewish machismo. "Abishai probably has her chained to the furniture," he mumbled aloud at 7:45. At eight he left for an Independence Day celebration at Dr. Romanetti's.

CHAPTER FORTY

Renata had planned to go upstate with Simone and Pierre the following morning and return to New York Sunday night.

Simone phoned Cordis at his office Monday in the afternoon to tell him that Renata was in the hospital. The connection was a poor one, and Simone was so upset, speaking rapidly in a mixture of English and French, that he found it hard to follow what she was trying to say. What he did hear was that Renata seemed to be in a delirium. He thought he heard Simone mention "recurrent pneumonia," which, if it were the case, sounded plausible.

A little later the head nurse on Pavilion A at St. Mark's Hospital telephoned him that Renata's physician was requesting that he consult on her case.

When Cordis arrived at the hospital a little after five, he was told by Renata's private duty nurse that Simone and Pierre had just left. Renata was resting comfortably for the moment.

"That sedation won't last long," the nurse said. "She keeps thrashing about so."

Cordis noted that her pulse was rapid and her skin warm. Her temperature was recorded as 100 degrees Fahrenheit on her bedside chart.

He went down to radiology to talk to the radiologist about her chest films; they looked at the x rays together, and the radiologist said he saw no evidence of pneumonia. Cordis returned to the third floor and filled out his consultation sheet. His impression was that the problem was medical, not psychiatric, and that there was no need for alarm—she was not "relapsing" into mental illness, which was what was on everyone's mind.

Later that evening he received a phone call from Pierre, who expressed his disappointment over missing him at the hospital. Pierre was able to fill Cordis in on some pertinent data. The three of them had gone to Poughkeepsie on Independence Day as planned. Renata took ill while they were packing for the return drive to New York, and rather than take her to a local doctor, they quickly drove back to Manhattan, where her family's physician had her hospitalized.

"Is there any chance that she could have been bitten by a tick or something?" Cordis asked him.

"*Je ne sais pas*," Pierre answered, momentarily taken aback by the question.

"We have to think of everything," the doctor said.

"*C'est possible*," Pierre muttered. "I suppose it is possible. But I have no way of knowing."

"Well, do you recall anything unusual that happened during your vacation? Too much sun? Strenuous exercise?"

"Pierre was silent for a few moments. "Renata came back from a morning walk yesterday coughing a good deal. She mentioned that a plane was spraying insecticide nearby."

"I see," Cordis said.

"Will she be all right, Doctor? She is so terribly restless lying in bed. Quite unmanageable much of the time."

"She's going to recover, Pierre," Cordis replied. "You and Simone are not to worry."

"Simone is a nervous wreck over this."

"Tell her Renata is going to be all right."

After his phone conversation with Pierre, Cordis called the family's internist.

"Well, young man," said the octogenarian physician, "what do you think of our patient?"

188

"I think she has a delirium as you indicated," Cordis replied. "A toxic delirium. You know, I checked up on her x rays, and they don't confirm the presence of pneumonitis. Pierre Delacroix was just telling me a moment ago that Renata had been close to a field being crop dusted yesterday morning. This could be parathion or malathion poisoning—"

"One of those organophosphate things?" the older doctor interjected, sounding alarmed.

"Yes, a cholinesterase-inhibiting pesticide. A poison designed to kill insects but spare higher mammals like us, so the manufacturer would have us believe."

"Where are you now?" the internist asked anxiously.

"I'm at home," Cordis answered.

"I'll have to get down to the hospital right away," Renata's physician said with urgency in his voice.

"Yes. You'll want to have a blood sample sent for a cholinesterase determination. She'll probably need some atropine sulphate i.v.. It's all medical management. Nothing psychiatric about it. A neuro consult might also be indicated—these things can turn into a peripheral neuropathy later on."

"Yes, of course," the old physician said. "Thank you for your timely assistance."

The following afternoon, Cordis received a call from the family's doctor while at his office.

"Her blood cholinesterase was depressed by thirty-five percent," the elderly doctor said, "confirming your diagnosis of organophosphate poisoning."

"Were both the plasma and the RBC cholinesterase activities down?"

"Yes. Renata is now recovering nicely. I'll keep her in the hospital the rest of the week to monitor her cholinesterase and adjust her atropine accordingly. I want to avoid complications like atropine toxicity and at the same time inadequate atropinization."

"You've got the situation under control, I can see."

"That was a topnotch consultation you turned in, young fella."

Cordis smiled at being referred to as a young fellow—at forty-four he considered himself middle-aged and felt older than that with his severe arthritis weighing heavily on his neck.

So, the young lady from the Maghreb has dodged another bullet, he mused, relaxing with a bottle of cream soda. The Fates seem to pursue her. Let me see, Hesiod named the daughters of the Night Clotho, Lachesis and Atropos. Clotho spins the web of life, Lachesis measures its length and Atropos cuts the thread of life. Which one of the Moirae hovers over

189

Renata? Probably Atropos. Renata's life seems interwoven with *Atropa belladonna*, the deadly nightshade, source of atropine. At least she's getting away from it now, so there's hope. Is it fate or destiny with her? Fate— whatever the gods decree—takes the future out of our hands, but we can fight for our destiny. *Our* God grants us that. Let it be said, daughters of Night, this one will work through to her own destiny.

CHAPTER FORTY-ONE

The following morning Cordis received a call from Celine Delacross.

"Edith and I have been visiting Renata at the infirmary daily since we learned of her latest illness and hospitalization. Our doctor says she will be able to go home by the weekend."

He was pleased to learn that she and her sister had made actual contact with Renata. He also noted that she made no mention of Beatrice.

"Yes. She's recovering all right."

"Dr. Cordis, we are leaving for France on Friday. Business, you understand. We expect to be gone quite a while. Renata will be in good hands."

"Oh." The news caught Cordis by surprise.

"For so many years," Celine Delacross continued, "I was led to believe that Renata's diagnosis was schizophrenia. *Mon Dieu*, what a hopeless diagnosis! No cure. Only those dreadful, mind-dulling pills. What do you call them?"

"Neuroleptics," Cordis answered.

"It's more than a disease," Edith stated, talking on an extension. "It's a curse."

"I thought I was doing the right thing for her," Celine Delacross said, "based on the best medical advice. Well, the advice I know now was wrong. I was wrong, and I can never make it up to Renata."

"The important thing is that now she has her chance," the doctor said. "This is her time, and all her suffering, if you care to look at this . . . well, we'll say theologically, has gone into the creation of her time."

"I wish I could accept that," the elder sister said.

"So do I," Edith added.

"Whatever you did, both of you, you did out of love, not malice, not selfishness. And the God who rules in heaven knows that."

"You are very kind, Dr. Cordis," Celine Delacross said softly.

"Know that in her heart she loves you," Cordis said. "Loves you all." He added Beatrice in his own mind.

"Doctor," Edith started to say, "I, too, want to thank you for your compassion, and I would like to ask you something."

"Ask away."

"When Renata was three years old, her one-year-old brother died. Do you think that particular trauma, part of her forgotten memories, could be the cause lying behind her subsequent mental difficulties?"

Cordis was surprised to learn about the brother, for he recalled that when Renata had filled out her general information sheet in January she had indicated she was an only child.

"I think the mind of the child has more plasticity than that," he responded. "I would say that the so-called original trauma hypothesis— the idea of a single event in infancy or early childhood as the direct cause of later psychopathology—has been overstated."

"Then how do you explain Renata's various episodes of mental illness?" Edith asked, pushing her point.

"She is of a melancholic disposition," he said simply. "She is well aware of that. So, given her nature, she's predisposed when stressed to the critical point to develop depression."

"A family trait," Celine Delacross said.

"In other words," Edith added, "that's her natural temperament."

"It's constitutional," Cordis commented, "and somehow linked to one or possibly more than one of her genes. We don't pay enough attention in psychiatry to temperament, believing too much that what we see in personality is derivative, that is, derived solely from experience."

"I understand," Edith said.

Now that he had the two closest of Renata's relatives available for historical data, he asked, "Was her mother any good at mothering?"

"For the first few years," Edith answered for the two, "she was probably an ideal mother, but after the baby boy died her problems emerged."

"Well, then," the doctor said, "we've ruled out the possibility of an anaclitic depression in Renata's case, one originating in the first year of life and stemming from a prolonged separation from the mother."

"Then exactly what is Renata's problem?" Edith pushed, "if she is not a schizophrenic and not the victim of a childhood trauma?"

"Hers is more an existential neurosis," Cordis answered.

"A neurosis of existence?" Celine Delacross said.

"That's a good way to put it," the psychiatrist responded. "Mind and body and soul are not in harmony. Not yet, that is."

"But you are going to get her there," the older sister stated emphatically.

"In due time," Cordis said. "All in good time."

"We will be gone longer than usual this time," Edith said, changing the topic and the general mood.

"We are in no hurry to return to New York with its ever-increasing crime and drugs and violence," Celine Delacross said.

Edith added, "In this new age of the young, Americans are living only for the present, forfeiting the future."

Her sister followed with, "In modern America the genitals are alive, but the heart is dead."

Edith came back with, "There is no passion—in its original meaning of spiritual suffering—in their soul, only violence."

Edith has depth, Cordis said to himself, and the grandmother can be very Gallic. They're actually an interesting pair to know.

"I do want to wish you bon voyage and a successful stay in your home country," the doctor said. "And do give my regards to Beatrice."

"Thank you, Dr. Cordis," the grandmother said, and he detected a note of sadness in her voice.

"Good-by, Dr. Cordis," Edith said, barely above a whisper.

CHAPTER FORTY-TWO

Renata was discharged from St. Mark's Hospital on Monday, the 16th. She phoned Cordis from the Delacroix's apartment to confirm her eight o'clock appointment for the following evening. With his newly reorganized schedule, he had moved her up to six, and she had no objection to that.

192

When she arrived, she looked gaunt and wan.

"I'm fine," she said, smiling languidly as she sank into her chair. "Just fine."

Cordis wondered if scheduling her for an office visit so soon after her difficult illness was wise. She's here, he said to himself. That's the reality.

"I think you're going to be all right," he said to her.

She nodded her head slowly, but did not speak for nearly a minute. Finally, she said, sounding sad, "I didn't get to see Grandmama and my aunts off at Kennedy."

"But you saw them regularly while you were in the hospital."

"Yes, and it filled my heart with joy to be reunited with my family," she said, perking up a bit. "I'll miss them, but I have my family back." She remained silent for about half a minute. "I understand it was you who correctly diagnosed my illness."

"I added my two-cents worth."

"Well, it saved my life." Her eyes filled with tears. "Thank you," she whispered.

"I can't have my patients die on me!" Cordis said laughingly. "Psychiatry is a bloodless specialty with a mortality rate of zero—close to it, anyway."

Renata smiled. "It's intriguing, just as I was decreasing my use of atropine, atropine suddenly became necessary to save me."

"Huge doses of it are required for insecticide poisoning of the type you suffered," he said. "No comparison to the small amount you have been taking for your stomach."

"Well, I'm happy to report that I've gotten rid of it. I threw my medicine bottle, dropper and all, away."

"Ah, you've turned away from the goddess Atropos."

Renata smiled, but said nothing for a few seconds, and when she spoke again she was solemn. "I feel as though I have had a close brush with death. I came near to dying . . . before I ever had the chance to find . . . fulfillment in this life."

When she did not continue, the psychiatrist said, "Now you have that chance."

She looked at him, studying his face, and then turned her gaze toward the Castel painting. "Do you really believe in this God of yours, Yahweh? That he exists?"

"God of the universe, who goes by many names."

"At least you have the One God," she commented. "For Catholics there are three of Him—the Father, the Son and the Holy Spirit, a.k.a. the Holy Ghost."

"I understand that," he said, nodding.

"Well, I'm glad you do because I don't. How do I reconcile myself to three Gods in One, this complicated scenario of the Holy Trinity?"

"Three is the most complete number under heaven," Cordis responded. "The spiritual world rests on the number three, just as the physical world revolves around the number four."

"Four is important in the physical world?"

"The world of living things is built upon the tetravalency of carbon. But that is another matter. Your concern is with the Trinity."

"You once mentioned this quaternary concept in relation to religion," Renata said thoughfully. "That's what we really need, because there's no room for a feminine presence—God the Mother—in the concept of the Trinity."

"There's the Marian presence," he countered.

"That's exactly it—she's not a part of the Trinity!" Switching her focus, Renata said, "You have a similar problem in Judaism—a patriarchal God with no feminine attributes."

"That's the older biblical God, the God of Mount Sinai," Cordis said. "With the rise of Jewish mysticism, the Kabbalah, early in the Christian era, God took on the attributes of Father and Mother. There's a word for God's female aspect and immanent presence the Kabbalists used—the *Shekhinah*. For the exiled Jews of the sixteenth century, the *Matrona*."

"Hmm," Renata murmured. "And what do you imply by immanent presence?"

"Much of God's presence in the world is female, i.e. Mother Nature, on Friday nights Jews welcome in the Sabbath Queen, et cetera."

"Yahweh with feminine attributes? How extraordinary!"

"If humanity, the highest expression of creation in the universe is divided into male and female, then there is something inherent in the Creator that is both male and female."

Renata was inclined to remain on the religious theme. "But you wouldn't pray to God through a statue of Our Lady of Guadalupe," she said, frowning.

"I wouldn't, but you can. The Virgin Mary, after all, is an archetypal figure, the mother of all humanity, not only of all Christianity. Through her you *can* reach to the Infinite One."

"Archetypal?" she said. "What are you specifically conveying with the use of that word?"

"As a psychological term, an archetype is, simply stated, an inborn disposition shared by all people which is part of our human inheritance."

"Is that Jungian?"

"Yes, it's from Jung."

After a pause Renata, still staying on religion, moved to the topic of miraculous events.

"Do you really believe that Yahweh could empower Moses to part the waters of the Red Sea and Joshua to stop the sun?"

Pointing to the Castel painting, Cordis said, "There you will find the Tetragrammaton—YHWH. We pronounce it as Yahweh, or Jehovah in German, but no one knows how the Tetragrammaton was pronounced in antiquity."

"It's a mystery," Renata said.

"Yes, the mystery of the Ineffable Name. Lost in the past. And with it has vanished the power that could work miracles."

"Do you believe that?" she asked, sounding incredulous. "It sounds very primitive."

He detected the sarcasm in her comment. "Primitive," he started to say, "in the sense of being early—this was an earlier time in history when people were tuned in to their God, when they found it natural—another meaning of primitive—to tune in to their God."

"So Moses tuned in to God."

"Was in tune with God."

"Was in tune with God," Renata repeated.

"So were others," Cordis said. "But Moses was special to the Almighty One. Moses possessed the power of the Shem, the key to the Ineffable Name, and so was able to function beyond the limits of time and space. Or, for the Kabbalists, he was so spiritually developed that he could manipulate the physical world—"

"Part the waters of the Red Sea."

"Yes. Just as Joshua, his disciple, was able to lengthen the day."

"Sure, he was the first to convert to daylight saving time."

"Jest if you must, but—"

"Oh, I take this very seriously. And Moses got the tablets of clay directly from God." She may have said she was serious, but she delivered her words flippantly. Now, in a more natural tone, she added, "We have mysteries enough of our own in Christianity. Miracles which need to be explained, clarified, interpreted. Like Jesus rising from the grave on the third day—"

"I'm familiar with that account."

"Is it a fabrication? If it is true, how do you explain it?"

"Psychology isn't concerned with whether it's true or not, but simply focuses on the fact that there is such an idea."

195

"That's eloquent, more like a lawyer's answer, but it doesn't answer the question."

"I can only refer you to what Jung, the Protestant minister's son, would have said. It's psychologically true inasmuch as it exists."

Renata sighed, letting out a bit of her frustration, and then continued with her line of inquiry.

"Am I supposed to believe the biblical story of the seven-day creation of the world?" she asked. "It's not a very scientific account of events, you know."

"It wasn't meant to be. There were no scientists in those days. Genesis tells us that the world has a history." Cordis stopped there and looked at her.

"And Adam and Eve—it's a rather naive little story of man's origin and descent."

"You've got to give it a meaning."

"For instance."

"Well," Cordis said, "Adam ate the fruit from the Tree of Knowledge, the sacred tree man must climb in order to ascend to God. When Adam and Eve left the Garden, they abandoned the mystical life to live in the world. Now, that's one interpretation."

"And Yahweh, a God quick to anger, punished Adam for his indiscretion."

"Nonsense! Adam was the apple of his eye. But that was then, this is now. We still, every one of us, must choose—to live in the world . . . or follow the spiritual path."

Renata then took a sudden change in direction.

"Is the Jewish mission in history over?" she asked.

"It is written that salvation comes through the Jews. Jesus said that to the Samaritan woman. That was then, and it may still be so now."

"Why do Jews go on rejecting Jesus as the Messiah?" she asked, becoming engrossed in the dialogue.

Rejecting Jesus seems to be your problem, Cordis said to himself. Answering her, he said, "In the Jewish tradition, God is incorporeal— God the Unseen, the Unknowable. Jesus the Son of God therefore is a contradiction."

"God is everywhere, yet God is nowhere," she said, nodding her head slowly.

"I agree with only the first half of that," the doctor commented.

"Isn't that the pantheistic view—God is in all things?"

"It comes through better when you reverse it. The true believer says, 'All is in God.'"

196

Renata sighed. "Even if I ever do come to terms with this Trinity concept, I don't see how I can accept a religion handed down to me in which a god-man, nailed to a wooden cross, cries out: 'My God, my God, why hast Thou forsaken me?' If he didn't believe in his own divinity at the end, how can I?"

"Ah, yes, those famous words," the psychiatrist said. Cordis sat up straight and rocked gently in his swivel chair. "You've got to know something," he began to explain. "Everyone present in the Valley of the Skulls that day knew what Yeshua, to give him his name in Hebrew, was doing: he was reciting the Twenty-second Psalm, the prayer of a lonely soul who through defeat nevertheless snatches victory. It starts out with the man describing his suffering and ends as a hymn of thanksgiving. But Jesus never got past the first line. At that point he expired."

"I have never heard it explained that way," Renata said, looking nonplussed.

"He was merely reciting from the Bible, not complaining about how unkind fate had been to him. After all, he was there, up on his cross, voluntarily. He was born to die, to suffer for the sins of humanity, thus giving people the opportunity for . . . redemption."

After a short silence Renata heaved a sigh and said, "You appear to have more faith than I do, mountains more. I somehow had the impression that psychiatrists were impassive scientists."

"There is the world of science and there is the world of faith," he said. "One belongs to the mind, the other to the human heart."

Although Cordis was a man of science, he was drawn to the ancient mysteries.

"Obviously, I'm deficient in faith. Some people suffer from vitamin deficiencies; I suffer from a deficiency of faith."

"Suffer?"

"I don't exactly agonize over it."

"You don't," Cordis said matter-of-factly.

"I was born into the Catholic faith just as you, I assume, were born into the Jewish faith. We're not responsible for our origins."

"I was borne—with an e—carried on the wings of an angel—into the faith of my fathers."

"Such faith I have never before witnessed," Renata said, sighing.

"Must I remind you of what is in your part of the Scriptures?"

"Apparently you must," she answered, "for I know very little of what is in either part of the Bible, yours or mine."

"John says: 'Everyone begotten of God conquers the world, and the power that has conquered the world is this faith of ours.'"

197

"I have been begotten, but I don't seem to be one of God's begotten."

"John adds: 'Everyone who believes that Jesus is the Christ has been begotten by God.'"

"Where does that leave you Jews and other non-Christians?"

"That's not your problem," he said forcefully. "You don't have to be concerned about the rest of us. There are others begotten of God who are not Christians. Your problem, your task, is to conquer your world."

"To do that I have to begin by believing in the Creator, as you also refer to your God, Yahweh. But being so full of doubt, I have to ask: Who begat the Creator?"

"Now you're going to get caught up in the infinite regress mess. The Creator is beyond time, in no need of explanation. In no need of existence, except in your mind, because he created you out of his own Mind."

Renata was visibly tired and chose to end the session at that point.

Cordis walked with her through the empty waiting room to the door to the hallway. Before opening it he said, "I'm surprised you haven't figured it out yet."

"Figured what out?" she asked, perplexed.

"Why Jesus was on his cross in the first place and how he rose from the grave."

"He died on the cross for our sins," Renata responded. "That's what I was taught as a child in Catholic school."

"That part's right."

"But it's true, I don't understand how he raised Lazarus from the dead and rose up himself after three days in his tomb."

"The explanation is actually quite simple," the doctor said. She stared at him, wide-eyed. "Like Moses," Cordis explained, "Jesus had the power of the Shem—he knew the Ineffable Name."

CHAPTER FORTY-THREE

The following week Renata, still looking a little pale, started off her session by returning to the subject of the Trinity.

"I'm really struggling with this concept of three Gods in One, three for the price of one. I need some help in coming to grips with it."

"Have you tried a priest?" Cordis asked.

"I haven't talked to a priest since my father's funeral."

"Well, let me see what I can dredge up for you," the doctor said. Cordis sat thinking for a while. "Seven is the holy number of the Hebrews—God rested on the seventh day and the number appears time and again in the Bible."

"Yes, I know," Renata said impatiently. "And the oedipal period comes to an end at the age of seven, when the child's superego has formed, and so on. But my question pertains to the number three, not seven."

She certainly has been reading, Cordis mused. Making up lost ground rapidly.

"I'll come to that," he said. "You see, the Pythagoreans, who saw in numbers the essence of things, considered seven the number for the whole cosmos, because it was comprised of three, representing the deity, plus four, the world. God and the world—the spiritual and the physical."

"How did three become associated with the deity?" she asked.

"Because they thought everything has a beginning, middle and an end."

"Um."

"The number three in relation to the Divinity pops up in many religions of the world," Cordis said. "Vishnu, in the Hindu tradition, is part of a trinity. He is Brahma, Vishnu and Siva, one but threefold—creator, preserver and destoyer, in that order."

"What you're saying is that the tripartioning of God is a very old concept," Renata commented.

"It may have its roots in Paleolithic times when ancient man began to try to understand the mysteries of nature—Mother Nature. He was closer to heaven than we may be today."

"Why is that?"

"God would never have allowed him to perish. Ancient man needed to get to us in order that we may get to the future. Past, present and future—the beginning, middle and end—which is absorption back into the Creator."

Renata nodded and remained silent for a few moments.

"There are a number of concepts in Catholicism I find strange and at odds with reality," she finally said.

When she did not continue after some ten seconds, Cordis said, "Can you give me an example of what you have in mind?"

"The Church acknowledges a phenomenon referred to as bilocation, the location of one body in two places at the same time. St. Clement and

St. Francis of Assisi, for example, were said to have had this special gift. A rather unusual projective ability, wouldn't you say?"

"Is that what it is—an extraordinary protoplasmic projective ability?"

"A slight correction," Renata answered. "The Church's explanation is that the material body is in one place and only apparently—that's the key word—present in the other."

"Apparently," Cordis said, repeating the word she had stressed.

"The second presentation is supposedly a vision or an apparition. Now, how does natural law explain bilocation?"

"Is it supposed to?"

"You're begging the question," she said.

"I can discuss the world of natural phenomena with some degree of confidence, but not the spiritual realm. Perhaps some people, like the saints you named, are extraordinarily endowed so as to be able to transmit or project a mental image of themselves to another location."

"Do you believe that's possible?"

"Well, with this bilocational gift, what only a few people, only the holiest, have been able to achieve up until now may become accessible to a greater number at some future time when we have gained greater mastery of the mind . . . and over our passions."

"That sounds like science fiction."

"Today's science fiction has a way of becoming tomorrow's science fact."

"Yes, I know," she said disdainfully. "A thousand years ago bubble gum was only someone's vision."

"If I may . . . look . . . you're looking for science to explain religion. But you can't apply the scientific method to explain a religious belief. Whether God exists, a religious belief, can never be presented as a scientific hypothesis—and it shouldn't."

"Why not?"

"You can't devise a scientific experiment to prove it. What you can do, however, is try to intermix science and religion."

"How, for instance?"

"Well," Cordis sat back in his chair and stretched his arms, biding some time to collect his thoughts, "here's a little sketch for you. Some five billion or ten billion years ago—who really knows when?—God kissed a very special star bon voyage and sent it on its inter-galactic way through time and space until it came to its appointed place in the universe. It would be called the Sun, and the rest is history. And now God is living out his existence in us, the human race."

"You put a lot of stock in humankind."

"Because God is here, with us, within us."

"Some prominent Christian philosophers have been claiming that God is dead."

"In the Buddhist scripture there's a passage: 'Struggle on, always remembering that God is not dead.' Now, who do you choose to believe?"

Renata nodded noncommitally. "You see God at the center of things, the hand behind all creation."

"Out there in the great cosmic swim where elementary particles struggle to be born, perhaps the presence of a creator may seem less necessary, but in the realm of living things God's guiding hand is indispensable; for even the so-called simple life forms—algae, amoebae, bacteria—are too complex to have evolved haphazardly."

"I was reading an article written by a physicist who said everything is made up of those simple particles, which have fallen into place randomly to produce the world and all the living forms in it."

"The essence of existence," the doctor responded, "is more likely to be found in the trenches of the body where enzymes do their work, rather than in the elementary particles of the physicist."

"This is getting too deep for me."

"Even a good Catholic should not have to live without the spiritual implications of scientific discovery."

"But don't forget, I'm a Catholic dropout."

"But not by conviction."

"No? By what then?"

"By neurosis. Through repression and neglect of the religious function of the psyche. Fouling it up gives rise to psychic disturbances. Using it properly, it serves as an integrating element in mental health."

"So you believe I have a chance of becoming a good Catholic again."

"The choice is yours. Life is a process of becoming. Through it—becoming—and maybe it's a word that needs to be capitalized—was created our consciousness. Through it in the end we will reach to God, back to the God who had us in his mind in the beginning."

"You're sure of that."

"I feel it in the very depths of my mind, where the psyche was formed."

"I wonder how I'm supposed to do that, I mean, make a start?"

"For a beginning, there is a passage from Luke you can cogitate on: 'I count all things worthless but this: to gain Jesus Christ and to be found in him.' For the ordinary Catholic, that's simple enough. For the Catholic who can go beyond the ordinary, it means in the end a return to the source, gaining reentry into the Holy Trinity."

"So," Renata said solemnly, "I began my session with the Trinity and

201

I end it with the Trinity!"

She had finished for the day, but she lingered on her way out to ask, "Do you believe in paranormal phenomena? Like Padre Pio's stigmata and his bilocationary gift?"

"Believe?"

"Yes, believe."

"Well," Cordis started to say, "a belief is something you accept on faith; what you *think* is something you subject to a more critical analysis based on fact."

"So you really don't think much of paranormal or supranormal experience?"

They were standing near the door to his office. Cordis stroked his chin, while his mind struggled to come up with a response which would satisfy his patient.

"The first century Neopythagorean preacher, Apollonius of Tyana," he said finally, "lost his concentration in a speech one day because in his mind's eye he saw the murder of the emperor in far off Rome several days before it happened, which he relayed to his attentive audience as though he were actually present as an eye witness. And what he saw did happen."

"A clairvoyant?"

"A rival of Jesus . . . until he faded into history. But to answer your question, yes, I think it's possible for some people to perceive events through channels other than the five senses."

Renata smiled and patted him tenderly on his jacket lapel. "Thank you for clarifying an important mystery of experience for me," she said, and with that the session ended.

CHAPTER FORTY-FOUR

Renata was looking much better when she arrived for her session on July 31st. Her face had filled out and her color had returned. She began with news of her family.

"Grandmama is well—she writes and phones. Aunt Edith likewise is well. Aunt Beatrice . . . well, she'll be all right."

"That's good."

She hesitated a bit, and then plunged back into the religious discussion.

"You mentioned that seven was the holy number of the Hebrews of old. God rested on the seventh day, and there's seven of this and seven of that in the Bible."

"Yes."

"But—and here's the flaw—the prophet Samuel went through all of Jesse's sons and found them wanting. It was the eighth son, David, whom he chose to anoint. You see, not the seventh."

So, she's been reading the Bible, Cordis mused. That's good. She thinks she's found a chink in the sacred structure that will topple the whole edifice.

"Well," Cordis started to respond, "you can make much out of the number eight. Turn it on its side and you have the symbol of infinity. Or two eyes that see and know all. God, who sees all down through infinity, saw to it that Samuel would find David." Not waiting a moment to give Renata a chance to comment, he continued, "And then again, the figure eight is one of the symbols of the Egyptian god Thoth—"

"Who?"

"The ibis-headed god Thoth, who pours the waters of purification on the heads of the initiated . . . much like Samuel anointing the head of David with oil. Thoth had infinite power, which was why his worshippers called him Thoth, meaning three times very great, which to the Greeks later on became Hermes Trismegistes, or Hermes the thrice greatest."

"So, you have come back to three, the number of the Holy Trinity, again!" Renata exclaimed. "How do you do this?"

"Do what?" he said, feigning innocence.

"These . . . these coincidences," she said, struggling for words. "You always seem to have some verbal trick up your sleeve."

"Nothing up my sleeve," he said calmly.

"Then what is it?" she asked exasperatedly.

"You are simply confronting the unconscious," Cordis explained, "and you have a genuine facility for doing so."

"Oh," she said.

"Are you familiar with the Egyptian pantheon?" he asked, wanting to tie together a loose end.

"I know about the sun-god, Akhenaton's Aten. The one represented by a solar disk. I read Waltari's novel, The Egyptian."

"Somehow, I thought you did," Cordis responded. "Knew about

Aten." He was thinking back to her Columbus-in-chains experience.

"How did you know that?"

"Through the unconscious," he answered. "I have a functioning unconscious, too."

Renata remained silent for a while and then said, "When I was a child, do you know what my friends used to call me?"

"No, I don't," he replied, surprised but pleased she was about to say something from out of her childhood.

"Rena," she said. "Which rhymes with hyena. Now, that I am not."

"Which? A Rena or a canine scavenger type?"

"Neither. I'm Renata. It's . . . dignified."

After a pause the doctor said, "It's your last name that's intriguing."

There was another brief silence before she said, "Yes, Delacross. Delacroix originally. *De la croix*. Of the cross."

"It perhaps has a history?"

"Our geneology goes back many centuries until it is lost in the mist of time."

"I know a doctor named Tangredi, very possibly from the line of Tancred, or Tancredi in Italian, who captured Jerusalem for the Pope during the First Crusade and became the Prince of Galilee, a title he favored."

"Ten ninety-nine," Renata said softly. "That was a good year for Christianity. I don't believe I can trace my line back quite that far."

So the lady from the Maghreb knows some history, Cordis said to himself.

"You may find that you have a pope or two among your ancestors," he said light-heartedly. "You never know."

"Maybe . . . maybe a long, long time ago we had ancestors who were involved in the work of the Church, in holy work," she said dreamily. She paused momentarily and then added, speaking her words quickly, "I don't know."

"In time you may find out."

Renata smiled and asked, "Do you usually resort to—what shall I call it?—religiotherapy with your patients, or am I a special case?"

"The therapy is tailored to the needs of the individual patient," Cordis responded. "And, yes, you are a special case."

After another short period of silence, Renata asked, "These numbers—three, four, seven—and your explanations, which you say come forth from the subconscious, do they have anything to do with what you have referred to as the Kabbala?"

"Yes, indeed," he replied.

204

Over the next fifteen minutes or so, Cordis gave her a quick history of Kabbalah. She was particularly taken with the most famous of all the Kabbalists, Rabbi Isaac Luria, and how he had come to be known as the Ari, which in Hebrew means lion. He had been given the surname of Ashkenazi to denote his German family background, and "Ari" was formed from the first letters of Ashkenazi Rabbi Isaac.

"Ari," Renata said. "I will remember that name."

Renata spent the remainder of the hour discussing her "immediate options": returning to college versus becoming involved in the Delacross business enterprise. When she was all through enumerating the pros and cons of each pathway, she was clearly leaning in the direction of the latter choice.

"I feel strong enough now, emotionally as well as physically, to stand on my own two feet," she said at the close of her hour. "And I have Simone and Pierre. Then again, should I happen to waver, I have you to lean on, don't I?"

"Of course," Cordis said reassuringly.

As she was leaving at the conclusion of the session, Renata paused to make one further comment.

"Jews don't have to contend with such theological esoterica as Logos, or the Word, and the trinitarian concept of God, which we were discussing last week. Jewish thought is so straight-forward, not at all tangled up like Catholic theology."

It was the Hellenized Jew, Philo Judaeus of Alexandria, from whom the first century Christian thinkers acquired the term Logos, but Cordis wanted to avoid opening up another new area of discussion with the session now over. He had allowed her to linger at the end of her previous hour, but he was opposed to "exit" therapy, that extension of the session after time had elapsed which some patients liked to engage in.

"You'd be surprised how complex and obscure Judaism can be," he said, smiling benevolently.

"Do you have anything in your religious readings as obscure as 'The Word of God became a man who lived among us,' for instance? That's the sort of obfuscation we have to contend with."

"Well, you see," Cordis said, trying to come up with a timely intervention, "in the beginning there was Logos, the underlying order of the universe."

"But it's used to designate the Word, whatever that means theologically."

"The power of the Word. God said, 'Let the world be!' and it was."

"And God told Moses that his name was 'I Am That I Am.' I

wouldn't call that obfuscation—it's simply primitive or rudimentary."

Cordis was patient with his "Bible novice," as he considered her. She was groping her way through Scriptures, but he was pleased to find that she was trying.

"But it's the same as Jesus, centuries later, saying, 'I am the way, the truth and the life.' But back to 'I Am That I Am.' In Hebrew it's *Eheyeh asher Eheyeh.* The key is in the verb *hayah*, to be, to become. The concept is in *becoming*—the capacity for change is what lies at the very core of life."

"And 'The Word of God became a man who lived among us' sounds reasonable to you?"

"Yes, of course. The spiritual became natural. Adam came from earth, and the second Adam, which is how Jesus is depicted, from heaven."

At that point Renata hugged the psychiatrist, and with tears in her eyes, said good night. What Cordis sensed was that she had reached a watershed.

CHAPTER FORTY-FIVE

As August came in, Cordis could sit back comfortably in his chair and say his career was shaping up well. He had succeeded in switching to half-time with the State, thus cutting in half the irritation he had to endure at the clinic. The bureaucratic way was not his way, and he disliked having to put up with automaton-like, pension-oriented state employees, most of whom he would never have hired to work in his own office. There was the nettlesome Miss Jones, the R.N. who would be Miss America; a coterie of subverting social workers, young and female, exercising the new feminist protest against the masculinist world order at every available opportunity, inciting patients to doubt and question the medication prescribed for them by their physicians; clerical and office workers, on the whole GED diplomates poorly equipped for the sensitive job of working with a mentally disturbed clientele, even in the peripheral roles they played; and the new clinic director, Dr. Armazón-Goldstein, who, in less than two months had endeared herself to no one, with the exception of Miss Jones, and had turned the clinic topsy-turvy with scatterbrained pet projects and an overpowering ignorance of what community psychiatry was all about.

Cordis had concentrated on building his private practice, which now kept him fully occupied every afternoon of the work week, making it possible for him to cut out evening hours altogether. His one exception was Renata, who preferred 6 o'clock to an afternoon hour.

Not everyone paid his or her bill on time or otherwise, and Pat O'Connell was the most glaring example among his deadbeats. Much to his surprise, O'Connell called him in the middle of July after no word from him in four months to report that the pargyline (Eutonyl) treatment had worked and had transformed his life! He was getting ready to travel to Dublin to "see the sights," which Cordis took to mean he was joining the IRA.

Howard Bergfeld, the psychiatrist working at Gotham State Hospital, finally broke off his long-running engagement to his fiancee and moved to Los Angeles, taking advantage of his license to practice medicine in California. His ides-of-March session with Cordis had not exactly galvanized him, but had spurred him on, over the next several weeks, to take decisive action.

Johann Klinger kept his fortnightly appointments, always arriving for them with Teutonic punctuality, but after half a dozen sessions had made no progress. Cordis found him to be a bright and engaging chap, but he was scotomatous when it came to looking inward at his own shortcomings, both as a family man and servant of Christ. He wanted the pope to end the Church's tradition of celibacy for priests and to admit nuns to the priesthood, subjects he returned to again and again, which had nothing to do with the issues confronting him in his life but served to divert him from them. With each passing session, Cordis saw less and less inclination on the part of Johann to be restored to his former station as an ordained religious functionary. On the secular side, Cordis viewed with increasing concern what he saw as his patient's pathological attachment to his eight-year-old daughter, a reverse Electra complex.

Most of his new referrals were young adults with drug problems, some with mixed drug histories and a growing group presenting with predominantly a marijuana addiction. There were others diagnosed as suffering from schizophrenia, manic-depressive illness and organic brain syndromes, and still others with an assortment of neurotic conditions. On the whole, he had a variegated patient population, the type of private practice considered ideal by his colleagues at the clinic.

At the clinic he continued to treat a steady stream of mainly schizophrenic patients discharged from the state hospitals into the community, where most clung tenuously to a marginal existence. Better to have invested the taxpayers' money in improving the mental hospitals than to have squandered the funds in community programs which were not working was the way he saw it. But he tried his best to help keep his patients out of the hospital and in the community — where life was so difficult that many a healthy New Yorker found the day-to-day struggle for existence arduous.

Joey Dee had missed his July 3rd appointment, showing up instead a week later in the afternoon. One of the other psychiatrists wrote him scripts for a month's Thorazine and Stelazine, and told Cordis that "this strange guy of yours wanted me to give him Haldol and Taractan because he liked their colors better."

Sarah Kay had survived her alcoholic complications of January, only to die from exposure during a cold snap in March — she was living on the Bowery, somewhere behind several garbage cans with newspapers for a blanket at the time. Larry Teek, living in the shadow of Huntington's disease, had come in for a visit in June, and after being loaded up with sandwiches, some castoff clothing, and a few dollars collected by the staff, was on his tragic way again into the hell that was his life.

Cordis attended Friday night services at his *shul* on the 3rd, and afterwards strolled over to Fr. Dominic's to chat a while. He had a house guest, Fr. Jules, a heavy-set, robust man of some seventy years whose starched white collar maintained its stiffness and spotlessness despite the heat and humidity and the dirtiness of the New York air. Fr. Dominic was pleased to see his psychiatrist friend and immediately offered a round of soft drinks.

"Fr. Jules is from Lille," the English cleric said.

"Oh yes," Cordis said, nodding, "General de Gaulle's home town."

Fr. Jule's eyes lit up. "Ah, so you know *le General* was a native son," he said in a thick French accent.

Fr. Dominic smiled benevolently. "You will find that Dr. Cordis knows a great many things."

"It was from Lille," Cordis said, "that the executioner came to carry out an act of justice that heaven cried out for and mortals had to perform. He came, at Athos' calling, to put an end to the life and career of the wicked Lady de Winter — Milady."

"Aha," said the French priest in recognition, familiar with the tale told by Alexandre Dumas in *The Three Musketeers*.

"He cut off her head with his great sword," Cordis continued, "over there on the left bank of the Lys."

208

"Yes, yes," the visiting priest said, nearly shouting.

"I told you Dr. Cordis would have something of interest to say," Fr. Dominic added.

They talked for the next two hours about Vatican II, the State of Israel, the Bible, American Catholics, American Jews, even the Huguenots of France. Fr. Dominic served a second round of soft drinks along with peanuts and pretzels.

In the quiet of Fr. Dominic's study, where a sense of peace and harmony prevailed, Fr. Jules was prompted to say, "Among men of good will, there is only a hair's breadth of distance between Judaism and Christianity and Islam for dogma and custom to squeeze through."

"Among men of good will," Cordis said, "the width may even be narrower than that. Here, I'll give you an example of what I mean. When St. Augustine says, 'My heart is restless until it rests in Thee,' he is of course referring to Jesus Christ. But if you interpret 'Thee' as God, his prayer can fit the Jew as well, or anyone else for that matter."

"Ipsissima verba!" Fr. Dominic said. "'My heart is restless until it rests in Thee.' As timely a quote as any for he who would seek union with the Lord."

Fr. Jules turned to another subject shortly after that. "I understand, *Docteur* Cordis, that you are a dream interpreter, the second Joseph."

"That was Freud," Cordis corrected him good-naturedly. "Yes, I have one patient in particular whose dreams are central to her psychotherapy. In fact, she is so fascinating that even though I don't know how her therapy will turn out, I'm thinking of doing a book on her case."

"You never mentioned that before," Fr. Dominic said. "When did that idea occur to you?"

"It's strange," Cordis answered. "I have to admit that. But back in the spring, I suddenly got the idea I should write a book about her."

"When did the thought come to you?" Fr. Jules asked, exchanging glances with Fr. Dominic.

"What was that?"

"Exactly when did the idea pop into your head?" he asked again.

"When? It was in the spring. May. Sometime in the middle of May."

"Dates are inscribed in heaven," Fr. Dominic explained to Cordis.

"The middle of May," Fr. Jules repeated, mulling the date over. "May seventeenth is St. *Thérèse de Lisieux's* feast day. The Little Flower. She was born one hundred years ago — eighteen seventy-three. Most propitious."

"It could have been the seventeenth," Cordis acknowledged. "I'm not positive."

"St. Dymphna's feast day is also around that time — the fifteenth," the French priest added. "She's the patron saint of the mentally ill, your specialty."

"It might just as easily have been on the other side of the fifteenth," Cordis remarked jocularly, playing the devil's advocate. To himself he added, He's bound to run out of dates.

"May thirteenth — nineteen seventeen — was when the Virgin Mary appeared to three small children in Fatima, Portugal, an event the Church celebrates annually."

"Well, hmm, this may develop into a heavenly project then," Cordis said affably.

"Nothing like having the blessings of heaven, my boy," Fr. Dominic added.

The conversation came to an end near midnight. Cordis walked back to The Adams, thinking all the way about what the priests had said about heaven's silent hand in shaping the course of human events. Fate may be the eternal cause of things, he thought, but destiny, with an assist from above, is in our own hands. It's not for me to shape Renata's destiny, but perhaps to document her story when it has unfolded so that others may profit from it.

CHAPTER FORTY-SIX

Renata phoned Cordis the following day to inform him that she was going to New Orleans with Simone on a business trip and would miss her August 7th and 14th sessions. He wished her well.

There were two issues on his mind at that moment concerning his patient. She was much improved, to be sure, but Cordis wondered if her improvement represented only a transference cure — a flight into health. With treatment improvement of this type, the patient's symptoms evaporate, but not because she resolves her neurosis; instead, she surrenders up her symptoms as a defense against the probing of the therapist into painful, unconscious material.

Well, if it's real improvement, he thought, she won't buckle under when confronted by the next stressful incident in her life; and life never ceases to present us with stresses.

The second concern he had went back to something she had said near the end of her previous session. It was a casual statement, one with no therapeutic relevance and thus calling for no commentary from him. She mentioned how much she had enjoyed listening to Richter's performance of Brahms' Piano Concerto No. 1 in D Minor the night before. But at that moment he had felt a sudden chill. Once again now, after her phone call, he felt an uneasiness he couldn't explain.

"It has something to do with Brahms," he muttered under his breath. "The feeling just won't go away."

Cordis even stopped off at Sam Goody's for the Brahms record performed by Richter—he wouldn't accept any other recording, not even Leonard Bernstein's. He played it several times, but nothing came to him. He read up on the life of the composer, searching for a clue to account for his disquiet. Brahms had been born on May 7, 1833, in Hamburg. His own mother's birth date was May 7, 1899. The numbers were interesting, but numerologically he could do nothing with them. Hamburg was where Antje Haag was living and practicing psychoanalysis. He thought again about that strange twist of fate: Antje Haag, the daughter of a German general active in Hitler's army, who had selected a "Jewish profession" for herself. He had written to her only recently.

He pondered the final work of Brahms, *Vier ernste Gesänge* (Four Serious Songs), composed shortly before his death, where the composer had turned to the Bible for his texts. The final song, dealing with the sadness of death, had been taken from the first letter of Paul to the Corinthians. So he turned to the New Testament.

He liked the part—borrowed from Isaiah and Jeremiah—where he thought the apostle is at his best with his intuitive insights into God's secret purpose: " . . . we teach what Scripture calls: the things that no eye has seen and no ear has heard, things beyond the mind of man, all that God has prepared for those who love him . . . the very things that God has revealed to us through the Spirit, for the Spirit reaches the depths of everything, even the depths of God . . ."

What riveted his attention was the familiar statement by Paul on death, based on a passage from Hosea: "Death is swallowed up in victory. O death, where is thy sting? O grave, where is thy victory?"

Death is near, he said to himself. But whose death? It wasn't to be Renata's. No, I don't feel it in my viscera. Whose then?

Early Monday morning, the 13th of August, at the clinic, Cordis received a phone call from Simone in New Orleans.

"I don't know how you did it!" she said excitedly.

"Did what?" he asked.

"How did you do it?"

"I've got to know what I did before I can tell you how I did it."

"Renata attended mass yesterday!"

"Ah, the fruits of the therapeutic process," he said calmly. "But I didn't do it. She did it."

"Do you realize she hasn't done that since her father died?"

"Well," the doctor responded, "she's worked through some of her critical problems." To himself he added, I guess she has!

"That's what you did!"

Two days later when he returned to The Adams after work, he found a message to call Harris, which he promptly did. Harris was not in, but he had left a number on his recorder where he could be reached—Pierre's number.

Pierre answered the phone and said simply, "Celine is dead. We received the news a few hours ago, and we're packing in preparation for a morning flight to Paris. Here, I'll let you talk to Harris."

"Aieee, compañero, sad news," Harris said.

"What happened—stroke, heart attack?"

"Apparently a stroke from what I understand," Harris replied.

"Whew, what a blow!"

"Renata and Simone are returning from New Orleans, and all four of us will fly to Paris tomorrow."

"Renata must be taking this pretty hard," Cordis commented.

"That's the thing," Harris said. "I wonder if you can see her early in the morning. It might be good for her."

"Of course."

"I'll bring her to your office myself at seven, if that's all right."

"That'll be fine," he responded.

Cordis sat by the phone motionless for a while. Finally, he dialed Father Dominic's number.

"Death has claimed the body of the grande dame whose grand-daughter would journey into the numinous," he said, selecting his words carefully.

"When did she die?" the priest asked softly.

"This very day."

"For a devout Catholic, which apparently she was, she could not

212

have picked a better day to die."

"What is it in the Gregorian calendar that is so special about this day?"

"August the fifteenth commemorates the dormition of Mary. This is the day tradition has it she was assumed into heaven . . . for those who believe in the mystery of the Assumption."

"I suspect she did believe so."

"Then blessed is she, for her soul may have been assumed into heaven on the coattails of the Blessed Mother this very day."

"Ascended into heaven with Mary?"

"Jesus ascended into heaven," Father Dominic said, correcting him. "The Ascension of Jesus is celebrated forty days following Easter."

"I get it," the doctor said, "the distinction. So, she may have bypassed purgatory."

"It is not for me to say. But as Saint Paul said: 'For as in Adam all die, so in Christ all will be made to live.' "

After his conversation with Father Dominic, he found himself rereading a letter he had received from Celine Delacross only a few days earlier. In it she expressed her regret over the way she had dealt with him in New York and hoped he could find it in his heart to forgive her. Much of the letter was devoted to Renata and the improvement she had observed in her granddaughter's health. She closed on a note from T.S. Eliot's *The Cocktail Party*: " 'Protect her in the tumult / Protect her in the silence.' "

CHAPTER FORTY-SEVEN

Harris and Renata were already in his waiting room when Cordis arrived at the office the following morning. She was dressed in dark colors and looked pale and exhausted. Harris appeared tired, and said he had been up much of the night.

Once in his office alone with her doctor, Renata cried freely. She was self-accusatory, which came as no surprise to him.

"This mea culpa approach," he said softly, "is unwarranted. Your grandmother died because it was her time to die. Not because of you. How old was she—eighty-five?"

"Eighty-seven," she answered through her tears.

"The Bible allots us three score and ten years. Celine Delacross had seventeen bonus years. When the Lord chose to call, she came. And it had nothing to do with what you did or didn't do."

"I could have been kinder to her these past months—"

"You have nothing to feel guilty about."

"But I feel a sense of guilt."

"Why? Because you took up the struggle to save your own sanity and secure a measure of autonomy for yourself?"

"But my victory is her death, and I can find no peace in that."

"When that last trumpet finally sounds," Cordis said, "mortality gives way to immortality. She is at peace now in the bosom of her God."

"I keep reliving these last months in my mind," Renata said, searching for a way to change the outcome."

"The process of undoing is a normal phase of mourning," he explained.

"I still blame myself."

"You will continue to do so for a while, for what you are going through is a normal part of any grief reaction," Cordis said. Then remembering what Father Dominic had said about August 15th, he thought he would share it with Renata. "Your grandmother could not have picked a better day to die. Imagine, she died on the Feast Day of the Assumption of the Blessed Virgin Mary into heaven. Since death is the final act of life, one can say that hers was a good death."

"A good death," Renata repeated, barely above a whisper. She stopped crying and sat quietly for a minute or so. Finally, she spoke again, "I feel . . . lost. I don't know what to do?" She looked up at the psychiatrist and held his eyes for several seconds. "What am I to do?"

"Keep your soul in your body and wait for better days," Cordis responded. The words suddenly had a familiar ring to them. "You know something," he added, "I think I may have quoted John Thomson, Francis Thompson's biographer. A particular thought that obsessed Thompson while he was wandering through the gutters of London was that he had failed in his filial duty."

Renata stared at Cordis for a few seconds and then said, "So, we are back to 'The Hound of Heaven' once more." She sighed deeply.

Cordis went over to his book shelves and found his copy of Thompson's poetry. He thumbed through it while returning to his desk.

214

"I like this," he said, "John Thomson's statement of the poem: 'God's pursuit and conquest of the resisting soul that would find its satisfaction elsewhere than in Him.'"

"And is that what I have been doing—running away from God?" Renata asked, staring at him.

"I think your recent attendance at mass—Simone told me of that—is a step in the right direction . . . for you."

Then he began to read "The Hound of Heaven" aloud to her. His voice was strong and his recital clear. The poem's powerful imagery is unmatched in the English language, and only Shakespeare ranks above this remarkable poet in English letters.

Renata was attentive throughout the reading, and when Cordis finished she remained silent and motionless for several minutes. Then she whispered, " 'Seek the Kingdom of Heaven, and the rest will be given to you.' Those were Grandmama's last words to me."

She rose from her chair and Cordis did the same. As he was opening the door to the waiting room for her, she turned to smile at him. Harris was asleep in a sitting position.

"Safe journey, old friend," the doctor said, patting him on the shoulder.

Harris quickly responded, "Then we are off."

Cordis put his arms around Renata, saying, "May the God of all watch over you and keep you safe till we meet again."

CHAPTER FORTY-EIGHT

Harris called Cordis on the 27th, the day he returned from abroad, and they had dinner that night at Lüchow's.

"Renata decided to return to Casablanca with Simone and Pierre for a while," Harris said soon after they were seated.

"A good choice," Cordis commented.

'Strange thing about that old lady," Harris said softly. "When she phoned me that she was going to France, she said it was to attend a funeral. She didn't specify whose. Only that she had to visit someone she had known all her life who was about to die."

"Interesting," the doctor said, nodding slowly several times.

"You know, things had been strained between the two of us ever since I participated in Renata's release from the hospital—"

"Participated?" Cordis interrupted, smiling. "That's the understatement of the day."

"All right . . . organized," Harris corrected himself, also smiling. "But I went to the airport to see the three sisters off. I know Death when he is present . . . and he was there—make no mistake about it. But I didn't know for whom. Was he there for one of them or for someone in France as Celine had said?"

How Oriental to personify death, Cordis thought. No American would come up with anything like that in ordinary speech. So, Harris and I both had a premonition of impending death.

"It reminds me of a story they told about Croesus—"

"Who?" Harris asked.

"Croesus, a king of Lydia in the sixth century, B.C.," Cordis explained. "Jungians just love these tales from antiquity. Well, the Delphic oracle told the king that if he crossed a certain river, he would destroy a large kingdom."

"And what happened?"

"Croesus did. He crossed the river and was defeated in battle. And so it was his own kingdom that was destroyed."

The old Japanese nodded approvingly and said, "In my philosophy, her time had come, and now it is for the living to carry on."

"Yes, it is now Renata's time."

"I have to tell you something, compañero," Harris said, looking earnest. "Over the years the old lady seldom went against my advice, but she did object to my recommendation of having you treat Renata. Celine Delacross, in her own way, was a good person. But she had a blind spot— this hatred of the Jews. I don't know how to explain it."

"A theological scotoma," the psychiatrist said laughingly, deliberately trying to sound obscure. "Her judophobia never bothered me—I have a protective shield around my psyche. But, please, go on, Harris."

"I kept insisting you were the best choice, until it drove her to do a background check on you. Yes, she could be spiteful."

"Ha," Cordis let out, feeling somewhat defensive.

"And she was thorough. She even showed me the report she got. First off, she complained you were too inexperienced—you had only finished your psychiatric specialty training two years ago."

"That's true," Cordis said, feeling even more uncomfortable.

216

"She did a good job. For instance, she also found out you were in the export-import business before and during your medical school days—"

"What!" the doctor shouted.

"And that you turned down the chance to introduce the first of those hand-held medicated inhalers for asthma into the United States market, a product distributed by Hico of Cologne, Germany."

"She found out all that?" Cordis said, incredulous.

"Yes," Harris replied. "As I said, she was thorough. That was her way in all matters pertaining to business."

"Well, it's true. I could have made a great deal of money with that product. But it was back in the summer of nineteen sixty, the time I met Antje Haag . . . in Amsterdam. I saw her again a few weeks later in Cologne, where I had to go to talk to the people at Hico; in fact, she went with me to their office. Yes, I could have had the entire American territory for the Hico inhaler. Could have gotten in on the ground floor. But I balked. It was only fifteen years after the War, and I found I just couldn't bring myself to do business with the Germans."

"And you sacrificed your entire financial security."

"Oh yes, I became pauperized."

"The old lady looked at it differently. She thought you were frivolous with money, and she was afraid you would sink your clutches into Renata and gain access to her fortune."

"How was I supposed to do that?" Cordis asked, finding it harder to conceal his mounting discomfort.

"She thought you would figure out a way to marry her."

"She seriously entertained such a worry, Harris? Wow!"

"There was more to it," the old Japanese responded. "That plus her hatred of Jews and the clouding of her judgement following a stroke she had. Well, anyway, it sounds very paranoid, doesn't it?"

"Well, let's call it . . . negatively imaginative."

"Later on, when she saw how much Renata had improved under your care, she changed her attitude toward you. In the end, she actually *liked* you. And I think she died happy."

" 'If that is not a happy death, then what death is happy?' " the psychiatrist said, borrowing a line from Eliot's Sir Henry Harcourt-Reilly. "You know, old friend, I had promised her at that dinner party that I would do everything within my power to restore Renata to health—physical, mental and spiritual health. So she went to meet her Maker knowing the process was well underway."

"I think she had a good death," Harris said with Japanese somberness. "Yes, a good death."

217

CHAPTER FORTY-NINE

The month was drawing to a close. On August 29th, Cordis was on the NBC-TV "Today" show. He and Dr. Mitch Rosenthal, director of Phoenix House, one of the nation's largest drug rehabilitation programs, discussed the drug epidemic that had been spreading across America since the early 1960's. Cordis concentrated his remarks on cannabis, his area of growing expertise within the field of drug abuse.

Later, at the clinic, several of the social workers had harsh words to say about his comments on television, accusing him of overstating the health hazards associated with smoking marijuana.

"When the clinic becomes The Retreat, then you can smoke all the pot you want in the potty room," he said to the pro-marijuana trio confronting him. "Until then it's verboten." It irked him whenever his nostrils detected the odor of marijuana smoke in the clinic's bathroom.

There was a new patient, Macko X. Devereux, for Cordis to see at 11 o'clock. He turned out to be the man who tried to mug him and Harris back in January! Much to Cordis' surprise, and satisfaction, he *had* entered a drug-treatment program, and had recently been referred to the clinic for help in dealing with a new drug problem: alcohol. Cordis had a name for the substitution of one drug of abuse for another—the laterality effect.

Macko had given methadone a try for three months, but decided, heroically, Cordis considered, to become completely drug-free.

"Methadone is just another narcotic," he explained to the psychiatrist, "only in this case sanctioned by society. I believe I can do better than just play the substitution game."

When Cordis heard that his patient was enrolled in a computer programming course, he decided to set aside the memory of that unpleasant winter night and work with Macko to the best of his ability—his initial impulse had been to shunt him to Dr. Judd Axelman, who had recently replaced Dr. Schlosberg.

"You and that little Japanese fellow really brought me to my senses," Macko said, thinking back to the night in January when he had encountered the two.

He considered physical courage the supreme virtue. Even his name had a martial origin, which he could trace back to African ancestors who had been illustrious warriors. When he happened to mention the movie *Zulu*, he was surprised to find that his doctor was familiar with the life

218

of Shaka, who had forged the Zulu nation in the last century.

"How come you know so much about Shaka?" he asked.

"I read a lot," Cordis replied.

Actually, he had heard about the legendary Zulu ruler years earlier while at St. Andrews from several of his African classmates.

"I'm gonna have to read more myself," Macko said.

As noon approached, Cordis said, "I think you ought to give Antabuse a try for a month or so to help get you started building up some sobriety time, and I also recommend that you get into AA. I'm going to be seeing you once a week at eleven on Wednesday's."

"Thanks, Doc," Macko said. "They hurled me into a pit when I was born, where I have remained all my life, but I'm beginning to realize that a lot of people have made it out of the pits."

Macko's insightfulness and motivation impressed Cordis. "That computer course of yours makes a great shovel," he said. "You're on your way up and out into the world."

Cordis didn't take Wednesday afternoons off to play golf, but was in his office seeing patients from two until five. Of the three young women with drug problems whom he used to see Monday evenings, only Sonja Olamstein, the CUNY student, was still in therapy. The foul-mouthed patient who had compared him to a dog never returned, and the young lady who had accused him of "only listening" dropped out after one more session. Neither one had as yet paid her bill. The Monday roster, now moved up to Wednesday afternoon, included Sonja and two new patients, one with a drug problem and another suffering from "religious doubts," as she had phrased her chief complaint—Renata was not the only Catholic patient he had with a conflict in this particular sphere.

Her name was Sylvia Blank, and she was a pretty blond in her early twenties. She did smoke an occasional reefer and had tried LSD once, but she claimed drugs were not a problem for her. Her faith was.

It was 4:15, and she was saying to Cordis, "The Bible—the New Testament—has Jesus preaching that if your hand causes you to sin, then you should cut it off, because you're better off with one less hand in this life than winding up in hell with two. The same holds true for your foot and your eye—pluck out your sinning eye, because that way you can still make it into heaven."

She was paraphrasing from Mark.

"It's designed to make a dramatic point, Cordis commented. "No one expects you to react so drastically to your own recognition of a suspected sin. In our society only schizophrenics go all the way like that—cutting off body parts to atone for sins real or imagined—and you're not schizophrenic. As a Catholic, you have the confessional for the resolution of sin."

She could see some merit in his interpretation, but as she proceeded it became clear that her religious problems were more broadly based. Still referring to the New Testament, again from Mark, she was critical of the manner in which Jesus answered the question about divorce put to him by several Pharisees.

She commented, "Jesus told them that God created man and woman, and they are to go out from their home to unite and become like one body."

"What God has joined together, let no man put asunder," Cordis said. "Yes, I'm familiar with that."

"Although society allows for divorce, my church does not."

"It provides an out through annulment."

Sylvia got to the heart of her discussion.

"I don't want to be blended into anybody," she said defiantly. "I want to be me. I'm a person with my own identity, my own individuality."

"So that's the crux of the problem, of the conflict."

She had a boyfriend, a regular mass-attending Catholic, who wanted to marry her, but she was going to college and was planning on a career.

"I don't want to be smothered in a holy union," she said. "I want more out of life than *Kinder*, kitchen and cooking."

"Another hard c—career."

"Yes."

"The two—a life of domesticity and career—aren't necessarily incompatible."

"Do you realize, Dr. Cordis, that the divorce rate is now one out of three marriages?"

"Yes. Going up to one out of two, I'm told."

"Few women are capable of juggling both lives. Still fewer, like Katharine Hepburn, make the wise decision to forgo marriage and concentrate on their career, because they don't believe a woman can manage both successfully."

"So we know how Katharine Hepburn handled her choices."

"You're supposed to help me handle mine," Sylvia said, raising her voice.

"Ah, I wish it were so simple," the psychiatrist responded. "You have your choices, but you must choose."

"I have so many, I don't know which to choose."

"From the existential perspective, we have many choices in this life,

220

but the ground into which we are thrown does limit us all."

"I'm free, white and twenty-one—and I want the world!" she said exuberantly, thrusting her arms out into the air.

"Still, you're a woman, and the ground of existence for a woman is not the same as for a man."

"Why is the *ground* necessarily different for a woman?" she asked, accentuating *ground* scornfully.

"Sex defines to an inescapable degree the possibilities of one's existence."

"But today's woman rejects the limitations and restrictions traditionally imposed on her."

"True, but women, and only women, still bear the babies, and men are still the fertilizers and the hunters, although dressed in modern garb and less noticeably pugnacious than their forebears."

"Well, my ground of existence may be different from a man's, but I don't see where that by itself imposes limitations on my goals."

"It does us all," Cordis said, "because throwness dictates who our parents will be in the first place. We have no control over our lineage, and that is the most important ground of all. Beginning with what you are, you must live out your destiny to authenticate your life."

"I am in the world to get everything I can out of life," Sylvia said. "That's what I'm authenticating."

"There are modes of being-in-the-world," Cordis said.

"Is that four words or a four-in-one hyphenation?" she asked.

"Hyphenated," Cordis replied, smiling for a moment. "It's existentialist talk."

"And what's the best mode?"

"You have to choose," the doctor answered. "You have already cast aspersions on the dual mode, that of two people who love one another—the 'I' and 'thou' becoming the 'we.'"

"What other choices do I have?"

"Another option is the singular mode, the one Katharine Hepburn, as you say, chose."

"Anything else?"

"You can immerse yourself in the crowd and live the mode of anonymity."

"Well, the 'I' and 'thou' becoming 'us,' two halves incomplete needing union to make each other whole, is now the old-fashioned mode and on its way out."

"It's the time-honored mode which your church still presents as a first choice."

"My generation has been raised on Sartre, not the Bible, and he stresses freedom. Thanks to Sartre, I can shout, 'I have my freedom!'" She did shout the words, and once again raised her arms in the air.

"Freedom without a sense of personal responsibility, which is what we're seeing today, will lead to social disintegration."

"The Constitution guarantees us the right to life, liberty and the pursuit of happiness. I'm availing myself of my rights."

"Right. But you can learn something about rights from the Barotse tribe of Rhodesia, who live by the concept of *Swanelo*, the balance between rights and duties."

The session went on in that vein for another fifteen minutes, with neither giving ground. It ended in a draw.

These Hunter College women are really something, Cordis said to himself afterwards. Tough as nails. God help the future of this country if all the women are being shaped this way!

CHAPTER FIFTY

Labor Day was on the 3rd, and two days later things got a bit out of hand at the clinic. Dr. Armazón-Goldstein was yelling at Dr. Arnold Grossman in front of the patients in the waiting room when Cordis arrived at 9:10. She was accusing him of cheating on the red-line sign-in sheets. The CSEA rep had lost the clinic's case, and emboldened by the outcome, the director was clamping down on late arriving staff. That morning Dr. Grossman had arrived before 9:00, but she was taking him to task for all the times he had been coming in after 9:15.

"It's embarrassing to have the boss lady chew you out with all the patients as onlookers," he said to Cordis afterwards, his cheeks flushed. "And it's anti-therapeutic."

"Obviously, coming in fifteen minutes earlier doesn't build up credit for arriving after nine fifteen in her way of thinking," Cordis responded.

"But to attack me on a day when I'm here well before nine," Grossman persisted, "that's plain bitchiness."

While they were carrying on their conversation outside Grossman's office, one of the young Puerto Rican typists came up to them with an issue of her own. The clerical workers had failed to get a promised raise, and they were talking about striking.

"Are you doctors with us if we strike?" she asked them.

"It's something to think about," Grossman answered diplomatically.

"If you try to cross the picket line, expect to be roughed up," she said tersely. "We're talkin' about a raise due us—blood money."

"State workers aren't allowed to strike," Cordis said coolly. "The Taylor Law prohibits it."

Cordis' phone was ringing, and before she could comment he was on his way to his office to answer it.

The call was from a community psychiatrist in Miami who said, "We've got a Joseph Dee here at our clinic who says you're his doctor. He ran out of medication and wants us to give him Taractan and Haldol."

"Give him some Thorazine and Stelazine," Cordis said, sighing deeply. "What the heck is he doing in Miami?"

"He has no money and he's living on the beach."

"Look," Cordis said, "buy him a plane ticket and send him back to LaGuardia. I'll take up a collection and wire you the plane fare by noon. Just make sure your people put him on the plane. Please."

Cordis had difficulty getting his fellow doctors and the other clinic personnel to chip in for Joey's plane ticket. They had other things on their mind—the talk about an impending strike, Grossman on the phone to complain about Dr. Armazón Goldstein, the director sulking in her office and screaming to someone on her telephone, an out-of-control patient in the waiting room who required manacling by Pete and then transportation to Bellevue—and few employees seemed to care about Joey, anyway. Cordis wound up contributig the bulk of the money himself, and after his session with Macko Devereux, a good one, stopped off at Western Union to wire the funds to the Miami clinic.

In the afternoon he resumed his dialogue with Sylvia Blank.

"Our psychology prof has us reading Sullivan," she said. "Can't stand the man."

"Who? Your professor or Harry Stack Sullivan?"

"Sullivan," she answered. "Do you know what he had to say about modern women—and in the thirties?"

"What?"

"He said the career-oriented woman was out to become 'a man

223

among men.' The nerve!''

"What?"

"The nerve!"

"Oh, I thought you said, 'the nerd.'" That elicited a smile from Sylvia. "Yes, I know. Sullivan on masculine-oriented females in his *Personal Psychopathology*."

"He may have a point or two," Sylvia conceded, "but today's woman doesn't want to wind up being only a baby factory."

"Does a man want to be only a war machine?" Cordis asked.

"Why do you bring that up?"

"That's been his role for thousands of years. Tens of thousands. In fact, it's been that way for so long, it's inscribed in his genes and thus carved into his brain. The same can be said for the historical, and prehistorical, path women have trodden."

"Don't misunderstand me," Sylvia said, appearing to give ground. "I'm not saying I resent the fact I've been designed for motherhood—"

"Constructed anatomically and physiologically for that prime role," Cordis interjected.

"But I want to do something in life besides contribute to the world's population."

"Yes, of course," the doctor said. "Another role. And there you have your choices. In your case, with your intelligence and beauty and sensitivity, you have more choices than most of your contemporaries." He was being generous by including sensitivity among her attributes.

"Thank you for the compliment," Sylvia said. "I'll take all the ego-stroking I can get." She paused for a moment and then commented, "You think of men as war machines?"

"Whatever God's design for us, he organized our development through nature. Survival—so that we would make it to where we are today—required specialization within the species. Much of that specialized functioning is now in the genes and tucked away in the brain. It won't just disappear because of one vocal group's existential disenchantment."

"Dr. Cordis, do you realize that NOW would label you a sexist?" Sylvia said, laughing.

"Naturally," the psychiatrist responded. "A sexist is a person—male or female—who is still able to acknowledge differences between the sexes."

"*Vive la difference!*"

"You know, another patient of mine once uttered those very words to me in this chamber."

"Well, Dr. Cordis," Sylvia started to say, returning to her major point of the previous session, "I don't think I can regulate my life according to the Bible's dictates."

"The Bible is for those who would live in a world governed by the laws of God."

"Who is to say what God's laws are?"

Cordis collected his thoughts and responded, "That's the contemporary position . . . and dilemma, an attitude which attempts to deny the past, the linkage in the continuity of man, or humankind, if you prefer. If you're involved in the Judeo-Christian tradition, then you can find God's laws in the Bible. That, at least, is one place for you to look."

"You mean, for example, the Ten Commandments."

"Why not?" he responded. "And you can count them off on ten fingers, if you've got the normal complement."

"Of course I have ten fingers," Sylvia said emphatically.

"See how normal you are!"

Cordis allowed the session to run overtime, since he thought Sylvia was beginning to show signs of being less dogmatic in her views, and he had no one following her at five. Besides, he enjoyed the give-and-take with women who were involved in the National Organization for Women. The women's movement was running wild in 1973, he felt, and there was hardly any response to it from the other half of humanity, save for capitulation.

CHAPTER FIFTY-ONE

September moved along quickly. There was no strike at the clinic. Grossman and Armazón-Goldstein avoided one another as much as possible; and the director added a second stripe to the red line drawn across the sign-in sheet. Joey Dee returned to New York, a fact confirmed for Cordis by his social worker.

Renata wrote Cordis about every ten days during the month, always saying she was well and was working on plans for the future. In the first letter she mentioned that she had received news of his appearance on the "Today" program and was "thrilled to have a celebrity as my doctor." The third letter in the series arrived October 1st, the day before he left for Europe on vacation: he had purchased his airline tickets to Madrid near the end of August, planning to stay with Maria Anastasia and her family for ten days.

Maria Anastasia had been Freddie Grutman's fiancee in the "old days" in Mexico. Although Freddie's body had never been recovered from the Matto Grosso, there came a moment when she knew in her heart that he was dead. Over the years she had kept in touch with Cordis by letter and by phone, always apprised of his whereabouts by the ever-resourceful Harris Hashimoto. She had a need to cling to the memory of Freddie, and in Cordis, who bore a remarkable resemblance to him, she maintained her link to her past.

In Mexico Maria had been a nurse. In Madrid she devoted herself to her two adolescent daughters and her foreign-service husband, while teaching English at the high-school level. Now middle-aged and plump, she nevertheless still had the same allure that had caught the eye, and heart, of Freddie in her youth.

"This is *El Hombre*, the man who loved the beautiful Ramona, there in the hills of northern Mexico," she said to her family at the dinner table. "He and the Freddie I have told you so much about could have passed for identical twins. What a fearless duo!" She then proceeded to recount several of the Chihuahua adventures of "our own Clint Eastwood and his double."

"Those stories sound so much better now than when they happened," Cordis said laughingly. "However, I think you have embellished them just a bit, for which I thank you."

"That, Doctor, is how legends are born," added Señor Anastasia.

"He's too modest, my dear," Maria said. "It was he—*El Hombre*—who dashed into a burning shack in Juarez along the Rio Bravo to save a small child. If that were to happen today, he would be on television and the mayor would honor him with a medal."

"We shall honor him with a toast," said her husband, and they all three took a sip of fine Spanish wine after clicking glasses.

"What happend to the beautiful Ramona—?" the younger of the two daughters started to ask, but her mother, switching to Spanish, adroitly changed the conversation to another topic.

The next day Maria took him on a tour of her school. They entered a large lecture hall where a history class was in progress and listened to a 15-year-old in the middle of her recitation.

" . . . and in eleven fifty [one thousand one hundred fifty is the way it is said in Spanish] the Count of Catalonia, Ramon Berenguer the Fourth,

226

married Petronilla, the daughter of Ramiro the Monk, chosen to rule Aragon following the death of his brother, Alfonso the Warrior. Ramiro then returned to his monastery and Ramon became King of Aragon and Catalonia."

"My gosh," Cordis whispered to Maria, "so accomplished at such a tender age."

"Ah, so you remember enough Spanish to follow her," she whispered back.

Another girl in the same age group was now reciting: "Alfonso the Learned retook the Kingdom of Murcia from the Moors in the year twelve sixty-six with the help of James the First of Aragon. He devalued the *real* to relieve poverty in the land, a move which led to economic ruin . . ."

"How extraordinary!" Cordis exclaimed as they slipped out of the hall. "I can't even fathom contemporary economic theory, and I'm three times her age."

"In America," Maria said, "anything older than fourteen ninety-two isn't history, it's archeology."

"Academically, our schoolchildren can't begin to compare to the students here," the doctor said.

"In one more generation you will see that education, not the might of arms, is the key to the future."

"*D'accord*," Cordis said in French, unable to think of the correct Spanish.

"Wrong language," Maria said and laughed.

Then remembering, Cordis quickly said, "*De seguro.* I agree."

"Now I shall set up your social calendar for your stay in Madrid," Maria said, walking arm in arm with him. "Harris mentioned recently that you date a steady stream of internationals at the United Nations. You should have come to Madrid sooner."

"Ah, so you keep that pipeline to Harris open!"

"He suggested I look around for someone suitable—that's how he worded it—for you. He doesn't want you marrying a Japanese and spending the rest of your life with a *mamasan*."

" 'Matchmaker, matchmaker, make me a match,' " Cordis sang out, from *Fiddler On the Roof*.

He was just beginning to enjoy his Madrid stay when war broke out in the Middle East on October 6, Yom Kippur, the Day of Atonement, the holiest day in the Jewish calendar.

"I nearly went to fight for Israel in forty-eight, when I was nineteen," he explained to the Anastasias. "Now, as a doctor, I would be even more useful—if it comes to that. The Arabs can afford to lose their wars; Israel

227

cannot survive one such loss."

Maria and her husband understood. On Monday, the 8th, Cordis flew back to New York.

CHAPTER FIFTY-TWO

Caught off guard initially, the Israelis retreated on the Egyptian front. Gradually they regained the upper hand and threatened to crush the main Egyptian army—Soviet-trained and equipped—when the Soviets made it known to Washington that they were ready to airborne troops to the region to save their client, which then brought the war to an end.

Sylvia Blank had interrupted her weekly sessions in order to prepare for the new college year, and now—on October 10th and following Cordis' return from Europe—resumed.

She was dressed in tight-fitting jeans and wore a pull-over sweater that accentuated her bosomy contours. She had not thus far in her therapy been sexually provocative toward Cordis, and he assumed she had dressed so alluringly for the benefit of the male students she encountered at Hunter.

Sylvia fidgeted with her cigarette case and asked Cordis if she could smoke, well aware of his no-smoking policy in the office. It was not long before she started asking him questions about whether marijuana had any health effects. She had previously denied any problem with cannabis, admitting only to infrequent use.

"You're taking pot luck with your ovaries," Cordis responded to her question about the action of marijuana on reproductive functioning.

"What does it do for the male?" she asked, resorting to avoidance.

"Not 'for' but to," Cordis replied. "It 'doth quench geniture,' as Dioscorides wrote in the first century, and it 'dryeth up the sperm,' as Galen noted the following century."

"But it doesn't affect the brain, does it?" she asked hesitantly.

"If it didn't, you wouldn't experience the high, would you?"

Sylvia had heard from more than one of his other patients—several

228

were friends of hers—about his views on marijuana, particularly its central-nervous system effects.

"So it's bad for your brain."

"The cannabinoids in pot interfere with protein synthesis, among other metabolic processes, going on in brain cells," he said. "Protein synthesis is necessary for the fixation of short-term memory into long-term memory, and even in short-term memory you have to have a registration step initially which cannabinoids—"

She wouldn't let him finish the sentence. "And marijuana interferes with that, too, is that it?" she said in an unsteady voice.

"Yes."

Regaining her composure, Sylvia attempted to go on the offensive. "This presupposes that protein synthesis in the brain is involved in the memorization process."

"Learning in the broader sense," Cordis said. "There are a lot of things going on in the brain affected by protein synthesis besides learning. And protein synthesis goes on all the time, everywhere in the body, not only in the brain."

"But you are able to present marijuana's role in adversely affecting memory only as an hypothesis," Sylvia said, stressing "only."

Hunter College obstinacy and belligerence, he thought to himself. "Supported by laboratory evidence," he said to her.

"From humans?"

"No, animal models."

"You mean rats, mice, monkeys, spiders?"

"In this case, *Tetrahymena*."

"What's that?" she asked quizzically.

"A protozoan. A good model cellular system for studying the action of tetrahydrocannabinol, or THC for short. The Zimmermans, up at the University of Toronto, have found that THC causes a reduction of DNA, RNA and protein synthesis in this little fellow."

"This little fellow," she repeated mockingly. "*Tetrahymena*. And so you're actually reasoning by extension, applying their data, the Zimmerbergs—"

"The Zimmermans," Cordis corrected her.

"Applying their data collected from a protozoan to the human brain. How do you know if this THC of yours will have a similar effect on, say, the laboratory rat brain? That would come a bit closer to reality than protozoan research."

"There are quite a few researchers who have injected known inhibitors of protein synthesis—puromycin and acetoxycycloheximide—into the brains of mice, and they have found a failure to learn.''

"Learn what?" Sylvia asked demandingly.

"The standard testing such lab experimenters employ. Like learning how to avoid an electric shock.''

"And if they do fail to learn to avoid an electric shock, why do they fail to learn?''

"These two chemicals in particular are often used by neurochemists in memory testing. They are known to prevent protein synthesis for several hours. And puromycin has been shown to cause electrical seizures in the hippocampus, a region of the brain associated with memory.''

"So you're reasoning by analogy," Sylvia said, "by extension. You're surmising that THC acts like puromycin and that other thing on the brain.''

"Acetoxycycloheximide.''

"Yes. Acet—whatever," she said, unable to pronounce the word. "That's actually jumping over a lot of necessary in-between experiments, I should think. And protein synthesis in the human brain is supposed to be the key to learning, is that right?''

"It's part of the process," Cordis responded. "Learning is far too complicated to be dealth with simplistically.''

"Your reasoning leaves much to the imagination," Sylvia said haughtily.

"There's clinical evidence to support the thinking that people who smoke pot compromise their learning ability," Cordis said, not yielding.

"Clinical?''

"What clinicians—practicing physicians—find in their patients.''

The Middle East is on fire and we sit here debating—that's what it amounts to—the issue of marijuana's harmful effects, something enlightened Arabs came to understand centuries ago, Cordis mused.

He was prepared to continue the discussion, but Sylvia returned to a theme from her previous session.

"Getting back to something we were talking about last month," she said, "ancient man clubbing his way into the present, you're saying that the Ice Age made us into what we are.''

"Yes, modern man is a product of the Pleistocene.''

"That's the cutting edge.''

"True. The glacial experience turned man into a carnivore hunting the wooly rhinoceros, mammoth, bison, saber-toothed tiger. Meat—topnotch protein—put meat on his own bones and advanced his brain. Had he remained in the savannah picking berries and eating legumes, his destiny would have been retarded.''

"The hunter is in his genes—in the males'.''

230

"It fell to the males to bring home the bacon, which the women cooked."

"In the lair where they were caring for the babies."

"Where they were caring for the very young, for whom survival was far more precarious then than it is now, for life was Darwinian."

"The fittest survived," Sylvia said. "And woman in her hearth— with her genes—felt right at home."

"Well, well, you're mastering Pleistocene psycho-physiology with nary a drop of perspiration."

"I don't think this thesis of yours will hold much appeal to the NOW membership," she said, shaking her head.

"Ah, but the purpose here is not to add fuel to the raging female-male feud," Cordis said, waving a finger in the air.

"No?"

"No, no. This has to do with God and man—mankind, humankind."

"I don't follow."

"God has been watching over us for a long, long time, waiting— " and Cordis paused.

"Waiting for what?" Sylvia asked, curiosity evident in her expression.

"For the human race to come of age . . . to become . . . godly."

CHAPTER FIFTY-THREE

Ruby Lokko had written Cordis in August that a magazine writer friend of hers from Kampala would be in New York in the fall and would like to talk to him about Dr. Robert W. Felkin, a 19th century British explorer in Africa. He arrived in October, and Cordis arranged to see him in his office on the 23rd.

"So you want to talk about old Bunyoro," he said to his guest.

Fred Banner was a short, chubby Ugandan whose dark brown skin glistened like a polished apple, and the bright colors of his shirt and tie shimmered when caught by the sunlight. Cordis found his urbanity refreshing.

'Ruby told me that you wrote an article about Felkin last year," he said. "Not many Westerners have heard of Bunyoro."

There are no clues to the medical glory of Bunyoro in the common works that cite the names of places. The various popular dictionaries and encyclopedias in use do not even list it. But in the last century this east-central African kingdom showed the world that there was a shining light in what was called the Dark Continent.

The Kingdom of Bunyoro-Kitara was a large and powerful African state which developed in the regions between Lakes Albert and Edward and Lakes Victoria and Kyoga. In its heyday during the sixteenth to the eighteenth centuries, its boundaries finally became overextended and the authority of its *kabaka* (king) began to weaken. Ascendancy passed to Buganda, a smaller state to the south, which expanded at the expense of Bunyoro-Kitara. Both Bunyoro and Buganda are today parts of the Republic of Uganda.

Cut off from the rest of Africa for centuries by forbidding boundaries, things began to change in this region in the 1840's, when the first Arab traders reached Buganda, there to trade in ivory and slaves. The first Europeans to visit Buganda were John H. Speke and James A. Grant, the British explorers who discovered the source of the Nile River at Lake Victoria in 1862. The Anglo-American explorer, Henry Morton Stanley, reached Buganda in 1875, calling it "the pearl of Africa."

In 1879 Robert Felkin, a British physician, visited the village of Katura, then in Bunyoro but now a part of Buganda. There, in the pre-aseptic era, only two years after Jacob Lister had moved to London to spread his gospel of antisepsis, Felkin witnessed a caesarean section performed by an African surgeon.

The patient, a twenty-year-old in her first pregnancy, half intoxicated with banana wine, was tied down to a bed by bands of bark cloth. Two assistants helped maintain her in the proper surgical postition. The surgeon washed his hands and the patient's abdomen with banana wine and then water. After muttering an incantation he adroitly made an incision from the umbilicus down to the pubis through the abdominal wall and uterus, so deft that the amniotic fluid gushed out with one swipe of the surgeon's knife. Bleeding points in the abdominal wall were touched sparingly with red hot irons by one of the assistants. The infant was removed, the cord cut, the baby handed to an assistant, and the placenta removed with skilled fingers. The uterus was not sutured, but squeezed manually till it contracted. A porous grass mat was secured tightly over the wound and the patient positioned so as to facilitate drainage of fluid from the abdomen. Finally, the wound was closed with seven well-polished spikes and string. Mother and child were doing well eleven days later when Felkin had to leave.

What impressed Felkin was that the operation was conducted by a long-practiced surgical team working smoothly and with unhurried skill. Lister and his assistants back in London couldn't have done better. Somehow, here in darkest Africa there was an appreciation of antiseptic surgery among the Banyoro medical men, perhaps even a pre-vision of aseptic surgery.

The Banyoro were a preliterate people. All that is known about their medical skills is what Felkin wrote and transmitted to Western doctors. Felkin was a religious man of unquestioned integrity. He never retracted his account of what he witnessed in the middle of Africa in 1879.

"Do you think it's true?" Banner asked after Cordis had recounted what he knew of the Felkin story.

"Dr. Henry Sigerist, the eminent medical historian," he responded, "includes Felkin's account in his canonical *The History of Medicine*."

Banner smiled and said, "But even the Bible is subject to scrutiny."

"Some things you've got to believe."

"In my research on Bunyoro," the Ugandan said, "I came across a *kabaka* by the name of Kabarega who commissioned Yangoma, well known for his medical skills, to make experiments in the interest of science in order to try to cure an epidemic of sleeping sickness. That was in eighteen eighty-six."

"Much like President Nixon asking the National Institute of Mental Health to seek out a cure for schizophrenia."

Banner laughed heartily. "Why, yes, of course!"

As they were saying good-by, Cordis mentioned to his visitor, "The knife used in the case of the caesarean section in eighteen seventy-nine was presented by Dr. Felkin to the late Sir Henry Wellcome and is now in the Wellcome Historical Medical Museum in London. You might want to stop by there on your way home to take a look at it."

CHAPTER FIFTY-FOUR

Sylvia Blank switched from weekly sessions to one every two weeks because of the cost factor, and she preferred the fifty-minute hour to weekly thirty-minute sessions offered her as an alternative.

She may have presented initially with a chief complaint of "religious doubts," but her problems, from the amount of time she was spending discussing marijuana, obviously went beyond theological considerations.

Sylvia began her October 24th session by asking Cordis about the "finger test" used to detect the presence of marijuana.

"There's more than one, actually," the psychiatrist responded.

"Is the procedure very technical?" she asked.

"Nothing to it," he said. "You extract the cannabinoids present on the fingers of smokers with a little chloroform, a commonly employed fat solvent, and then develop a color by adding a particular reagent to the extraction. The intensity of the color is then measured by a colorimeter, a simple-to-operate lab device, which tells you how much cannabinoid material you have."

It was the old analytical chemist speaking, and he relished the opportunity to talk chemistry, something he rarely got to do in his practice.

"That's it?"

"Yes. So you see, you can establish the presence of marijuana, a qualitative test, and also determine how much of it is there, a quantitative test."

"Those cannabinoids you mentioned," Sylvia said.

"Yes. In addition to THC, the psychoactive component, there are several dozen of these chemicals present in the hemp plant, and I doubt if any of them are up to any good."

"Well, if you wash your hands after smoking a joint," she angled, "you can get around the problem."

"You've got to wash your mouth out also," Cordis retorted.

"I thought you were describing the finger test."

"It works for saliva, too."

"Then just rinse your mouth out after smoking."

"If you have the presence of mind while high to do so. After an hour you're safe—it can no longer be detected in saliva or mouth washings."

"What's the time limit for the fingers?" she asked, exhibiting the thoroughness of a cross-examining lawyer.

"About three hours. There's another reagent, by the way, they use that can detect cannabinoids in dead bodies, like those found floating in the river . . . even days later."

"You mean dead men tell their tales," Sylvia said laughingly. "I've heard about that test. It gives a positive reaction with something as commonplace as coffee, so it's inadmissable in a court of law."

"What are you . . . preparing for the bar exam or a chemistry quiz?" he asked jovially.

"I hate chemistry," she responded in a similar vein. "I dropped my freshman course after one week."

"Well, you had the old Duquenois test in mind. We've got better testing methods these days, but, given the current state of the art, cannabinoid testing is still inadequate."

The more sophisticated methods, such as radioimmunoassay and gas chromotography-mass spectroscopy, which would assume prominence in the '80's, were in the making in 1973; but Cordis didn't want to turn the session into a lecture on analytical chemistry, so he stopped there.

"What art?" she asked.

"The art I practice: medicine."

"I thought it was a science."

"The practice of medicine is an art, a very old art, which now incorporates what is useful from the realm of science."

"And here I thought you were a psychiatrist," Sylvia said looking nonplussed.

"First I'm a physician," the doctor responded, "then a specialist in the area of psychiatry."

"Thanks for straightening me out on that," she said cheerfully. "You know, I only recently figured out the difference between an intern and an internist."

Even for an intelligent person like Sylvia Blank, Cordis had found widespread confusion surrounding the psychiatrist's identity.

After a short pause, Sylvia continued, still staying on the marijuana theme.

"Do they do much marijuana research on humans?" she asked.

"If you can get the volunteers," he replied. "Certainly in psychiatry you need human subjects, given the subjective nature of the effects of pot on the mind. Research animals don't tell you what's going on inside their cranium. If Rhesus monkeys could talk, maybe they would tell us that rock 'n' roll music is murder to listen to without pot."

She snickered and said, "See, even you have found something good to say about marijuana!"

235

"Save the sophistry for your schoolteachers," Cordis retorted. "From what I have been able to gather, I would say that pot is neuronicidal—it kills brain cells. Every time you light up a joint, you destroy a few of those precious cells within your skull. And as far as we know, they don't grow back up there once they're dead."

"It's a small matter," Sylvia retorted. "You have billions and billions of brain cells in your head you never use, anyway. You may kill a few with marijuana—if it's true, as you say—but marijuana makes so many brain cells you've never used before come alive."

What a tough cookie to crack, Cordis said to himself. "The proper nourishment of brain cells," he said to her, "does not include the repetitive introduction of cannabis and other noxious chemicals into their substance. All these so-called recreational drugs which have hit the contemporary scene are psychotoxins."

"Your thesis is powerful, Dr. Cordis," she said calmly, "but your supporting evidence is weak."

She won't admit it, but I have to think she smokes the stuff regularly, he mused.

"Your God has endowed you with free will—that's what the Garden of Eden tale was all about—and you are indeed free-willing it," Cordis said.

The mere mention of God changed Sylvia's countenance.

"You have invoked the Deity," she said glumly, "and the Garden of Eden, where his retinue romped, not unlike Zeus, ruler of the heavens, and his Olympians. Which is the true heaven: the Garden of Eden or Olympus?"

"It's convenient for now to conjure up a cosmic dwelling place for the Deity," Cordis replied, "until the time we can fathom him at a deeper level."

"Very abstract, Dr. Cordis," Sylvia said with a note of bitterness, "and all very abstruse—I mean, some of the statements in the Bible. For instance, last night I was reading John, and Jesus says, 'It is easier for a camel to go through the eye of a needle than for a rich man to enter the kingdom of God.' Well, heck, who is heaven for—beggars?"

When she didn't continue, Cordis said, "In the first place, Jesus liked to use hyperbole. He's not talking about the eye of a sewing needle. Second, he's referring to excess baggage—worldly goods and concerns. If you want to enter his kingdom, shed yourself of earthly matters and turn to the spiritual. As for a camel threading its way through the eye of a needle, they would lock the main gate into Jerusalem at night in Jesus' time, and if you wanted to enter the city after dark, you had to squeeze

236

through a postern gate, too low for a camel loaded with driver and goods to pass through. But stripped down and on his bent knees, the camel could manage to make it through."

"Ah, so that's what John Ten:Twenty-five is about!" Sylvia exclaimed, her eyes brightening.

"That's it," the psychiatrist said, smiling inwardly, as he noted that Sylvia could state chapter and verse.

"But, still, it seems impossible to gain entry to his kingdom — Jesus'."

"John goes on to say: 'With men it is impossible, but . . . all things are possible with God.'"

"Well then, you tell me, who can be saved?"

"You need the grace of God to be saved," Cordis answered. "The kingdom of heaven is a gift, not to be considered in the same breath as your Constitutional rights."

The session ended there, with Sylvia smiling contentedly as she left. Cordis felt that what they were discussing was beginning to make an impact on his patient.

CHAPTER FIFTY-FIVE

Dr. Romanetti had rented out a large private dining room at his favorite Italian restaurant in the West Village for a Halloween party. Everyone came dressed in costumes — as witches, skeletons, hobgoblins, even as Dracula and Frankenstein. Cordis wore his business suit and a black mask that covered his eyes.

Romanetti's wife Rita, dressed as one of the Furies, greeted him warmly but chided him for not getting into the true spirit of the occasion, whereupon he opened a package he was carrying and said, "This is a brand new bedsheet. I can make a slit in the middle, and turn myself into a ghost, or you can take it home with you and use it in good health."

She accepted the gift, laughing, and led Cordis to the punch bowl.

It was a typical Romanetti gathering, with clinic staff, friends of his from the Italian community, and several Gotham State Hospital doctors present. Salvatore had had a run-in with Armazón-Goldstein at the clinic in September, and she had recently managed to have him transferred to the hospital.

He latched onto Cordis as soon as he spotted him, and reviewed the strategy he was pursuing to get his clinic position back. Salvatore had been hired by the State when the clinic was part of an independent agency answering directly to Albany. But in 1970 all the state-run community clinics were absorbed by the state hospitals, and the Soho clinic came under Gotham State's control — "suzerainty," he called it. His legal position was that his contract had been drawn up with the old independent agency, not Gotham State, and therefore it was a contractual violation to have dispatched him there without his consent. He reasoned that he had made a commitment to follow a career in community psychiatry, and had he been interested in public hospital psychiatry he would have prepared himself accordingly by taking the Psychiatrist III examination, not required in the clinic, where he had functioned as a Psychiatrist II. "I would be running Gotham State if I had chosen hospital psychiatry," he had stated to a number of people on several occasions since his unwanted and, to him, unjust transfer.

It was a sound argument, which Cordis was hearing for the third time. The only problem was that Salvatore was unable to locate his original contract and the agency had long since been shut down. Cordis could only repeat what he had been saying: "Sal, you've got to come up with the contract; otherwise, you can't make your case."

Dr. Al Tate walked in dressed as a skeleton, accompanied by a date wearing a Wicked Witch of the West mask. Naomi Rothstein, garbed as a witch, cornered Cordis to ask advice on a personal medical matter. Mrs. Rosenberg, supposedly dressed as Lilith, in Semitic lore an evil spirit preying on children and in Jewish mythology the first wife of Adam long before the coming of Eve, sang "Bei Mir Bist Du Schön," a golden oldie.

When she finished singing, Cordis asked her how she knew what Lilith looked like, and she answered, "Who knows — who cares? She was just another *skicksa* — there were no Jews yet!" She had already had too much to drink, and the evening was still young.

Dr. Judd Axelman, dressed in a Count Dracula cape, came over to talk to Cordis. He had replaced Dr. Schlosberg, as already mentioned, and had a full item, that is, was working full time.

"I saw this odd fellow, Joey Dee, near quitting time today. He kept asking me — begging I should say — for Haldol and Taractan, but I followed your order sheet and kept him on CPZ and Stelazine. Was that all right?

CPZ is short for chlorpromazine, the generic name, and Thorazine is its tradename in the United States.

"Fine, fine," Cordis answered. "Thanks for taking care of him. I'm going to have to buy the guy an alarm clock or figure out some way for him to learn the difference between a.m. and p.m."

Tate's date, a graduate of Tuskegee Institute in Alabama, commented to Cordis at one point that she had never been out with a white man before or to an interracial party and was surprised to see how well everyone got on together.

"That's because everyone here is middle-class," Cordis explained to her. "You see, the problem in America isn't so much racial as it is class."

There were prizes, a comedy sketch, and a good deal of singing. At eleven Cordis left, not waiting for the "witching hour of midnight," when Frankenstein and his bride would be crowned king and queen of the night.

He took the subway home, shuttling over to the East Side where he was to catch his train to the 86th Street station. It was 11:50, and he was waiting on the platform at 42nd Street when he became aware that a ring of five young, tough-looking blacks was forming around him. He felt vulnerable: he was without his umbrella, which made an effective defensive weapon. He brightened up a bit when he saw his train pulling into the station, which was well lit, something in his favor, although there were only a few passengers on the platform. Not that he could count on anyone for assistance in the event of trouble, which he was expecting to be the next event in his life.

Just then, with the apparent menacing human ring only yards away, he heard a loud and familiar voice, "Hi, ya, Doc," and Macko had his arm around his shoulder as a protective shield. "I see we're taking the same train northbound."

"Good to see you again so soon," the doctor said, heaving a sigh of relief. Cordis had had Macko, whom he now saw every two weeks, in on the 24th.

"Well Doc, I get off in Harlem," Macko said as they entered the train, "where I park my carcass."

The incident would later remind Cordis of a somewhat similar one which had happened to Philippe Pinel, the great French psychiatrist who opened up the modern era of psychiatry at the Bicetre Hospital in Paris in 1792 by casting off the chains of the mentally ill. He was cautioned against unchaining one particular giant, but he did so anyway, believing that kindness would win out over madness. It worked, and the patient was eventually able to leave the Bicetre. One night several years later, Pinel was walking down a darkened street in Paris when he was set upon by a

239

thug—but out of the shadows came the giant to his rescue! The story is not apocryphal.

While they were on the train, Cordis told Macko about Parkyourcarcass, a character on the old Eddie Cantor radio program, since he had used the word "carcass" and had set off a train of associations in his own mind. He had time to tell Macko about Bert Gordon, the Mad Russian, another one of Cantor's mainstays, and to talk about Jack Benny, Fred Allen, George Burns and Edgar Bergen and his Charlie McCarthy, but all too quickly it was time to get off at 86th Street.

While walking the rest of the way to the Adams, he found himself singing "Bei Mir Bist Du Schön," which he had first heard in 1937 on the Eddie Cantor program. It was the Sammy Cahn song that would make the Andrew Sisters famous—and himself.

Entering the Adams, he muttered under his breath, "New York is now jungle town."

CHAPTER FIFTY-SIX

There were no letters from Renata during October.

I wonder what's happening with my absent patient, Cordis mused, sitting in his office the first day of November and rereading the last letter from her. Who knows if she is planning to come this way again. Maybe she can't get out of that Muslim country. America is Israel's ally. For the Arabs, the enemy of my enemy is my friend, and the friend of my enemy is my enemy. Perhaps she's stuck there . . .

On November 5th a letter arrived from Renata informing him of her scheduled return to New York on the 16th. She asked if he was still keeping her six o'clock Tuesday hour free and, if not, she would take any hour he had available. Cordis immediately wrote her that the hour was still hers.

Cordis had cut his office work down to three afternoons a week, Tuesday through Thursday, a concession to his arthritis and his need to have time for himself. He had his regular patients, those who had been with him for months, as well as referrals for one hour consultations and some who had decided to drop out after only one or two sessions. Renata Delacross and Sylvia Blank were the only patients receiving what Renata had referred to as religiotherapy. Whether such an approach was more suited to Catholics was a matter open to question and investigation — he would not generalize from two cases. For the majority of his patients, clinic and private, Jew and gentile, young and older, religion was not a vital force in their treatment nor, for that matter, in their lives. Perhaps the situation would have been different in the South or Midwest, areas within the "Bible belt," but he was finding New York, with all its religious shrines, not to be a spiritual mecca.

In the course of her session of November 7th, Sylvia Blank made the statement, "The Supreme Court declared abortion to be a legal right earlier this year."

Cordis was inclined to come back with, "What do the 'Holy Nine' have to say about the legality of marijuana?"

"Abortion," she said testily. "I'm talking about abortion now, not marijuana."

"Is that some kind of a personal matter with you?"

"No, I have never had an abortion, and I don't need one." Sylvia rendered her words angrily. Then calming down, she added, "All I said was that the highest court in the land says abortion is legal."

"Okay, the Court says it's legal, but does the Court say it's right?"

"If it's legal it's right. But look, this isn't a moral issue. Their decision is a legal one—abortion is a legal issue."

"So you say."

"What is there to a ten-day-old fetus? It's only a cluster of cells no larger than a pinhead. Even at thirty days it's only a speck, a tiny blob, not a real human life."

Cordis heaved a sigh. She's arguing such an important issue, he said to himself, and doesn't even know the first thing about it—the difference between an embryo and a fetus.

He sat quietly with his eyes closed for five or six seconds and said, "The Talmud teaches that before birth the soul knew the entire Torah, the heart of the Bible, but forgot it on its passage into the world that begins beyond the womb."

"So what!" Sylvis said. "What's your point?"

"The fetus and possibly even that earlier little blob you and the Supreme Court would allow to be cleaved away so readily knew all that was necessary to know about the world."

"Christ! What has the Talmud have to do with me? I'm not a Jew!"

"Yes, of course," Cordis said, smacking his lips. "Very few people are Jews; most people are not. But the Talmud is available to any noble soul wishing to study it."

After what was a particularly long silence for Sylvia, some fifteen seconds, she spoke again. "I know you think marijuana is dangerous to health," she said, "and I know you know that I smoke more than an occasional joint; but what do you think—do you think I should stop?"

"I don't tell people what to do," Cordis answered, his voice louder than usual. "I give you information, explanations, interpretations, options. Especially options. But not advice. If advice is what you want, write to Ann Landers. It's a lot cheaper."

"You think it's bad, don't you?" she said, biting on two fingernails.

"Bad in what sense?" Cordis responded. "It's bad for one's health. Is it bad for your soul, your immortal Christian soul? Well, I leave that to the theologians. As for buying and selling the stuff, I leave that to the magistrates."

"We always seem to go from pot to the religious in these sessions," Sylvia commented.

"Our interest here is in change, transformation," Cordis said, leaning forward in his chair. "If you must deny the medical evidence about pot, then perhaps what you need is a spiritually generated internal transformation, or a conversion in the New Testament sense—*metanoia*, a turning to God to produce change for the better. Or as Flannery O'Connor, the Catholic novelist and short story writer from Georgia put it, you have to turn inward toward God and away from your own egocentricity—you have to see the selfish side of yourself to be able to turn away from it."

Cordis knew that his approach was like a thunderbolt and chancy, but he had confidence in his own intuition. Intuitive techniques are generally frowned upon by those doing therapy, mainly because "intuitive powers" is something that cannot be taught to other therapists. Not too many doing analytic-type therapy are capable of imaginative insight, but Cordis felt he was carrying on in the tradition of Wilhelm Stekel and Sandor Ferenczi from the Freudian school, and Jung and his associates from the other major camp of dynamic psychotherapists.

Tears welled up in Sylvia's eyes. "I'm so desperate to find . . . peace," she said softly, "to make my peace with God." She sighed deeply and reached into her purse for a handkerchief.

"Give it time," Cordis said soothingly. "Good things come to those who wait . . . and work on their salvation."

"Must I retreat from the world to the refuge of the nuns to find the peace I seek?" she asked, more like in the manner of a soliloquy.

"Ah, but you have more choices than that," the doctor said. "You

242

can be in the world and still find peace. The choice is yours. As Moses approached his end, he told his people: 'I set before you life or death, blessing or curse. Choose life, then, so that you and your descendants may live, in the love of your God.' "

"Work on my salvation," Sylvia said slowly. "That's a purely theological term—salvation—isn't it?"

"Is it now?" the psychiatrist responded. "It also means deliverance from difficulty. Look it up when you get home."

By the time she left at 4:50, Cordis was weary, but he still had one more scheduled patient, Johann Klinger, who had a preference for the 5 o'clock time slot. Fr. Dominic was financing his therapy out of a special fund, and was prepared to continue paying for him until the end of the year. Cordis had reached a point where he thought it was a waste of church money and was set on making this the last session.

"In the six months you've been coming to see me, the doctor started off, "you really haven't had your heart and mind in this."

"Oh," Klinger said, looking surprised. "I wouldn't say that."

"Well, we have to go by what we've accomplished, very little, and what we haven't, a whole lot," Cordis said softly. "I thought we were off to an auspicious beginning back in the middle of May. You began on May fourteenth, the day before the feast day of St. Dymphna, the patron saint of mental health, but it's been downhill ever since. I think you need therapy and—"

"Why do you say that?" Klinger asked, interrupting him.

"Your relationship with your young daughter is unwholesome, to say the least, and you really need to work through that conflict."

Dymphna was the 13-year-old daughter of a pagan Celtic chieftan, in the 7th century, who tried to seduce her after the death of his wife. She fled to Belgium, but her father caught up with her. Still she resisted his incestuous advances, and he killed her by cutting off her head. She became the patroness of the insane when a number of cures among the mentally ill of Gheel occurred, attributed to her intercession.

"And what do you see as my problem?" Klinger asked unemotionally.

"The Dymphna syndrome, or a Dymphna complex—an abnormal interest in your eight-year-old daughter. It's an issue which needs to be addressed."

Even with such prodding, the ex-priest failed to make a bit of progress during his hour, and at 5:45 Cordis suggested that perhaps he would prefer to be treated by another psychotherapist, perhaps a Catholic. Johann rejected the suggestion and was content to terminate treatment

243

with Cordis, exhibiting his usual courtesy as he bowed out.

Later that evening Cordis reached Fr. Dominic by telephone and brought him up to date on Johann Klinger.

"It appears we have lost another priest," the cleric said.

"A long time ago," Cordis responded. "He never revealed the faintest flicker of interest in returning to the priesthood. He's a lost soul with a silently aching mind. I did my best—but he never made any effort to get inside himself."

After the 11 o'clock news, Cordis found his mind wandering back to the end of his session with Sylvia, when he had quoted to her from Deuteronomy: "Choose life, then, so that you and your descendants may live, in the love of Yahweh your God, obeying his voice, clinging to him; for in this your life consists, and on this depends your long stay in the land which Yahweh swore to your fathers, Abraham, Isaac and Jacob, he would give them."

Israel had beaten back the onslaught of its Muslim neighbors one more time. The homeland was safe . . . for the moment. But it would be so only if its people remained just and clung to their God, the God of their fathers.

Pray, O Israel, for thine own survival, he prayed. Keep God's commandments, and you will live and increase in numbers, and God will bless you in the land he gave to your ancestors.

Israel needs prayers, he said to himself, as he dialed Fr. Dominic's number again.

"Father, please pray for Israel, and ask your parishioners to pray for Israel!"

CHAPTER FIFTY-SEVEN

In 1973 the American Psychiatric Association was beginning work on a major revision of the psychiatric nosology, and a number of groups outside of psychiatry and medicine were looking on with keen interest, among them, and most noticeably, the homosexual community. Homosexuality as a psychiatric disorder would be declassified, and henceforth would be considered an alternate sexual preference. No psychopathology would be associated with the state as such, although the homosexual could have emotional problems related to or apart from his mode of sexuality.

Cordis had followed Freud's classification of the sexual aberrations, which placed such disorders into one of two categories: sexual object distortions (homosexuality, pedophilia, bestiality, et cetera) and sexual aim distortions (exhibitionism, voyeurism, sadism, et cetera). That classification would disappear once the new *Diagnostic and Statistical Manual* would come out.

Miss Jones and Dr. Grossman were engaged in conversation when Cordis walked into the staff lounge at 8:45 on the 9th for a morning cup of coffee. Their discussion centered around one of Grossman's homosexual patients, whom he was treating for depression.

"You'll never cure him—change his sexual orientation," Miss Jones was saying. "It's something you are, not something you have. And why try to change all these people? Homosexuals are among the most talented, most creative people in society. Their incomes are above the national average and they pay a lot in taxes. So leave them alone."

"You make it sound as though there's a gene for each carried on the same chromosome," Cordis chipped in, while sampling his freshly brewed cup of coffee.

"I can't accept that the condition is genetic," Grossman said forcefully. "Following your line of reasoning, Miss Jones, you would deny them the availability of analytic treatment, and the condition is amenable to psychoanalysis."

There was a vocal group of analysts in New York who resented the impending psychiatric declassification of homosexuality and was resisting the proposed change. Among these were the noted analyst Irving Bieber, who regarded homosexuality as a heterosexual dysfunction or inadequacy, and Charles Socarides, who feared that now the pre-homosexual child or adolescent would be denied treatment at a time when it could be nipped in the bud, so to speak.

"It's an alternative sex style, nothing more," the clinic nurse said, "not an affliction calling for ten years of psychoanalysis."

"Nonsense!" was Grossman's rejoinder.

"History has left us no records of the existence of a viable society in which the preferred mode of sexuality and its institutional structuring was essentially homosexual," Cordis contributed.

Miss Jones laughed challengingly. "You're forgetting those old

245

Greeks," she said.

"Theirs was still basically a heterosexually-oriented society," Cordis responded.

"What about the Amazons?" she offered.

"Even that noted author on the classical world, Edith Hamilton, author of *The Greek Way*, considers them to have been a mythical race," Cordis said.

"The excesses of a free society," commented Grossman, finishing up his coffee. "We're beginning to look like ancient Greece near its end, where democracy finally failed when everyone decided to take control of the Senate," he added smilingly, as he left to see his first patient of the day.

Cordis had a homosexual patient that morning, a young man of nineteen who had only recently come to recognize his true sexual orientation, to use the term that was becoming popular. He hailed from a small town in Nebraska and despite living in Greewich Village, Manhattan's haven for artists, bohemians, and more recently, homosexuals, felt lonely and isolated.

He sat in the psychiatrist's office, tearful and agitated. "I'm lost," he said, "and frightened. My body has betrayed me, and there's nothing I can do about it."

Over the next thirty minutes Cordis learned that his patient accepted what he was and wanted counseling from a homosexual spokesman, but had no idea how to proceed. Earlier, Cordis had been reading a recent edition of the *Village Voice* and had noted that its classified section carried a list of homosexual organizations. He gave his patient the newspaper and advised him to contact one of the groups. The young man was overjoyed— a whole new world had opened up for him when he learned that there were others who were groping with the same issue confronting him.

How remarkable! Cordis thought afterwards. What appeared a minor intervention to me—all I did was give the guy a newspaper—may have saved his life. He had been talking suicide until he learned there was help for him.

At eleven Cordis saw a paranoid in his early twenties who had been doing odd jobs for a groom at Belmont Racetrack until the previous week when he threatened to kill the groom's wife because he thought she was mistreating one of the racehorses. He was mistaken in his interpretation of events, of course, but that was not unusual for him. The records accompanying him stated that he had no known history of violence.

"And how were you going to kill her?" Cordis asked, a harmless, routine question under the circumstances.

"I was gonna cut her head off with a butcher knife and dump her in

246

the river," he answered, smiling inappropriately.

"Which half? The head or the torso?"

The patient's social worker from the referring agency, a middle-aged Puerto Rican named Mrs. Romero, tried unsuccessfully to stifle a laugh, and then uttered something in Spanish which only served to release a belly laugh. Cordis himself had to chuckle over what he now recognized was a bit of inadvertent gallows humor.

At the conclusion of the hour-long session, with the patient removed to the waiting room, Cordis told Mrs. Romero that he didn't think her client would harm the groom's wife. It was a judgement call. He couldn't be sure, but based on what he had learned during the interview, there was nothing indicative of a tendency to violent behavior.

"You can't lock up everyone in New York making threats," Cordis said to her. "The ACLU will be all over you with accusations that you're interfering with free speech, the First Amendment. Just keep him away from that racetrack."

Cordis started him on Mellaril and suggested to Mrs. Romero that she have him return weekly to the clinic for follow-up.

"Is it safe to have this man walking around society?" she asked worriedly.

"New York is no longer a society," Cordis responded. "It's a jungle. But given all the civil rights mental patients now enjoy, we would never be able to 2-PC him at this point—get two physicians to certify that he is a danger to others and therefore should be hospitalized. He has to act first."

"Supposing he *does* try to kill her."

"That would constitute an act," Cordis said. "Then the legal machinery would go into action, and he would wind up in Bellevue or at Gotham State."

"This is crazy!"

"That's law."

As Cordis was getting ready to leave for the day, Dr. Armazón-Goldstein rang him up and asked him to stop by her office. She shut the door behind her and immediately launched into a censorious tongue-lashing, accusing him of exposing a client to uncalled-for ridicule—she had passed by his office earlier and had overheard his comment that had Mrs. Romero laughing so vigorously.

Cordis didn't see the issue her way. "It was a good hour," he said to her, when she had finished with her diatribe. "Very productive and helpful to him."

"We don't humiliate our clients here the way you did, Cordis," she said.

247

"Look, Armazón-Goldstein," Cordis retorted angrily, "when you've gone through medical school and have your M.D. degree, then you can voice your opinion about the quality of my work. Until then, just stick to your office chores and shuffling your papers."

He left in a huff and headed straight for The Adams, to follow up on several professional opportunities he was already in the process of exploring.

CHAPTER FIFTY-EIGHT

Cordis was at the front desk of The Adams at 7 a.m. the following Monday with an overnight bag, giving the clerk his schedule for the next few days. He was on his way to LaGuardia to catch a flight for Syracuse to interview for a position with Syracuse University's Student Health Service. As he was saying good-by, a telegram arrived for him. It was from the director of Student Health telling him not to come!

He was taking several days of hastily arranged vacation time, and he now returned to his apartment to ponder his next move. At nine he phoned Syracuse University, and after a while the Student Health Service secretary located the director for him. The director was apologetic, speaking barely above a whisper.

"I'm not supposed to be talking to you," she said. "There are all these AA and EOE rules and regulations I'm supposed to follow. I'm sorry, but I can't talk to you further."

"What AA—" Cordis started to ask.

"I can't talk further," she said, still whispering, and hung up.

Cordis phoned Simon Avika, LL.B., M.D., who usually covered for him when he was out of town.

"Sy, what is this AA and EOE?" he asked.

"The new federal hiring guidelines," he answered. "Affirmative Action and Equal Opportunity Employer. Haven't you heard of the EEOC?"

"No."

"The Equal Employment Opportunity Commission. Where have

248

you been?"

"I was out of the country for ten years and obviously missed the revolution—the social revolution."

"The country's changed with the civil rights legislation," Sy said. "Hiring practices now give preferential treatment to women and minorities. The WASP's have had it and—"

"And we Jews are now lumped in with the WASP's. That part I know."

"Nobody cares that you spent thirty years struggling to get where you are," Sy said. "Move over, buddy, and make room for the women, blacks and Puerto Ricans. They have entitlements."

A little later Cordis phoned Florida State University in Tallahassee, where he had an application on file also.

"I've reviewed your credentials," the Student Health director said, "and I like your background. Come on down for a visit."

"When?" Cordis asked.

"Anytime you're ready," he replied.

"What about if I left today?"

"That'll be fine," he responded.

Cordis exchanged his plane tickets at LaGuardia, and by supper time was in Tallahassee. He spent a pleasant two days visiting the campus and meeting with the director of the Student Health Service and his staff.

"You're my first choice for the position," the director told him, "but we're under great pressure to hire a woman for this job."

"Yes, I know," Cordis said. "AA and EOE"

He flew back to New York on Thursday, the 15th. The following evening Renata called him from the Delacroix's East Side apartment. She was excited, and she thanked him for keeping her hour open. "I'm just dying to see you again," she said closing out the conversation.

She looked healthy, poised, even vibrant, as she hugged Cordis in the waiting room of his office the following Tuesday evening.

"Once seated she said, "I'm in New York for a couple of months to close out Grandmama's house, and while here I want to complete my therapy. Perhaps I should have stated my objectives in the reverse order."

"I'm glad to see you again, regardless of whether therapy is first or second or lower down on your list of things to do in New York," Cordis said. Then he added, "When did you decide to return?"

"The day I wrote you," she replied tersely.

"I see."

Renata devoted her session to filling Cordis in on her activities since that grim day in the middle of August. Some of it he already knew from her letters. Much of her hour was spent detailing events in Casablanca dealing with the Yom Kippur War.

He was relieved to learn that she had not been penalized for her association with a Jewish doctor in the United States.

"In my fantasy," he said, "I had images of the natives burning down your house and forcing you to subsist on bread and water."

"My dear, dear Dr. Cordis. It was nothing like that."

"Okay, that's good." Deep down, however, Cordis felt she was holding back.

At one point she said something that intrigued him.

"This was the first time," she said, "anyone in Casablanca could remember an Egyptian army going into battle without the hashish wagons rolling along with it. Maybe that's why the troops were able to perform better under Anwar Sadat than they had ever done for Nasser."

He was surprised to hear that she had been "devouring Freud, Jung, Adler, Wilhelm Reich, William James, et cetera," as she put it while in Morocco. It made him wonder if her pursuit of psychology went beyond therapy to perhaps a budding professional interest.

This is a new and self-confident young lady, Cordis marveled. She has been tested these past three months and has come through.

"You've come a long way since we last met," he said.

"Where I am is where you have helped me to be," she responded. She smiled and looked at him for what seemed to him the longest time—until he had to break off eye contact.

She had once alluded to Eliza Doolittle of *My Fair Lady*. He suddenly felt like Professor Higgins.

Cordis scheduled her for the following Tuesday, the 27th, at her customary hour, thinking it could be her final session. It seemed to him that the only thing left to do now was to go over her plans for the future . . . and to say good-by.

CHAPTER FIFTY-NINE

Simone and Pierre arrived in New York two days after Thanksgiving, and Simone immediately phoned Cordis.

"Well, your charge is doing fine," the doctor commented after the introductory pleasantries.

"Not all that well, Doctor," said Simone, sounding glum.

"Oh?"

"I didn't expect her to get over her grandmother's death right away, naturally, so I have been minimizing her sullenness of the past few weeks. But there is something going on besides the normal grief over the death of Celine."

"What are you getting at?" Cordis asked. "Are you hinting that she might be depressed again?"

"It's not like her to be . . . like this."

"I saw her earlier in the week, and she appeared fine. Certainly not depressed."

"Yes, she is capable of covering up well for an hour if she has to," Simone said. "But that's not the problem. She started smoking that . . . you know, those things again in Casablanca, and more than ever."

"Ah, cannabis," the psychiatrist said. "So you think there's something going on besides mourning." There was no response. "Hello, Simone, are you still there?"

"Yes." There was another silence, and then Simone said, "Hasn't Renata talked to you about the great trauma of her life?"

"Well, apparently there's something you know that I don't know which she hasn't gotten around to disclosing to me."

"I hope it comes out soon, because there will be no peace in her life until the issue is laid to rest."

"I see."

"No, you don't!" Simone said, raising her voice. "There is another matter, one which looms even larger." There was another silence.

"Yes? Simone?"

After yet another silence, Simone blurted out tearfully, *"Elle t'aime!* She is in love with you! Don't you know that?"

The next thing he heard was the click when Simone hung up. Cordis sat quietly for a while, wondering what to make of what he had just heard. There is some deep, dark secret in Renata's past, but surely that will come

251

out eventually in therapy, he said to himself. So my timetable is off—there's still some work to be done before we say good-by. As for the patient thinking she's in love with her therapist, that's a common event in the course of any good therapy. It's transference, not real love, and the patient will eventually grasp the difference—with the proper explanation.

He dismissed Simone's bombshell by focusing on the least important point he could find. So, he mused, Simone tutoyered me!

Simone had switched from the formal pronoun, *vous*, to the informal *te*—*Elle t'aime* instead of *Elle vous aime*.

CHAPTER SIXTY

Sylvia Blank stopped by the clinic the first thing Monday the 26th. She had decided, mainly because of finances, to try to manage on her own for a while, but wanted to borrow Cordis' copy of the newly published *Marihuana—Deceptive Weed* by Gabriel Nahas. Since she lived in the West Village, Cordis had agreed to bring the book to the clinic for her convenience.

After she left, Cordis said to Grossman in the staff lounge, "I hope Armazón-Goldstein doesn't accuse me of seeing my private patients on clinic time, like Mansoni once did." He was recalling the incident involving Pat O'Connell earlier in the year.

"We have to do something about this woman," Grossman said softly. "I understand she's divorced, but she still keeps the Goldstein half in her name."

"Probably has used the full name throughout her professional life and doesn't want to change it now."

"Supposing she marries again to a guy, let's say, named Smith," the analyst said. "Do you suppose we'd have to call her Dr. Armazón-Goldstein-Smith?"

"I can think of better names to call her," Cordis responded.

"Did you know that Goldstein was a black Jew from Harlem? She has three kids, and they're a mess, I hear."

252

"We all have our *tsooris*, Arnie."

Tsooris is the Yiddish word for troubles.

Joey Dee was in the waiting room. He had been scheduled by Dr. Axelman to see Cordis on Friday, the 30th, so coming in three days earlier and in the morning was something of a therapeutic triumph in itself.

Cordis sat in his office thinking about Joey. "Every case is unique, yet similar to others," Eliot wrote in *The Cocktail Party*. But Joey's case was *singular*. The pieces didn't fit together to form a meaningful, consistent unity. Parts of it Cordis could explain away readily enough, but the whole, that which could furnish it coherency, eluded his grasp.

Certainly, Joey could be spending hours pouring through dusty old tomes, or the latest paperbacks for that matter, doing homework just for him, and then spewing out his erudition in the privacy of his office. And that was part of what was bothering him. No one else seemed aware of Joey's extraordinary talent for scholarship, or so it appeared. He didn't employ his natural endowment for any useful purpose as he went drifting aimlessly along in life. Then again, one can say such is the world of the schizophrenic. Furthermore, Joey was so asociable, Cordis could never get him near the day center to interact with another human being at the clinic.

Joey's facility with numbers—remembering the time spans of the yugas with ease and assuredness—was inconsistent with what Cordis would have expected from someone demonstrating his marked degree of withdrawal. To prepare his lessons at home was one thing; to be able to perform so capably in the clinic setting was something else—approaching, Cordis thought, the remarkable. One effect of his unusual scholarship was that it had driven his psychiatrist to library encyclopedias to check up on threes, fours, fives, et cetera.

Joey was wearing a torn overcoat splotched with food stains, and he looked like he hadn't shaved in more than a week. Cheerfully, he handed Cordis the typical brown bag, and even before the doctor could open it, launched right back into his numerological mystery game, picking up where he had left off months ago.

"Four an' t'ree are magical numbers," he said. "Four plus t'ree add up to seven."

Yup, Cordis said to himself, that's where he left off. It's amazing! He resigned himself to a long siege of sevens.

Joey started off with the Seven Wonders of the Ancient World. Interestingly, he could only enumerate four: the Great Pyramid of Khufu, the Hanging Gardens of Babylon, the Mausoleum at Halicarnassus, which he pronounced as "Halicases," and the Colossus of Rhodes. Cordis was hard pressed to come up with the other three: the Artemision at Ephesus,

Phidas' statue of the Olympian Zeus and the Pharos at Alexandria.

"You complemented da half I knew, Dr. Cordis," Joey said.

His psychiatrist wasn't sure whether he heard him say complemented or completed.

"What about the 'Eighth Wonder of the World'?" Cordis asked, smiling.

"Dere was an eight' wonder?" Joey asked in amazement.

"Well, he was more modern," the doctor replied. "Vintage nineteen thirty-two." Joey looked perplexed. "King Kong, the 'Eighth Wonder of the World,' " Cordis bellowed. Joey's puzzlement deepened. "You know, the overgrown gorilla that fell in love with Fay Wray—Beauty and the Beast, Hollywood style," he added.

"But he wasn't real, was he?" Joey asked anxiously, a man in need of an answer.

"Just a movie, pal," Cordis responded. "And I thought you had seen them all." He shrugged his shoulders. "There's another eighth wonder of the world," he continued. "Charity Hospital of Louisiana. When Huey P. Long built the hospital in New Orleans in the thirties, that's how they referred to it."

Joey's quizzical look began to fade as he grasped his doctor's latest tactic. Realizing that Cordis would be adding an eighth wonder for each one he disallowed, he said, "Yeah, but I was talkin' 'bout da Seven Wonders o' da Ancient World. Dese new ones ya got don't count."

No longer stymied, he was off again on his sevens. There was a tour of the body's seven spiritual centers as devised by Edgar Cayce, the Sleeping Prophet, and then a mechanical listing of the seven deadly sins: "Pride, ire, envy, avarice, gluttony, lecherie, acidie."

"Hold it," Cordis said, waving his writing hand in the air. "What's with this acidie?"

"It means slot'," he responded. "It's in Chaucer."

"Sloth?"

"Yeah, slot'. It means laziness."

"Ah, yes." Cordis smiled as he recalled how he had read through parts of the Canterbury Tales in preparation for a session with Anna Bee in April.

"Let me compliment you on your fine taste in literature, my good fellow," Cordis said.

"T'anks, Dr. Cordis."

When Joey started on the seven senses, Cordis stopped him. "I thought there were five senses," he said.

"Five?" Joey said, filled with disbelief over his doctor's apparent ignorance.

"Yes," Cordis said. "Sight, hearing, smell, touch and taste. As a physician I'm telling you that these are the five physiological senses."

"But ya left out two," Joey protested. Cordis suddenly got the feeling that the pupil was lecturing the teacher. "Understandin' is da sixt' sense an' da sevent' sense is speech," he added. "It's in da Bible."

Cordis tried to conceal a sigh of relief, for he thought Joey was going to invoke paranormal cognition and who knows what else as the extra two senses. He was also uneasy over his reference to the Bible. If he knew only the Old Testament, he could go on and on with sevens.

It was getting near noon, quitting time for Cordis on his part-time contract with the State, and at this point he started writing Joey's prescriptions for Thorazine and Stelazine.

"I'll see you again in four weeks," he said, "not sooner, not later, but four weeks from today. Four weeks is twenty-eight days, which is four times seven—excellent numbers. Today is the twenty-sixth of the month, two plus six, not bad numbers—six is two threes. Four weeks from today will be the twenty-fourth of December—two plus four, a remarkable number—and it will be the day before Christmas, a most notable event. So I will see you on the twenty-fourth day of December in this the year of your Lord, nineteen seventy-three, a sequence chock full of magic numbers."

Joey laughed good-naturedly, realizing that Cordis was putting on an act for him, and said, "I'll be here on da right day an' in da mornin'."

To get Joey to voice a promise with conviction as he had done was a gain of sorts; and he had picked up his scripts for Thorazine and Stelazine without a squawk to boot.

Cordis now got around to opening Joey's brown bag. The BIC's and the oranges were there—the pens were still blue.

CHAPTER SIXTY-ONE

When Renata returned the following week on the 27th, Cordis steered the conversation onto the topic of depression.

"Well, I'm still grieving over Grandmama's death, but I don't consider that the same as depression. There is a difference between the two, isn't there?"

"Yes, a period of mourning is to be expected after the death of a loved one," Cordis replied. "Depression, on the other hand, is an illness."

"How long is the mourning process supposed to go on?"

"My rule of thumb is Freud's mourning calendar: he set an arbitrary time limit of two years. If unresolved by then, mourning is considered pathological."

"I mourned over my father's death for years, it seems, so I guess you would call that pathological. It didn't end until I started coming to see you. That cured me—you cured me."

"You cured yourself," Cordis said, "and you did it without antidepressants. You marshalled the forces within your mind to restore various aberrant neurotransmitters back to their normal states."

"I did? Isn't that odd, I never thought of it that way."

"Well, take it from your doctor. You moved those key neurotransmitter molecules, whose names aren't important, back to where they belonged in your brain."

"Fine. But now, how am I to distinguish between the mourning process and a recurrence of depression, something we both know I am prone to?"

"If you have any thoughts of suicide," Cordis answered. "That's usually related to depression."

"You psychiatrists!" she said. "You're always worrying about suicide."

"That's very true," the doctor responded.

The two things psychiatrists are concerned about the most are: paranoids who may act on their delusions/hallucinations, and depressives who make suicidal attempts, especially successful ones.

"Don't you know that to a Catholic suicide is the great moral and unpardonable sin?"

"You should also know that suicide is man's ultimate hatred of God," Cordis said.

256

"Why would suicide be an act of hatred toward God?"

"To kill oneself," the doctor began his response, "is to kill a part of God, for we all take our source from God. By choosing to end one's life prematurely, one denies God the chance of fulfilling himself through that particular individual."

"God needs me to find fulfillment?" Renata asked, cocking her head.

"The human race represents God's means of achieving fulfillment, for we are the only creations in existence capable of communicating with him."

"There are trillions of stars in the heavens—more than there are bacteria in my bowel constituting my normal flora—and some of them undoubtedly have planets with life forms, some with life forms more advanced than we are."

"How do you know that?" Cordis asked.

Renata looked at him with exasperation and responded, "You don't believe God would create such a vast universe just to put us at the center of all things, puny creatures that we be!"

"Why not? I find no contradiction in a God who fashions a universe so vast that we cannot begin to measure its dimensions just to bring man into being."

"Well, you certainly have faith in the Creator, which I know you do. I share that faith, too. But your view of humanity's role in the scheme of things sounds like a minority view."

"Existence takes on meaning if you think this way," the psychiatrist said. "For instance, you can then say that God created earth to accommodate man, because he anticipated his coming."

"Don't forget woman in your scenario," she said contentiously.

"Yes, both, of course. Created he man and woman in his very image."

"You mean, God has blond hair, blue eyes, a vermiform appendix, testes and a uterus? Months ago you were telling me God is incorporeal."

"In his image means in his mind's eye. He had man in mind all the time. That he took two or four to five billion years to evolve him after having made earth is inconsequential. Time, after all, belongs to God."

"The time dimension belongs to God," Renata said, following him carefully.

"Yes, we cannot begin to fathom the meaning of a billion years. We live out our meager three score and ten years, and then in death we are reunited in timelessness, with the one and only operator of the time machine of the universe."

"So, you believe there is immortality in death. As a Catholic, I do."

"There is eternity in death," Cordis responded. "Immortality is that part of you which you leave behind for future generations to remember. You can find that in the Book of Sirach: 'A good life hath but few days, but a good name endureth forever.' "

"What are you really getting at?" Renata asked.

"God is eternal and the source of all things eternal. Man is mortal, but also the source of his own immortality possibly—by his deeds does he live on."

"You are implying," Renata continued the line of thought, "that eternal and immortal, although sharing some attributes, are not the same."

"That which is eternal has never come into existence, for it has always been," Cordis explained, leaning back in his swivel chair. "God is eternal. That which is immortal lives forever, but had a beginning."

"What about the soul—our immortal soul?"

"It is actually part of the eternal, because after death the soul is reunited in God—it returns to its source."

Renata was now caught up in the dialogue. "If God is so almighty," she said, "why does he need a universe at all?"

"In order to create mankind," he replied. "I should really be saying humankind."

"But what purpose does mankind, I mean, humankind, serve?" Renata asked, blushing over having to correct herself. She was excited.

"God's purpose."

"Which is what?" she asked, continuing to press the doctor.

"To fulfill his design."

"But how?" she screamed at him good-naturedly.

"Well," he started out, buying time to organize his thoughts, "there are three things—three because it is a number with latent numinosity—we are meant to do here on God's earth." To himself he said, Now, let me try to figure out what they are.

When he did not continue after a few seconds, Renata said, "Yes, don't keep me in suspense!"

"Here . . . here are the things we are to do. First, to do what is right in the eyes of God; second, to acquire wisdom in the sight of God; and third, to come to see that God is the light of the universe." There, that's three, he said to himself. Pretty good.

"The light of the universe," Renata repeated.

"Yes, for without God darkness and emptiness would cover the vastness of space—there would be no universe at all."

"Well, Dr. Cordis," Renata said, "listening to you expound like this is exciting, even thrilling. But I'm not sure I can buy all of it."

"I'm not selling anything," he retorted. "You've been asking me to propound on the purpose of existence—Thank God you haven't limited me to twenty-five words or less!—and I have given you my best effort. The time will come when you'll probably be able to find the answers to your cosmological searching yourself—come up with better answers than mine."

"Hell may have frozen over by then."

"No need to wait—I see hell as a very dark and cold place . . . right now," the psychiatrist said. "You would do better to concentrate your journey where the light of God can enter."

"Hell has always been depicted as an inferno," Renata said. "A very well lit up place I would think."

"Hell is in the void of space," Cordis responded. "The soul that cannot get back to God lingers in that cold nothingness. Sometimes it is referred to as Gehenna in the Jewish tradition."

At that point Renata got up from her seat and said, " I must use the ladies room."

"By all means," he said. "God speed."

She returned after an absence of five minutes, during which time Cordis made a phone call . . . to avoid self-examination, for he knew very well that he was skirting the key issue: his would-be personal relationship with his patient.

After seating herself again, Renata asked, "And where does one begin the great cosmic search?"

"They say that awe of God is the beginning of wisdom."

"Which in your language means awe of the universe."

"Something like that," the doctor said. "And now you *are* beginning."

"By the beard of Allah, maybe I am!" Renata said, using a home-grown phrase, and she laughed.

"It is not by his beard nor his aftershave lotion that you will recognize the presence of God," Cordis said solemnly. "God is beyond ordinary means of perception."

"I know," Renata responded. "God reveals himself only as he wants to—via the numinous."

"Ah!" the doctor exclaimed. "And only a short while ago you were trying to convince me you had no talent for God-searching."

"I remember what the novelist Joseph Conrad once said: 'God is for men and religion for women.'"

"Well, as you know, novelists write fiction. You can't believe everything they write."

"Do you believe there's equality in God-searching then?"

"Now you know one of the great truths of this life," he answered.

After a short pause, Renata asked him, "Do you think this journey of mine, this far journey as you have referred to it, will take me to a distant place where I will discover my innermost identity . . . and my soul?"

The doctor shrugged. "It is only after the journey to a distant place that the inner voice which guides our quest is revealed to us. The Hassidic Rabbi Eisek traveled from Cracow to Prague, where he heard the dream of a palace guard and learned the secret to a hidden treasure he was seeking." Cordis paused a moment for effect. "It was buried in his own house."

"Is that my soul or my destiny you're referring to?"

"The soul-seeker must ask the question: What have I done for mankind lately? To participate in a part of mankind's salvation is the way you search for your soul."

"Um," she muttered, nodding her head thoughtfully.

"As Horace Mann said, 'Be ashamed to die until you have won some victory for humanity.' "

Renata stared at him, and she had tears in her eyes. She had to bite her lip before she could regain her self-control to be able to speak again.

"Thomas Mann. Not from your Talmud?"

Cordis shrugged. "Maybe Mann got it from the Talmud."

As she left his office that evening Renata hugged him and whispered, "God be with you; God is with you."

Now alone in his office, Cordis sat back down at his desk and reviewed the session. He shook his head repeatedly to express his dissatisfaction with his performance, grading himself no higher than a C and tempted to lower that even to a D. He had failed to carry out his initial intent, a systematic inquiry into the presence or absence of depression. She wasn't depressed. That was evident, but he hadn't gone about it systematically. Instead, he had allowed himself to get sidetracked into philosophical folderol. All because he couldn't face the nitty-gritty issue disturbing his own equanimity: what he felt for Renata.

CHAPTER SIXTY-TWO

"I enjoyed our little detour into philosophy last week," Renata said, starting out her next session, on December 4th. "Too bad it's all so speculative—philosophy, I mean—with no real substance to it."

"Goethe once said it's more important for a philosophy to be interesting than to be true," Cordis responded. They both chuckled at that point. "However," he continued, "whatever it was we were discussing last week, I thought it was closer to theology than to philosophy."

"Maybe we can call it psycho-theology," Renata said, tongue-in-cheek. "What about mystico-psychiatry? The psychiatrist as priest—in your case rabbi."

"What about analytical psychology? Jung's school. And of course, the school of Sir Henry Harcourt-Reilly. My approach isn't all that special, you see."

"I find it more interesting—and pertinent to my needs—than discussing id impulses and the superego's development," she said, in a swipe at the Freudians.

The doctor nodded. You're sounding chipper these days."

"And why not? I'm receiving Communion again."

"Yes, the Eucharist is the most potent medicine you can take."

I don't find the slightest evidence for a depression, he said to himself. Simone was seeing something else. What?

"Do you realize I hardly take any medication anymore—for anything!" Renata voiced jubilantly.

"Well, as I said, you've got the Eucharist. What about marijuana? Do you still smoke those reefers?"

"I smoked them for a while in Casablanca, that's all. It's no problem now."

I don't get it, he said to himself. If I didn't know it, I would never associate Renata Delacross with marijuana. It's an incongruity.

Renata didn't smoke marijuana for pleasure. The only thrill she ever derived from "grass" was the one time she "heard lights and saw sounds," as she had related it to him in an earlier session. His response had been, "So what? Rabbi Ben Simeon bar Yohai and his followers in the second century experienced synesthetic phenomena like that strictly through meditation—without recourse to hallucinogens."

"Do you ever eat it—as hashish?" he now asked her.

"Ugh!" She made a face. "Never."

In the 19th century, hashish was eaten, usually as an electuary, from Araby, where it had originated, to Paris, where a group of intellectuals were devouring it in a similar fashion.

The history of hashish—hashish is a stronger form of cannabis prepared from a different part of the hemp plant—dates back to the end of the 12th century, when a Sufi religious leader, Shaykh Haydar, introduced it. The Sufis were an ascetic sect who sought mystical ecstasy; and hashish intoxication found a ready place within their practices. The Sufis tried to maintain a monopoly on the drug, but it eventually passed into the public domain. Hashish became known as "the wine of Haydar"— wine itself was prohibited under Muslim law—and "the wine of the bankrupt."

By the 13th century, the use of hashish was common in Arab lands. It took root at the Gardens of Cafour in Cairo, where its use got so out of hand the governor of Cairo finally closed the popular recreational area in 1253. It was to no avail because the cannabis faithful took their drug to hashish inns in the suburbs, until in 1324 the powers that be shut down the inns and burned the cannabis fields. Twice more in the 14th century they tried to eradicate its use, but it had become part of the fabric of life in Egypt and much of the Arab world.

Napoleon conquered Egypt at the end of the 18th century, and after surveying the scene before him associated the stagnation among the populace with the widespread consumption of hashish. He, too, issued a proclamation forbidding its use, but like his interdicting predecessors also failed. It was Napoleon's troops who brought hashish to France when they returned home. But its use would never spread beyond the confines of *Le Club des Hashishins*, the Club of the Hashish Eaters, in Paris. One of its luminaries, Theophile Gautier, ecstatically proclaimed: "Ah, to taste the joys of Mohammed's heaven!" Charles Baudelaire, another member, waxed lyrical in his praise of the drug for a while, but in the end said: "One who has recourse to poison in order to think, will soon be unable to think without taking poison."

In his review of *Easy Rider*, a low-budget Peter Fonda-Dennis Hopper film of 1969 dealing with a pair of rebellious pot-smoking motorcyclists making their way aimlessly across the United States, Vincent Canby of *The New York Times* used the term "grass curtain." Yes, a Grass Curtain was beginning to surround America in 1973, until it would become a vise choking the vitality out of the nation between its seductive jaws.

"In the fourteenth century, there was an emir of Joneima who had the teeth of anyone caught eating hashish pulled out," Cordis said to Renata, attempting to continue his inquiry into her marijuana-using history."

"Quite a draconian measure," Renata commented. "But take my word for it: marijuana is not my problem."

If she had said "not a problem for me," he would probably have let the matter go. By saying, "not my problem," she was suggesting there was another problem calling for his attention. But whatever that might be, he felt it involved cannabis in some way. He would not press her further on the subject of marijuana . . . but made a note in her chart to try again the next week.

He was doing no better with the supposed transference issue. Transference can be defined as the patient's projection of deeply harbored feelings, thoughts and wishes onto the therapist who figures as a representation from her past. Accordingly, Renata would be transferring to Cordis the magical powers and omniscience she had lavished earlier in life upon her father.

It's all an unrealistic overevaluation of her therapist, he said to himself. Nothing more. But is it? And what about the counter-transference? That's the problem now!

Near the end of her hour, Renata showed him several Christmas cards she had bought. One of them had a kaleidoscopic design which produced different colored images as the viewer moved his head about.

Cordis tilted his head back and forth enjoying the changing colors and patterns. Then he said, "Interesting how you can get a different picture simply by altering your angle of view."

"Um," she murmered only.

"Did I ever explain the difference between an illusion and a delusion to you?"

"No, you never did."

"Well, then," he started, while scratching his chin, "a delusion is a fixed false belief. No matter how you tilt your head, you always get the same incorrect view of a reality. But with an illusion you have enough sense to check for its correctness, usually bringing to bear another sense or senses to clarify your misperception."

"My dear Dr. Cordis," Renata said in a shaky voice, her face blanching and her hands beginning to tremble, "some things never were, others shouldn't be and still others cannot be." Tearfully, but with her characteristic poise and dignity, she got up and without another word, left.

CHAPTER SIXTY-THREE

The following week's session started off slowly, with Renata making no reference to what had happened at the end of the previous hour. She talked about the weather, her efforts to dispose of the Manhattan property, and then mentioned her plans to visit her great aunts in France for Christmas.

"That's a sound plan," Cordis commented. "Are Simone and Pierre going with you?"

"No, they have to go to New Orleans." Then she asked, "Isn't there a major Jewish holiday soon also?"

"Hanukkah," Cordis replied. "This year it begins on the twentieth."

"It always falls out around the time of Christmas, doesn't it?"

"The twenty-fifth of Kislev in the Jewish calendar," he answered, and then proceeded to explain the difference between the Hebrew and Gregorian calendars.

The Jewish calendar is based on a lunisolar year of 354/355 days with a metonic cycle of 19 years, in contrast to the Gregorian calendar with its solar year of 365/366 days. In the Gregorian calendar January begins 10 days after the winter solstice, and in the Jewish system Tishri begins with the first new moon after the autumnal equinox. The Christian winter of 1973 overlapped with the year 5734 in the Jewish chronolgy. For Jewish traditionalists, year 1 represents the year of creation, but for modernists it signifies the dawn of civilization, not the beginning of the world.

"I think we once talked about that holiday," Renata said. "That is, you did."

"Yes, I did. It commemorates the victory of the Maccabees over the Syrians twenty-one centuries ago."

"The Jews have always been a brave people," Renata said. "But weren't they foolhardy to take on the might of Rome following Christ's death. They lost that war and their country."

"They were always courageous," Cordis affirmed, "and in that war of seventy A.D. you're referring to, they drew inspiration from the Numantians. Four thousand Numantians—in north-central Spain—held off eighty thousand Roman troops in the second century B.C."

"How extraordinary!" she said. "Did they win?"

"They resisted Rome for twenty years before capitulating. But they became a symbol of greatness in defeat."

"Ah," Renata said, dragging out the word. "So, we're back to symbols."

"Nothing that is symbolic is ever lost," he said. "Always remember that."

Cordis felt the session wasn't accomplishing anything, and he was getting ready to bring up the marijuana issue again when Renata, suddenly somber-faced, intoned, "I remember something Kierkegaard said." She paused a few seconds. "Do you know what he said?"

"He said a lot of things in his time."

" 'Life can only be understood backwards, but it must be lived forwards,' " she quoted.

Cordis had been doodling in her chart while chatting with her since the hour began, but now he gave her his full attention.

"Please continue," he said, wondering what she was leading up to— and hoping it would be something important.

'I will try to start at the beginning."

"Always a good place to start."

"Now, let me see." She paused and sighed nervously. She took another deep breath and let it out slowly. Her breathing was becoming labored, and he was concerned that she might start hyperventilating.

Take it easy," he said soothingly, trying to calm her. "Take it slow and easy. You have all the time in the world. Nothing is going to happen to you."

"All right," she said shakily, the words sticking in her throat. She coughed a couple of times. "I'm all right." She sighed deeply again, and now appeared to be recovering her composure. "This is very difficult. Few people have ever heard what I am about to relate to you."

Something crucial was about to occur, and he fidgeted in his chair, trying to get as comfortable as he possibly could so that he wouldn't miss a word of what she would say.

"Don't rush. Take your time."

She waited a few seconds before continuing. "Do you remember reading Omar Khayyam when you were in high school?" she asked.

"Omar the Tent Maker?" he said, surprised to hear the name brought up. "Sure. 'The Moving Finger writes and having writ moves on. Nor all thy piety nor wit . . . ' et cetera, et cetera."

"Yes," she said, looking very serious. "Well, while he was writing the 'Rubaiyat' and reforming the calendar, his best friend, Hasan-e Sabbah, was founding the Assassins, an Ismaili sect which engaged in a policy of political assassination against its enemies: Abbasids and Seljuqs. He began by seizing the fortress of Alamut, an Abbasid stronghold near Qazvin in

265

northern Iran, just south of the Caspian Sea, in the year ten ninety. His followers were fed hashish and were furnished the most voluptuous women imaginable after returning to Hasan's mountain fortress following one of their political murders, like the well-planned killing of the Seljuq vizier, Nizan al-Mulm, in ten ninety-two."

Perhaps it should be mentioned that the spelling of Arabic names used here are as they appear in Dr. Cordis' notes, and these vary from one standard reference to another.

"Very interesting," Cordis said. He found her knowledge of the period impressive.

"There's more to the story," Renata said. "My part of the story." Her breathing became labored once more. "Between Teheran in the Interior Plateau of Iran . . ." She paused. ". . . and the Caspian Sea Coast to the north are the Elburz Mountains, where . . . Hasan had his fortress . . ." She stopped and remained silent, trembling noticeably.

"Take your time," Cordis said softly, repeating the sentence several times, as he got up and walked over to his refrigerator. Removing a bottle from it, he returned to his desk, holding it in one hand and two drinking glasses in the other. "Here, have a drink," he said, pouring out the contents into the glasses. "Black cherry soda. Guaranteed to calm the nerves."

Renata took a few sips and said, "Thank you." Smoothing out her dress, she indicated she was ready to continue with her narration.

"You were telling me about the mountains where Hasan had his fortress," Cordis said.

"Yes, the Elburz Mountains . . . where I was held prisoner—held a slave—for two months during the eighteenth year of my life."

Cordis found it difficult to hide his emotion over this dramatic revelation, but managed a controlled response.

"Please, go on," he said softly. "Remember, take your time."

Renata sat stony-faced as she continued with her story.

"I was seventeen when I fell in love with a man nearly twice my age. It was in Casablanca, and he was a Muslim. Very suave and well-educated. Of course, the family warned me and expostulated with me, but I was smitten and obstinate. I had never loved a man before—mine had been a sequestered life up until then. If there ever was a time in my life when I was psychotic, it must have been then—if you can consider being madly in love a symptomatic psychosis." She forced a feeble smile.

"Some people might," the doctor said, smiling in tune with her.

"Well, against the entreaties of the family, I went with him for what was supposed to have been two weeks, to the mountains, only a stone's throw from the Caspian coastlands. For ten days it was sheer delight, and I felt as though I were indeed in an earthly paradise, or as close to Eden as you can possibly get. We made love in his mountain chateau every night. We dined elegantly. Sipped the finest wine—at least I did. Being Muslim, he didn't drink. During the day we swam in the Caspian Sea or went boating. What a halcyon refuge! It's not like the Sea of Galilee—there are never any waves."

"You've been to the Galilee Sea then."

"Never. That's where Jesus walked on water. Well, I was soon in rough waters of my own—when my period started."

She stopped and sipped a little soda. He waited half a minute for her to resume, and finally prompted her with the words, "How so?"

"Oh, sorry," Renata said. "I was momentarily lost in my past. Well, to go on, in the Islamic world a woman is held to be ritually polluted during menstruation—and for that matter for forty days after childbirth. It is this ritual uncleanliness, incidentally, which is used by Islamic men to limit their women's activities—an unclean woman cannot participate in the public and religious life of the community."

He recognized that she was loading up her account with unnecessary details, in an attempt to postpone the inevitable, when she would finally have to say what she had to say.

"So, you were saying that you found yourself in hot water when your period started."

"Yes, anyway, he used the occasion of my menses to scream at me: 'You unclean whore of the streets!' and even more evocative epithets. I was . . . I was dumbfounded. I had believed I was living a storybook romance. The reality was sudden and harsh. There I was, the inexperienced, chaste Christian maiden, now deflowered, out in the middle of God knows where, in the clutches of a satanic, satyric infidel." She took another sip of soda. "I had no escape. He locked me in a tower. Every night I would hear his footsteps as he came up the stony steps to have sex with me—even during my period!" She began crying, and Cordis, leaning over his desk, passed the box of facial tissues to her. After dabbing at her eyes and blowing her nose several times, she continued. "He beat me. He screamed at me. He called me an unclean bitch. When visitors came, he would tie me up and gag me. At other times, he would bring them up the steps to peer at me through a peephole in the door." She lowered her head. "I could hear them joke about me, the rich little Christian princess."

Tears were streaming down her face, and she didn't wipe them away. Cordis remained attentive in his silence.

267

He waited several minutes, and finally asked her, "How did you survive?"

"I have heard it said that memory is the only paradise from which we cannot be expelled. So . . . I relived the happiest moments of my life again and again in my mind."

"How did you manage to escape?"

She stopped crying and said, "It seemed to me that he—or maybe he was part of a ring of smugglers—was holding me for ransom or that he would sell me into slavery. Telegrams came from Grandmama and Simone, imploring me to telephone or write. He was sending them telegrams in my name—'Having a wonderful time' and all that—but they wanted to hear my voice or see my handwriting. Their telegrams went to an address down by the Caspian. So, in effect, I was being held incommunicado."

"Kidnapped sounds more to the point."

"Yes, I agree," Renata said. At that moment she leaned forward in her seat to retrieve the glass of soda she had placed on his desk top—and swooned. She barely missed hitting her head against the side of his desk, as her limp body made contact with the floor.

Cordis rushed over to her, and lifting her up in his arms, carried her to the analytic couch. She was still unconscious, but he was relieved to see that there were no bruises or lacerations on her face and scalp and no apparent injuries elsewhere. He elevated her lower limbs using the cushion from her chair and rubbed her wrists vigorously. A few seconds later she regained consciousness.

"What . . . what happened?" she asked, dazed, gazing at the doctor's face less than a foot away from hers.

"You keeled over in a dead faint," he answered.

"I did?" Renata said, sitting up on the couch.

He backed away. "Yes, you passed out."

"How utterly Victorian!" she laughed. She checked herself for injuries. "I appear to be in one piece."

"No broken bones," the doctor said, "and no cuts or bruises."

"Well, land sakes alive! as Scarlett O'Hara would probably have said at this point. You know, I can't recall ever having fainted in my entire life!"

"As long as you don't make a habit of it," Cordis said, "you're excused one faint."

Renata stood up and tested her equilibrium.

"I'm all right," she said. "Doctor, I think this session has come to an end."

He went downstairs with her and hailed a taxi. As the cab sped away, he remained at the curbside, musing. It's like an old-fashioned cliffhanger. How does she escape from the clutches of this Simon Legree?

Returning to his office, he took a few sips of his black cherry soda and reviewed his notes of the session. The more he probed, the more his imagination ran wild.

Supposing someone—maybe the cleaning lady—had come into the office while he was carrying Renata. Supposing she came to while in his arms—what would have happened? Supposing it wasn't a genuine faint but the ploy of an hysteric who wanted him to do just what he did.

He had been taking refuge behind the analyst's jargon—like the term transference, ignoring the possible reality—that what she felt for him was real. After all, he wasn't her gastroenterologist or her gynecologist or her dermatologist, yet this young woman had offered up her body's filth to him—her bowel contents, her vaginal discharges, her skin lesions—and he had not rejected her, but instead had smiled kindly, talked softly, and always encouraged her.

He shook his head and said aloud, "This is a very delicate situation I find myself in."

The sofa in the waiting room opened into a bed, and he decided to spend the night just where he was. He got very little sleep, and what little he got was punctuated by a number of distressing dreams. The last one found him and his old buddy, Freddie, as they were in their youth, wading knee deep as though in slow motion through the sands of the Sahara, until they saw, looming ahead, a huge dark tower. Now he was alone, and the entrance to the tower was barred by seven-foot guards carrying oversized scimiters. Rockets were going off in the background—Freddie had deployed to the rear, diverting the guards from the main gate. He climbed up the stony steps to the top of the tower, and there in a small dungeon he found her. She could have been Snow White. There was no time to waste. He carried her in his arms down the steps and out across the drawbridge. Finally safe, he bent over to kiss the sleeping beauty—and suddenly she was a little girl crying out: "Daddy! Daddy!" He awoke . . .

CHAPTER SIXTY-FOUR

"You were asking me last week how I escaped from my prison in the Elburz Mountains," Renata said, starting off her session on the 18th. She made no reference to her fainting episode.

"Yes, I'm more than mildly curious."

"Well, it was my godfather, Harris, who rescued me. Harris, the old private detective of another time. He freed me after two months of that living hell. He fractured a few jaws and shot up a few people in the process. Harris, the judo master from the Kodakwan in Tokyo."

"The one and only," Cordis said. "I'm well aware of his skills on the mats."

"He's Sam Spade, Philip Marlowe and the Saint all rolled into one when the occasion calls for it," she said. "He was shot in the chest during the rescue, and I didn't know anything about his wound until we were safely back in Casablanca. He could have died."

Cordis nodded sympathetically, noting the calmness with which she delivered her words. "And what happened to your ersatz lover?" he asked.

"For years I wanted vengeance. In my fantasy I would see him hanging by his wrists in the public square, or having his hands lopped off on the chopping block, or his testicles sheared off in public view. Of course, these are Muslim punishments, and I'm only an unclean infidel. So who am I to ask for Islamic justice!"

"You wanted your pound of flesh."

"But didn't I! I wanted him dead for what he had done to me. I know that somewhere in the Bible God says: 'Vengeance is mine!' But I wanted this man dead." Renata paused and sighed. "Well, our Casablanca police and the officials in Teheran were supposed to be looking for him, but nothing ever happened."

"And what happened to you after your dramatic rescue?"

"Oddly enough," Renata replied, "I suffered no obvious effects from the ordeal."

"You held together."

"Yes, I held together extremely well. Everyone expected me to fall apart, to have a delayed reaction. I don't know why I was spared a serious nervous collapse."

After a silence of about ten seconds, Cordis commented, "You said you were spared, suggesting a power outside yourself had done the sparing."

"I was a fallen-away Catholic at the time, and I didn't believe God had interceded on my behalf. I guess some young girls would have wound up in an asylum after such mental and physical suffering."

"But not you."

"In retrospect, I now realize how strong I actually was. For that matter, how strong I am."

"Good for you."

"But you must hear the next part of my story," she said with a broad grin. "The family thought I should take advantage of my U.S. citizenship and attend university in California. It's only when I came to America that I started going to psychiatrists. Naturally, my relatives thought the Iranian experience had finally caught up with me—the long-awaited delayed reaction to the nightmare in the mountains. But I went crazy, if indeed I did—and now I don't think I ever did, thanks to what I have learned about myself in these sessions with you—because . . . well, because I found myself in a crazy, mixed-up society which I did not understand, surrounded by a few thousand seriously maladjusted students there in Berkeley whom I did not understand, struggling to get on with people who did not and could not begin to understand me."

"There's a touch of irony in that."

"It's worse. My father—God rest his blessed soul!—had said to me when I was little, something I always remembered, 'When you grow up, go to Berkeley, California, for your university education. There are so many Nobel laureates walking the ground there, it has become hallowed.' By the time I got to Berkeley, it was hollow. Hah! It was theatrical farce, not higher education."

"Your father was right," Cordis said when she paused. "I can recall its great reputation in the forties. But that was another time."

"Well, in the silly sixties Berkeley gave us, 'Don't trust anyone over thirty,' the drug culture and a new children's crusade, the flower children, along with social revolutionary theory."

"Practice also," the doctor added. "They put some of that revolutionary theory into practice."

"I almost joined them," Renata said, eliciting a look of surprise from Cordis. "Not for their purpose, though, but for my own."

"And what purpose was that?"

"I had joined a gun club and became expert in the use of several types of hand guns," she replied. "Since the police in my region of the world were doing so little with my case, I thought I would hunt the fiend down

271

myself during summer vacation."

"Really?"

"Absolutely," Renata stated, "and I even thought of joining Students for a Democratic Society to learn how to set off bombs and use weapons which packed more of a wallop than hand guns. In fact, I began to fantasize myself as a female Che Guevara."

Ernesto "Che" Guevara, an Argentinian doctor, had played a key role in Fidel Castro's revolution. Afterwards, he extended his revolutionary plans to the interior of Bolivia, where he was killed by government forces in 1967. He became a cult hero to some segments of American youth.

"Did you join SDS?" the psychiatrist asked.

"No, I didn't. One day I had a vision of St. Joan—more a dream, what I have come to learn you psychiatrists refer to as a hynopompic dream, between sleep and awakening—and she told me simply that this was not the way. So I desisted."

"God had been sending you messages all along which you chose to ignore," he said.

"Now I know better," Renata said. "He's been hounding me from Heaven." She smiled.

The doctor also smiled. A nice reference to Francis Thompson's poem, he thought.

"Well, you've certainly learned something," he said.

"But I was a misfit at Berkeley," Renata said. "I didn't date and I kept guns. No one wanted to room with me, except for one or two lesbians. And, oh yes, I acquired one of their habits: smoking marijuana, which I had never been able to let go of . . . until now. There, you now have it: my true confession. I think all that marijuana dulled my sense of scholarship—I was ineffective as a student."

"You were raised to be a scholar, not a coed," Cordis commented, avoiding any further talk about cannabis. If she would stop using it now, there should be no lasting effects, such as her occasional memory lapses.

"That's true," she said. "I wanted to be a scholar."

"And then what happened to you?"

"The family gene for melancholia, or whatever, was finally activated in nineteen sixty-nine, leading to the first of several hospitalizations. Thank God, Harris was always there, because without him Grandmama and my aunts would have allowed those psychiatrists to perform shock treatments on me. It was bad enough getting the wrong pills, that Thorazine, and being misdiagnosed as schizophrenic. Well, Grandmama bought an apartment in San Francisco, and when I went back to classes I never lived on campus again."

"And then what happened to you?"

"In between hospitalizations I had a succession of psychoanalysts," she said, "and they were no help either. I had four of them in four years, but only for short periods of therapy. They each had the same objective in mind: to bed me down. But you know about that, or heard about it."

He nodded. "Yeah," he said simply.

"The world is full of lechers," Renata said, "with and without higher degrees. Men are what they are. Don't you remember—R for rapacious? Mother Nature has made them that way—slaves to the power of their testosterone."

"And what about women's sexuality?" he asked.

"In general? Mine?"

"Yes, yours."

"I don't know what I am," Renata replied. "I'm neither involved heterosexually nor homosexually. I have been . . . psychologically at least . . . neuterized."

"And what are your hopes?"

"In the male-female tangle?" she said. The doctor nodded yes. "None at the moment. You may be preparing me for a nunnery." She laughed.

"Can you take the vows of poverty, chastity and obedience?" he asked with a grin.

"The poverty part would be hard to handle," she answered. "I am, after all, a millionairess, and it's only recently that I have begun to appreciate that reality."

"Interesting," the doctor murmured.

Renata fell silent for a while, and then rose to her feet, saying, "I must got to the ladies room."

When she returned several minutes later, he could see that she had been crying.

"Are you all right?" he asked quietly.

She nodded. "I'm fine, just fine," she said, smoothing out her dress and fidgeting in her seat. "Now where was I?" she continued. "Oh yes, doing the Cordis association test. Woman's major function is to try to civilize the male, and not to compete with him at every level. This is indeed a strange country: the women want to be men, and the men want to remain boys. There is no place here for a great love, *un grand amour, en francais.*"

"*C'est vrai,*" he responded. After a pause, he said, "You know, I get the impression that you can now leave that dreadful experience you suffered in Persia behind you."

"Persia is derived from a Greek word," she started to correct him. "The Iranians prefer to call their county Iran, meaning the land of the Aryans."

"I stand corrected," he said.

"Well, I feel good, relieved, talking about the Iranian nightmare. But it's not entirely over yet. I cannot find it in my heart to forgive that . . . bastard," she said calmly. It was the only time in the course of her therapy that she had resorted to an off-color word.

"We be one with others always—emulate the Trinity," the doctor said. "What's happened to that concept?"

"I know, we are all brothers and sisters together," Renata said, "one human family. But there are limits to forgiveness. I now go to mass again, and I'm thankful to be restored to my faith, but I admit, I'm not Christ-like. I cannot forgive that rotter who so misused me."

"Um," he muttered. "Of course. Forgiveness is a process, not a single act. A process requires time."

"Maybe one day . . ."

"But not this day," he said, smiling.

"Yes, not this day." She returned his smile.

"One thing to remember, God forgives you your sins, so the time will come when you will be able to do the same for those who have sinned against you."

Renata nodded, but said nothing.

She was leaving for Paris in two days, and planned to return to New York on the 2nd of January. She asked him if he could see her on the 3rd, a Thursday, and he agreed to it.

"Merry Christmas," he said to her, as her hour drew to an end, and he embraced her.

"Happy Hanukkah," she said, kissing him on the cheek. "I'll see you next year."

There had been no dramatic emotional catharsis. The material she had brought forth had never been repressed, only suppressed. Like lancing a boil, the poison had been removed, but the wound produced by the procedure would itself require time to heal. At least he now knew the identity of the shadowy form in her Snow White dream and why she smoked marijuana—identification with the aggressor, one of the mechanisms of defense of the ego, always an unconscious process.

She cried again! he said to himself. He sighed deeply and buried his head in his hands . . .

CHAPTER SIXTY-FIVE

The Christmas season had arrived, and everyone at the clinic was in good spirits, with the exception of the brooding Armazōn-Goldstein. In half a year she had succeeded in alienating the entire medical corps at the clinic, which was still the clinic, not The Retreat or any of the other de-medicalized names she and the administrative group had been considering.

Joey Dee arrived about an hour early for his 11 o'clock appointment on the 24th.

And people say miracles don't happen anymore, Cordis mused when he spotted Joey sitting quietly in the waiting room. His schedule for the morning was light, so he was able to see him ahead of time.

Joey's clothes were tattered and his lengthy hair uncombed. He had shaved, however, and his face bore the evidence of several razor nicks, which he had covered over with Mercurochrome.

Cordis accepted his brown bag offering with the oranges and the BIC's, and expressed his appreciation. Examining one of the pens, he mumbled, "Still bringing me blue BIC's."

"I'll bring ya black ones next time," Joey said with a broad grin.

Maybe—behind that smiling face—I hurt his feelings by criticizing his gift, Cordis said to himself.

"Sit tight," he said to Joey. "I'll be right back." He picked up his coffee cup and went to the staff lounge, returning promptly with a tray load of Danish and two cups of coffee. "Here, Joey, eat, drink and may your Christmas be merry."

"T'anks, Dr. Cordis," Joey said, his face beaming, and he plunged right into the doctor's offering. He took larger than average bites out of the pastry and made porcine noises drinking his beverage.

Cordis nibbled on his Danish and sipped his coffee, observing Joey with a heart full of pathos.

"Well, Joey, I forgot to get you a Christmas gift, so I hope this will do."

"T'anks, Dr. Cordis," Joey repeated, his mouth chewing and talking at the same time.

When he had finished, he said, "Dr. Cordis, da ancient Israelites had twelve tribes," and he started naming them.

Half way through his enumeration, Cordis shouted out, "Wait a minute!"

Joey had jumped from sevens to twelves, bypassing other key numbers, such as eight, nine and ten, especially ten, the basis of the decimal system. Eight is a number Cordis thought Joey could have manipulated easily enough, since it is 4 times 2, containing his favorite number repeated twice. If you turn 8 over on its side, you get the mathematician's symbol for infinity. Cordis could visualize the Sleeping Buddha—with his Eight-fold Path—in the position of infinity. There is so much he can do with eight. Why has he skipped eight and everything else to jump to twelve?

"Did I say somethin' wrong, Dr. Cordis?" Joey asked innocently.

"You've done fours and threes and then sevens," Cordis explained, "because seven is four plus three. But why the dickens are you now starting on twelves?" The answer suddenly struck him like Newton's falling apple, even before Joey responded.

'Four times t'ree makes twelve," he replied.

Of course, definitely on course, Cordis mused.

The doctor then heard all about the twelve Titans of Greek mythology and poor Hercules, who had to purify himself at the court of King Eurystheus of Tiryns, which Joey couldn't even approximate in pronunciation, for twelve years during which time he performed his famous twelve labors. He listened to Joey tell him about the Delphic Amphictyony of Ancient Greece, originally a league of twelve tribes. Joey pronounced Amphictyony no better than Jimmy Durante would have.

"Da twelve-tribe federation o' Israel was an amphictony also," Joey added.

"Touché!" Cordis exclaimed. "You've discovered the duodecimal world for yourself."

Joey acknowledged his beneficence. "And dere was da twelve Indian tribes o' da League o' da Iroquois," he continued.

Cordis was smiling and his head bobbing in approval up until that point, but the smile turned to a frown and his head became still. "Repeat that," he said, sounding troubled.

"An dere was da twelve Indian tribes o' da League o' da Iroquois," he said, exactly as before.

"What did you say?" Cordis asked, sounding gloomy. "What was that?"

"Da twelve tribes o' da League o' da Iroquois," Joey repeated again.

This was Cordis' first awareness of an error in Joey's numbers game. He looked at him with surprise—and suddenly he sensed that their strangely played out game of numbers was coming to an end.

"What's da matter?" Joey asked, also sensing that something was amiss.

"I don't know much about Hindu Indians," Cordis responded, "but I know a little about American Indians."

"Ya do?" Joey said ingenuously.

Two years earlier, when he had been bedridden with an acute and particularly painful attack of arthritis, he had read and in some instances reread James Fenimore Cooper's novels.

"You see, Joey," Cordis began to explain, "in the sixteenth century Hiawatha, the Mohawk, got the five tribes of the Mohawk, Oneida, Onandaga, Cayuga and Seneca to form a confederacy or league, the famous League of the Iroquois. There were five tribes, Joey, not twelve."

"Not twelve!" Joey said pathetically.

"Five," Cordis repeated softly, aware that he had uttered a number Joey disliked. To try to mollify his anguish, Cordis moved quickly to six. "Then in the eighteenth century the Tuscarora came up from North Carolina to New York, and it became the League of the Six Nations."

Perhaps, Cordis mused, he can still squirm out of this through the device of six times two.

"Roman law was codified in da Law o' da Twelve Tables," Joey retorted, his voice unsure.

He was referring to the Lex XII tabularum.

"The old Romans engraved or painted their laws on tablets of wood," Cordis said. There was close eye contact at this stage. The doctor's words were soft-spoken but emphatic. "Wood rots, Joey, because termites feed on it and the four winds and all the many rains help beat it back into pulp."

Joey mopped his brow with a dirty, torn handkerchief and ran his hands over his face and hair several times.

"Where did I go wrong?" he asked, sounding bewildered. "Where did I fail?"

Slowly, and with a good deal of sympathy, Cordis said, "Joey, you apparently didn't read William King's *Art of Cookery*."

"Cookery? Cookery?" was all Joey could articulate.

"Yes," Cordis said, and paused before delivering what were the crucial words. "*Crowd not your table: let your numbers be*
 Not more than seven, and never less than three."
He had one more statement for him, but it was anticlimactic. "You should have stuck to sevens, pal, or threes and fours."

The game was finally over, but now Cordis waited to see what Joey's reaction would be.

"I should have stuck ta sevens," Joey said. Speaking as though mesmerized, he continued, "Da hues o' da rainbow are red, orange, yellow, green, blue, indigo an' violet." He got all seven of them correct.

"ROYGBIV," Cordis said, pronouncing the old mnemonic he had learned in high school physics for recalling the colors of the visible spectrum in decreasing order of wavelength. He sat still, breathing the air of silence for half a minute, deep in thought. ROYGBIV, Roy gbiv—Roy gives and Roy takes, he said to himself. Roy is the Anglicized form of Rex. Can that be it? Is he equating his psychiatrist with the king, the omnipotent father figure, or possibly God? Does he see me, Rex, as the instrument of his salvation?

As he had done in a previous session, Joey turned to the yin and yang cosmological philosophy of the Chinese.

"You must blend Yin an' Yang, Dr. Cordis," he said, still in his trance-like voice, "in order ta achieve peace an' purity." He paused and looked at the psychiatrist beseechingly. "Celestial Whiteness is how I know it!" he shrieked. And then he sobbed for about a minute, into that dirty, torn handkerchief of his. When the tears were over, he looked up at Cordis and forced a smile.

The doctor started to write prescriptions for Thorazine and Stelazine, all the while feeling, sensing, knowing intuitively that the denouement to the drama was close at hand.

"Please gimme Hadall and Tractan, Dr. Cordis," he said, almost inaudibly.

"You mean Haldol and Taractan," Cordis said, pronouncing the names of the drugs in his best Professor Higgins manner.

"Please don't gimme dem blue pills an' dose orange pills, Dr. Cordis. I need da red ones an' da green ones, Tractan and Hadall."

They sat in silence for what seemed an interminable length to Cordis, as he pondered the case of Joey Dee. Finally, he started nodding his head as he began to see the light. When he saw it clearly, he said, "Joey, do you know anything about Newton's three laws of motion? What's meant by electromagnetic wavelength?"

Joey looked at him with a blank expression. "Awh, Dr. Cordis," he said, looking embarrassed now, "I did well in history an' English an' subjects like dat in school, but I was no good at science."

Cordis had been reading up on the visible spectrum and the colors formed by blending different pigments, and was finally able to put the information he had gathered into action. It was the former which held the key to the puzzle.

He had already written Joey's prescriptions, but now he tore them up.

278

"Yes, Joey," he said, "stop the Thorazine and Stelazine. From now on you will be taking three Taractan tablets during the day and one Haldol tablet at bedtime, for a total of four tablets a day."

"T'ank you, Dr. Cordis," he said, bubbling over with joy. "T'ank you. Yer an understandin' doctor. Ya understan'."

"Yes, I understand," Cordis said, tears welling up in his eyes.

He had been able to look deep into the mind of his patient and glimpse his rainbow of hope. And this is what he had come to see and understand. Joey kept bringing him oranges and blue BIC's, and he kept giving him Thorazine and Stelazine. Thorazine and Stelazine were effective medications, but they were not meant for Joey. Thorazine, in all its milligram strengths, is an orange tablet, and the several different strengths of Stelazine all come in the form of blue tablets. His offerings to his doctor were of orange and blue, and he could *not* accept orange and blue tablets, Cordis' offerings to him, in return, for both gifts would then extinguish each other, just as blue and orange light, which are complimentary colors, extinguish one another by producing white light, or "Celestial Whiteness," as Joey called it. Restated, he had to offer Cordis blue and orange, the necessary colors, but when the doctor reciprocated with blue Stelazine tablets and orange tablets of Thorazine he unwittingly cancelled out Joey's colors. White, formed in accord with the laws of physics, had wiped out or neutralized white in his mind's colorful eye. Thus, he went another color route. Haldol tablets, which are red, and green Taractan tablets also blend, for they too are complimentary colors producing white light, Celestial Whiteness, or yin-yang balance in another sense. Here Joey had finally found the long sought non-obliterative complimentation, subjectively perceived as it was. As Childe Roland had come to his dark tower, so had Joey finally found the tower of light.

In the ancient rabbinic writings, not only is the Shekinah the female representation of God but also, in a better known sense, a visible manifestation of the divine presence—the Shekinah Light. Leo Shaya writes that to the Kabbalists creation stemmed from God's luminous fullness, the light of his divine radiation spreading to fill the universe. God remains incorporeal in the Jewish tradition, but Light stands as a sign of his presence. For example, Exodus describes the skin of Moses as being *radiant* when he descends from Mount Sinai—he was full of the Lord God.

The idea of the luminous presence of God pervades other religions as well. Jesus was transfigured, i.e., became luminous before Peter, James and John (Matthew 17: 1-2). Mircea Eliade points out that the chief god of one Tatar people is called White Light, and among the Ostyak, a Finno-Ugric people of western Siberia, their word for God has the meaning of

279

luminous, shining and light. Likewise the mystic Sufis saw God as Light, from which the Prophet was created.

Somehow, Joey knew about God's luminosity, at a level beyond the unconscious, in some unknown deeper recess of the mind, perhaps where mind and soul meet. Pills are good—man-made molecules can help heal the sick mind. But Joey, with his pleading for Haldol and Taractan to produce White Light, was actually asking for God's intercession!

"Merry Christmas, my friend," Cordis said to Joey. "God be with you."

"Yer my frien', too, Dr. Cordis," Joey responded, picking up his scripts for Haldol and Taractan. "I wanna wish ya a merry, merry Christmas!"

Cordis sat motionless with his hands cradling his coffee cup. God chooses the least among us to reveal his glory, he mused.

CHAPTER SIXTY-SIX

Cordis had Christmas dinner with Harris and several mutual friends at Harris' home in Queens. The old Japanese was a master cook, and he served as tasty a turkey roast as Cordis had ever eaten. After dessert, when the others had gone, he told Cordis that Renata had actually had a difficult time in Casablanca, contrary to her denial to Cordis. His book, A Psychiatrist Looks at Medicine, was dedicated to his parents, Jacob the Good and Rebecca the Kind, with a Star of David for each. A Delacross business rival spotted it and spread rumors that Renata was an Israeli spy, hoping to damage the House of Delacross. Renata was detained by the police for a while, but Pierre was able to hold the family's business enterprise intact, weathering out the Yom Kippur War nervously but without any significant financial damage.

Cordis received an embossed Christmas card the following day from Madam Bee, her first communication to him since returning to Alma-Ata. There was no word from Zelda Amado in Israel, and Cordis wondered whether she had finally succumbed to her cancer. He did receive a nice letter from Rosa de la Luz, the NYU student, who was now in San Antonio.

There was a card from the young homosexual Cordis had helped at the clinic simply by steering him to the classified section of the *Village Voice*. He attached a note to his card, thanking Cordis for "saving my life—I was ready to end it all that day."

Cordis thought, How fortunate! The only time I ever read the *Village Voice*, and I only had it to see how their book reviewer had dealt with Nahas' *Marihuana—Deceptive Weed*. The reviewer, pro-marijuana, had lambasted both the book and its author.

George, the patient who kept pickled cockroaches in his room, sent him a seasonal card—he had managed to stay out of the hospital all year. A victory of sorts, Cordis mused.

Sonja Olamstein sent him a Hanukkah card from Los Angeles, where she had moved the previous month. She added she was off marijuana for good.

The lady with the pressure sensation around her head he had seen for Division II in the winter turned out to have chronic sinusitis and had followed up with ENT treatment. She also sent him a card. In her case a solution was forthcoming, but most patients with carebaria have their sympton dismissed as neurotic. The subject intrigued Cordis, one more area he felt where the psychiatrist needed to work closely with other specialists, such as the ENT physician and the neurologist.

Sylvia Blank, still reading the Nahas book, phoned him during Christmas week to let him know she was engaged to be married.

"Maybe I will have a few babies after all," she said gleefully.

"Then you join with God in the co-creation of life," Cordis said to her, "and you help carry the human race forward toward its destiny."

A card came from Father Jules, the French priest who was visiting Fr. Dominic in May. He had gone "on loan" to a Louisiana parish, one in Acadiana, for a year. Cordis had heard him say mass during his stay in New York and was impressed by his eloquence and the depth of his sermon. They had had dinner together, and Fr. Jules told him how he had mastered Chinese in preparation for going to China, only to have the Communist takeover cancel out his missionary career. How he had wanted to go to China! Perhaps, Cordis mused, in Cajun country he may yet touch one soul . . . perhaps a Chinese . . . God writes with crooked lines.

Cordis exchanged seasonal gifts with Father Dominic, and had dinner with him several days after Christmas.

Fr. Dominic had not forgotten Renata—Cordis never referred to her by name, incidentally—and from time to time he would inquire about her. The psychiatrist would state that she was making steady progress, and the priest would end the conversation by saying he would continue to pray for her.

During their dinner, Fr. Dominic said to the doctor, "It has taken me all these months of nineteen seventy-three to squeeze out one final, elusive meaning hidden in your dream of January."

"And what is that?" Cordis asked, surprised and touched that his friend was still giving so much thought to the dream.

"With a little bit of latter-day Kabbala, I found another message hidden away in the Cologne street address: 3-7-9 Koln Strasse, Germany. Germany wasn't included in your dream, but add it to the address and drop out the Koln. What have you got now?"

"3-7-9 Germany."

"Correct."

"But what have we got?"

"What are the possible permutations with 3-7-9?" he asked. Without waiting for a response, he went on, "Three squared gives you nine possibilities. If you select out the sequence 7-9-3, it yields the words 'keep my,' in our Furstian system. Add to that the first syllables of Germany, which is 'German,' but reverse them to produce the word 'manger,' you arrive at the message: Keep my manger." There was a brief silence, which the cleric broke by adding, "Christ was born in a manger."

Following another short silence, Cordis said, "I know he was born in a manger. That's a fine message fathomed from the unconscious . . . for a Christian. But I'm a Jew. What am I doing with a Christian message revealed through Kabbalah?"

"Don't be so modest, my friend," Fr. Dominic said, "and don't shrink from your task. You're a go-between, a nexus, a living connection between the two faiths constituting Judeo-Christianity. The Lord has spoken to you in your dream—you have to consider that possibility—not in the usual garbled symbolism of dreams but in the mystical, kabbalistic language of your ancestors."

Cordis was deep in thought. Finally, he said, "You may have touched the heart of the matter with a finger pickled by fate."

"Faith, my boy, not fate. I was able—made able, I should say—to touch the heart of the matter through faith."

Cordis' father had died in 1965, during the Twelve Days of Christmas and at the very end of the eight days of Hanukkah, and Fr. Dominic had become, in essence, a father figure for him. He wished he had such a relationship with his rabbi, but he was thankful for what he had.

The Romanettis had a New Year's party, but it was listless and even gloomy. Sal had lost his bid to have his transfer to the hospital voided, and rather than continue with the State had resigned, with only nine years of service time, far short of what was required for a pension. He was now working at a community clinic in Nassau County, about an hour's drive each way in heavy traffic.

"Rex," he said, the muscles in his face twitching, "they won't get away with it!" He was unsteady on his feet, and Rita had to help him to sit down. "Enough vino, Sal," she said worriedly.

Cordis had a job disappointment of his own. The previous day he had heard from Florida State University's Student Health Service. The director wrote him 3 short paragraphs, and in each of them stated, "We have now hired a female psychiatrist."

On the 2nd of January he had dinner with Flora Rheta Schreiber at her Lower Manhattan apartment. Her book *Sybil*, about a multiple with 16 personalities, was a sensation and already she was anticipating it would be made into a successful movie. Daniel Schneider, author of *The Psychoanalyst and the Artist*, joined them. The two "contemporary" psychoanalysts Cordis admired most were Dan Schneider and T.S. Eliot's Sir Henry Harcourt-Reilly.

Dan's surname was a reminder of the past when Germans assigned Jews names according to occupation, viz., *schneider* = tailor, just as Flora's family name, Schreiber, in German means "writer," or in her case "scribe," a noble occupation in ancient Israel.

"Coincidence," Flora said.

"It is through coincidence that God communicates to us . . . if you are of a mind to listen," Cordis responded.

"You've got to write, Rex," Dan said to him. "That's the way to get ahead in our work."

"I'm working on a book idea right now," he responded. "About a beautiful young Christian woman raised in the Muslim world, kidnapped and held for ransom by an Arab fiend. Her story reads like a novel."

"Good," Dan said. "Good."

"He's had so many interesting patients," Flora said. "I have asked him several times why he feels this particular one merits a book."

"It's hard to explain," was all Cordis could say.

Renata had phoned him earlier on the 2nd, and would be in for her session the following evening. He spent a sleepless night, tossing and turning for several hours and finally got up to make himself a cup of

Sanka. An old Spanish hymn kept running through his mind: *"Señor, ten piedad. Señor, ten piedad. Señor, ten piedad. Ten piedad de nosotros."* [Lord, have mercy. Lord, have mercy. Lord, have mercy. Have mercy on us.] It was a slow-paced melody, and he could see, in his mind's eye, several old Mexican women dressed in black, praying with their rosaries and singing the hymn. He sat in his living room drinking his coffee slowly, and found himself transported back to Mexico many, many years earlier.

He and Freddie were up in the mountains in the north of the country in a small village. A rabid wolf had been terrorizing the community for days when they arrived. The villagers looked with awe upon the two tall, strapping strangers, with their dark beards—who appeared to be identical twins.

Cordis especially caught their eye: he was wearing a University of New Mexico sweater bearing a lobo (wolf) logo.

It was Cordis who killed the wolf—shot him six times in midair in the dead of night as the mad animal hurtled down on him, mouth dripping saliva. The villagers torched the beast's path with kerosine and burned the carcass. All night they danced around a bonfire, with Cordis, drunk on tequila, singing, "Who's afraid of the big, bad wolf, the big, bad wolf!" again and again, until he finally lapsed into deep sleep.

The campesinos entertained them for several days, and then Cordis took ill. Freddie wasn't ready to leave, so Cordis took his jeep to drive the twenty miles to town to see a doctor. He drove along a dirt road until he had to stop to throw up, and at that point five of the villagers drove up behind his jeep. He was glad to see them at first, but then realized they were not there to offer help. They surrounded him, armed with knives, and he was in a fight for his life. Calling upon all his skills learned from Harris, plus some innovative moves dictated by the occasion, he fought them well but finally succumbed. Two of them tied him to a tree and stuck broken branches in his hair. Cursing and laughing at him, Cordis heard them say: *"El rey de los judios."* [The king of the Jews.] The last thing he remembered was the two of them lifting their three unconscious companions into their car and Freddie's jeep and driving off in both of them.

He had no idea how long he remained tied to the tree. The next thing that crossed his consciousness were the sounds of a barking dog and a little later a woman screaming. He opened his eyes and saw what appeared to him to be a beautiful angel, but whose face was filled with horror and pity at the sight before her. A man appeared, her father, who gasped at what he saw. He untied Cordis and carried him to his car about a hundred yards away on the main road.

The next thing he remembered were the old Mexican women in black praying for him and singing *"Señor, ten piedad."* He survived a severe case of typhoid fever—before the introduction of chloramphenicol.

When he was well, he asked Ramona why she had screamed that day she found him tied to a tree.

"Your arms were outstretched and the branches in your head resembled a crown—for an instant I thought I had come upon Christ crucified!"

His time came to leave and return across the border to the north. The priest said to him in parting, "You have had a most remarkable experience—do not forget our Savior, with whom you are now joined forever."

And so his life shuttled back and forth between Albuquerque and the north of Mexico . . . until Ramona died.

His reverie was over. "Intriguing," he said aloud, "how much Renata resembles Ramona."

CHAPTER SIXTY-SEVEN

Cordis sat at his desk thinking while awaiting Renata's arrival for her 6 o'clock appointment on January 3rd. Therapy is like a game of chess in one respect—there is an opening game, a mid-game and an end-game. Here we are, near the end, the most difficult part of the psychic-interlacing experience, for we must each now handle the issue of separation.

Renata looked her best ever, health-wise and feminine-wise. Cheerfully, she got the session underway by stating, "I have some bad news and some good news. Which do you wish to hear first?"

"Whichever you choose."

"The bad news," she said, changing her facial expression toward the other side of the mood scale for the moment, "is that Aunt Beatrice is in a *maison de sante.* Strange, but what the family always feared for me happened to one of them. She is quite mad."

"I'm sorry to hear that."

"She's taking Largactil, which is the French name for Thorazine."

"I hope it works for her."

"They say she may improve," Renata said with a note of optimism in her voice. "There is hope for her."

'Good."

"Now for the good news. I was returning to our house last week after visiting Grandmama's grave when I was visited by a member of the Savak, the shah's secret police. He had come from Paris to inform me personally that my kidnapper, that caitiff, had been found and was dead." The doctor's eyes widened. "They shot him," she continued. "He had been part of a drug-smuggling ring, and ironically he was killed there in the north of Iran, in the Elburz Mountains, not far from where Hasan-e Sabbah had his headquarters nine hundred years ago."

"Astonishing!" Cordis said. "What a Christmas present!"

"Yes. Now I have a sense of, a feeling of . . . relief. Now I can get on with my life."

"That time has come," Cordis commented.

There was a pause and then Renata said, "Dr. Cordis, when I am with you, I feel the distance between Judaism and Christianity narrowing, dissolving and forming one unity. How do you explain that?"

"Christianity, of course, has its origins and roots in Judaism," Cordis responded. "When Jesus says something like 'You must love your neighbor as yourself,' he is repeating what is written in Leviticus."

"Is that right?"

"Yes. Chapter Nineteen, Verse Eighteen."

"The Ten Commandments links us, too," Renata said.

"Yes, and they represent one of the dividing lines."

"But both faiths accept them in their entirety."

"True," Cordis said. "However, to the Jew the Ten Commandments are an obligation, a duty, and after that he must accept them because they are sacred—they come from God."

"I don't see anything wrong with that," Renata said, looking puzzled.

"Well, you see, the Christian follows the Ten Commandments out of love, not obligation—and that is the difference."

"Ohh," she said, dragging out the word.

The rest of the hour was spent in inconsequential talk, until near the end when Renata said, "I read the Helen Waddell novel, *Peter Abelard*, on the flight back to New York."

"That's an oldie," Cordis commented, smiling. He was familiar with the story of this famous pair of 12th century lovers.

"But timely . . . for me," Renata went on to say. "What Abelard said to Heloise: 'Because I loved you beyond measure and longed to hold you for ever,' will always hold meaning for me. Those words were the undoing of their love. Because . . . nothing can be forever."

"Nothing is forever," the psychiatrist said, his heart suddenly heavy.

"Nothing lasts forever," Renata continued. "Life flows on a river of time, a river flowing on and on, never pausing, never stopping, unlike our lives, which have to come to an end somewhere in time."

"Does that bother you?"

"No. I accept it. I understand that the river of which I speak is symbolic of God, who alone is timeless. Everything else belongs in time, and knows a beginning and an end." Her eyes were watery.

Cordis bent his head over her chart pretending to be reading something so that she couldn't see his own tears. He blinked rapidly several times and shut his eyelids tightly to try to cut off the flow from his tear glands. Noisily clearing his throat, he said, "You know, your next scheduled appointment is for Tuesday, which is the eighth, but in going over the records I notice that the very first encounter I had with you last year was on January tenth. Maybe you would like to swich your next—and final—session to Thursday—"

"A grand idea!" Renata said before Cordis could finish what he wanted to add. "By all means, let us acknowledge the magic of the calendar."

CHAPTER SIXTY-EIGHT

Cordis ate an early supper on January 10th and then napped for a while. He wanted to give himself every advantage to be at his best for what he considered would be a trying hour emotionally. He then settled into the patient's chair with a copy of Freud's *Civilization and Its Discontents* in hand and Smetana's *Moldou* playing softly in the background. He found it difficult to concentrate on his reading and just listened to the music.

Renata was five minutes early. She looked especially radiant on this the occasion of their final scheduled meeting. He reflected that she always reminded him of the stunningly poised Moroccan Jewesses he met at the University of London's B'nai B'rith Hillel House during the early sixties when he would come down from Dundee in Scotland on his periodic visits. Renata had carriage, charm, breeding, culture, all the poise and composure the truly ideal woman possesses . . .

Recognizing that he was lost in thought, Renata said, "Dear Dr. Cordis, my dear Dr. Cordis, you are a strange combination: a blend of Romantic man and biblical man."

"Living in a world which has little use for either," he responded.

"It is indeed a world of so little faith."

"In that case," the doctor said with a smile, "we have God practically to ourselves."

There was an awkward silence, with both of them not knowing what to say next. Cordis felt like Toscanini must have felt during his final performance, when the incomparable conductor completely lost his way.

Renata broke the quiet. "The main benefit I have derived from my therapy with you has been the restoration of my faith—my religious faith and even my faith in humanity. I won't say I'm prepared to try to save humankind, but I'll do everything in my power to help preserve it."

"In that there is wisdom," the psychiatrist said. "Yes, when it comes to us—on an individual basis—salvation proceeds only from on high."

"I wear the cross around my neck every day," Renata said, lifting up a simple cross from behind her blouse.

"Let that be the symbol of your God," he said solemnly.

The session continued to move along with starts and stops. As far as he was concerned, the hour could extend past 6:50 if necessary. The way it was going, it wouldn't be necessary—only he didn't want it to end.

Half way through the hour Renata said, "I plan to concentrate on business, my business empire. It's fascinating and . . . invigorating. But I plan to go on reading everything in sight. I want to know everything!" Her last sentence was delivered with exhilaration.

"That's interesting," Cordis said. "You know, the sages say that the rabbis of old believed the fetus already knew everything, but on its way down the birth canal into the world its memory was wiped clean, and so in life it has to start all over again."

"What an enchanting thought!"

"It's more than that. It's part of the proof that God exists."

"We discussed that last year, dear Dr. Cordis," Renata reminded him, "and you concluded that God's existence is beyond the reach of science—we can know Him only through faith."

"I agree. But there is another argument—"

"More philosophy?"

"Yes, but applicable. We start by saying that God knows all."

"Yes," Renata said, drawing out the word, "God is All-Knowing."

"And we say that everything knowable is possible. Everything God knows we can know one day—in the far, far future. Theoretically, at least."

"You mean philosophically—the field of study without substance."

"But it's possible, no matter how far-fetched it may sound. To know everything is to become like God. Only *like* God. We can never become God—only absorbed into God, which is the final act of existence and of the evolutionary process itself."

"It's something to think about," Renata commented, putting on a serious face.

"Everything that will ever be known is locked away in the human brain. So, all we have to do, philosophically, is reverse the argument: God is stored in each and every human brain."

Renata was paying close attention. "Ahh," she let out.

"During the twelfth century," the psychiatrist continued, "there circulated through the Jewish mystical community of Provence a kabbalistic work called the *Book of Light*, the *Bahir*, which instructed disciples seeking after God to look within, 'for it is in the heart that God inhabits.' Of course, God dwells in the hearts of men, but He has built His Throne within the cranial vault, the brain. Seek Him there as well."

Renata found herself unable to speak for ten or fifteen seconds, so overwhelmed was she by what she had just heard. "Your argument is unique," she said, nodding her head slowly. "I've never . . . I've never heard anything quite like it."

"No, it's not a unique view," he said. "Poets and writers always seem to get there before the scientists. Joseph Conrad knew it. In his novel *Heart of Darkness*, he wrote: 'The mind of man is capable of anything, because everything is in it, all the past as well as all the future.' And your lady in the attic, Emily Dickinson, understood it as well: 'The Brain is just the weight of God . . .' and so forth."

After a prolonged silence Renata said, "This leaves me breathless. I have chills running down my spine."

"Just keep looking within," the doctor said. "The deeper you penetrate into yourself, the nearer you come to the ultimate reality about yourself."

"I will," Renata whispered.

As 7 o'clock approached, Renata was not ready to let go. He was.

"We have traveled a long road together," he said, "and now it is time for you to go in your direction and for me, mine."

"It's hard to take that first step away from here," she said, her jaw quivering, as she fought to hold back her tears. "It's hard to let go, to say good-by, perhaps never to meet again."

"We now have a cosmic connectedness—sanctified by the great Einstein himself. There's a concept in quantum mechanics referred to as 'entangled states,' officially the EPR effect. Einstein showed that two particles, at one time in contact but now separated, remain mysteriously connected though miles, even millions of miles apart. He may have been talking about the spin on particles in a two-particle system, but it seems to fit the human condition as well . . . at least in special cases."

Renata let out a deep sigh and could respond only, "Oh, my!"

"So we will always be connected in some way," Cordis said, and stood up. The hour was over, the therapy at an end.

Renata began to stand up, but then hesitated, and sat down again. "There's one more matter I need clarified," she said.

Tears welled up in her already reddened eyes, and the doctor could see in her face that she was agonizing over something.

"Yes?" he said softly. He was standing motionless, bent over his desk.

"At times during the therapy I have imagined you to be the psychiatrist Sir Henry Harcourt-Reilly in Eliot's *The Cocktail Party*. What do you make of that?"

"The workings of a healthy imagination," he said laughingly, "and nothing more."

"You don't ever see yourself as Harcourt-Reilly?"

"Not really. No, not at all."

Renata bit her lip and said, "That is disturbing, very disturbing, because then I must believe that one of us, you or I, is Celia Coplestone."

At this point she was sobbing, and she reached for the tissues on his desk.

Celia Coplestone is Eliot's protagonist in the play, *sent* by the psychiatrist to a faraway place, where she is martyred very near an ant hill by the natives she has come to serve.

Cordis came around to her chair and helped her to her feet. "Sir Henry was not a very good psychiatrist," he said, "if I may judge him by professional, not Eliot's, standards. For that matter, it's not a very good play either." He began moving with her slowly across the office. "You know that Eliot wrote dreadful poetry in French."

"Yes, I know," Renata said between sobs. "His French left much to be desired." She sniffled several times and forced a laugh.

"I don't expect either one of us to play the martyr on some distant shore," the doctor said reassuringly.

"Oh, that does make me feel better. So much better." She stopped crying, and then spoke what were for her the most difficult words of the entire therapy. "It is time to say good-by."

"Yes, that time has come," he said with a heavy heart.

Embracing him, Renata said, "How do I say good-by? How do I thank you? You who have been doctor, teacher, father, brother to me and—yes—I must say it, speak the words aloud if only for this one time— the man I love."

He cupped her face in his hands and said, "You go out from within these walls and give to the world what is in you from God. And know in your heart that a great love is out there somewhere waiting for you. My task is done."

Renata kissed him, not on each cheek in the French manner, but a lover's kiss.

"Now I had better go before I am no longer able to go," she whispered. "I am leaving New York in three days."

"You go on a good day."

"Yes, a good day."

"Sunday's mass, I am told, celebrates the baptism of Jesus. On that day you are born into your future."

He went with her as far as the hallway door, and she continued on from there alone. She stood, gazing at him tearfully, for what seemed an interminable length, as he struggled to hold back his own tears, and then she moved forward another ten steps to the elevator. It arrived almost immediately, as though a watchful angel wanted to spare both of them any further heartache. She turned her face one last time toward him and smiled.

"*Vaya con Dios*," he heard her whisper through her tears.

"*Vaya con Dios*," he echoed back, the tears streaming down his face.

Had her parting kiss lasted a second or two longer, all would have been lost. He would have held her in his arms and told her how much he loved her. But a Providential Hand had parted them in time.

He stood there in the doorway for another minute, before returning

291

to his desk. He smiled as he looked at her chart, and then he made a final entry: JANUARY 10, 1974. RENATA DELACROSS. THERAPY COMPLETED!

FINIS

EPILOGUE

Sylvia Blank went on to study medicine and specialized in pediatrics; she did marry, and has two children.

Edith Delacross died in 1975, and her sister Beatrice followed her several months later.

A. "Harris" Hashimoto died in his native Japan in 1977 of leukemia.

Father Dominic died in 1977 of pneumonia complicating a long-standing history of chronic obstructive pulmonary disease.

Pierre Delacroix died in 1985, and Simone in 1987.

Renata Delacross built her already successful business into a conglomerate. She subsequently married and has three children. The first she named Taj, for her doctor. Her explanation may appear convoluted, but kabbalistically it is straightforward. The proof of a successful psychotherapy is evident when the patient is able to love, to work and to play, or *amar*, *trabajar* and *jugar* in Spanish. Permuting the first letters of the three verbs yields *t*, *a* and *j*. A taj is a tall conical hat worn by some Muslims, but the Farsee word also has the meaning of "crown." Renata remembered what Cordis had said about God's Throne, and in Taj she had her living *connectedness* with her former psychiatrist.

Rex Cordis married Cecelia Therese Chen-Wu, granddaughter of Chen Pao-Shen, chief tutor to Aisin-Gioro Pu Yi, the last emperor of China, and descendant of the legendary Chen Loi-Ling, Supreme Judge when the Ch'ing Dynasty was in its glory.